GREEN DAY

american idiots & the new punk explosion

ben myers

Published in 2005 by
INDEPENDENT MUSIC PRESS
Independent Music Press is an imprint of I.M. P. Publishing Limited
This Work is Copyright © I. M. P. Publishing Ltd 2005

Green Day: American Idiots & The New Punk Explosion
by Ben Myers

British Library Cataloguing-in-Publication Data.
A catalogue for this book is available from The British Library.

ISBN 0-9539942-9-5

Every effort has been made to contact and credit correctly the photographers
whose work has been used in this book - however a few were unobtainable.
The publishers would be grateful if those concerned would contact
Independent Music Press.

Cover Design by Fresh Lemon.
Edited by Martin Roach.

Printed in the UK.

INDEPENDENT MUSIC PRESS
P.O. Box 69,
Church Stretton, Shropshire
SY6 6WZ

Visit us on the web at: www.impbooks.com

For a free catalogue, e-mail us at: info@impbooks.com
Fax: 01694 720049

GREEN DAY

AMERICAN IDIOTS &
THE NEW PUNK EXPLOSION

by Ben Myers

Independent Music Press

CONTENTS

ACKNOWLEDGEMENTS

Thank you to everyone involved in the research and writing of this book, and to all those interviewed. The author would also like to extend special gratitude to Emma Van Duyts and Phoebe Sinclair at Warners UK for being extremely accommodating (and buying lunch), Andrea Graham for knowing more about Green Day than anyone else, Ian Winwood for kindly donating valuable interview transcripts and providing insight, Lisa Johnson in LA for the many suggestions and all-round encouragement, the Myers family, Davey James, Kara Cooper, Anthony Luke, John Robb, Caroline Fish, the staff and *Melody Maker* 1996-1999 and *Kerrang!* for the opportunities, Martin, Kaye and Alfie Roach, and Richard, Lee and the illustrious Captains Of Industry bands (www.captainsof.com). Thanks also to Green Day and their management, who have always proven to be very accommodating people and whose music has taken me to places I never thought I'd see. I hope this book does their story justice.

Extracts from some of the author's own interviews have previously appeared in other forms in *Melody Maker* and *Kerrang!* and a number of fanzines and websites. These encounters took place over a number of years in Milan, London, Los Angeles and Nottingham.

This book is dedicated to Mark Robinson, forever teenage.

Ben Myers, April 2005.

AUTHOR'S NOTE

Wherever necessary I have occasionally adopted a first person narrative approach where my own eyewitness accounts are concerned or else have injected some of my own recollections into this book. While I recognise this might, on occasion, read like a literary indulgence, I hope that readers might appreciate the reality of encountering bands – as opposed to the toned-down, edited highlights that might appear in magazines or TV. The truth is in the peripheral detail – the unspoken glances, the tone of voice. This, then, is an interpretation.

Also, because Green Day and their music have featured in my life in one capacity or another for the past fifteen years – on the radio, on a stage, in the flesh – as they have with millions of others, it's almost impossible to remain impartial. And quite dull.

To that end I have included the odd personal anecdote to provide a wider context and illustrate the effect that the band have had on those anonymous fans like me around the world.

Besides, all music and writing is personal – it is how the individual reacts to it that matters. This is my take on it. It's neither better nor worse than yours. Just different.

PART I: THE BEGINNING

"Go west young man, go west!"
Advice given by Indiana newspaper writer John B.L. Soule in 1851, later adopted as a mantra for nineteenth century American migration.

Oakland, California, has a rich and colourful history and that colour is predominantly gold. The land that surrounds San Francisco's Bay Area was first settled upon some 1200 years BC and inhabited by transient tribes for centuries upon centuries before Spanish explorers became the first Europeans to visit the East Bay in 1772. Within thirty years the Mission de San Jose had established themselves in the settlement of Fremont and imposed Spanish jurisdiction over the area that would one day be called Oakland. A man named Don Luis Maria Peralta was awarded a 44,800 acre land grant from the King Of Spain that spanned most of present-day Alameda county; the first non native-American dwelling was built in 1821. And that was that for a number of decades. The Spanish had staked their claim for this corner of California and their legacy still looms strong today, not least in street names and surrounding towns. The white man had arrived to irrevocably change the area forever.

Quite how much the landscape, economy, psyche and pyschogeography of Oakland would be changed over the coming decades – or indeed the coming two centuries – could never have been predicted, but in 1848 change it did.

When James Marshall, described as "a dour, paranoid carpenter from New Jersey", discovered a pea-shaped lump of gold in a sawmill ditch in Coloma, near Sacramento in January 1848, the course of American history was changed forever. "Boys," Marshall told the group of labourers who were helping him build the sawmill, "By God, I believe I have found a gold mine."

Times were hard and nothing captures the imagination of the poor quite like the accidental discovery of gold. What followed was one of the biggest mass-migrations on record as 90,000 people flocked to California from all over the country – and from places as far-flung as Chile and Mexico – in the two years following Marshall's discovery; the average journey took five months. California, as we know it, was born.

By 1854 the total of migrants numbered over 300,000 optimistic prospectors – one in nine of every American citizen. The census of 1850 found that 73 percent of California's population was between the ages of 20 and 40, and 92 percent were males. These people came not to settle, but to take. The mortality rate was high, as many young men died from accidents, disease or conflict with their neighbours. Among the first places they flocked to was one of the largest towns, San Francisco, and its surrounding Bay Area. The influx spread sideways and new settlements appeared across Oakland. In the stampede, California became a state of strangers, of prospectors – and more likely, failed prospectors – ensuring that it was a place quite unlike anywhere else in America.

But before the Gold Rush, Californians were occupying themselves with other pursuits, one of the most popular being rodeo, a pastime that combined practical elements of the frontiersman's life with a showy machismo-based form of entertainment, and which spawned a town of the same name, Rodeo (pronounced Row-day-oh) in Contra Costa county, a suburban county in San Francisco's Bay Area. Rodeo was like a primitive precursor to rock 'n' roll, a chance for young men to show off their physical and sexual prowess in the most obvious and no-brainer way possible – by wrestling livestock in the dusty Californian dirt in front of excitable crowds of ranchers, farm-hands, livestock owners, rustlers, hustlers, thieves and their families. It was – and in many areas of the country remains – a great American tradition. America loves its meat and rodeo was just one more by-product of an alternative economy to gold, that of beef. Welcome to cowboy country.

And it was here – on a dusty plain or in a newly built pen or on the back of a bucking bronco – that the American Dream was born.

Resting some fifteen miles north of hip college town Berkeley, the actual town of Rodeo is home to less than 9000 people and a little over two thousand families. It is a town born out of the livestock round-ups of the late 1800s, when in March of each year the cattle that had roamed freely on the unfenced plains were rounded up ('rodeo' comes from the Spanish word 'rodear', meaning 'to wrap up, to circle, to encompass'). The town was officially founded in 1890 by the Union Stockyard Company on land once a part of Rancho El Pinole, for the sole purpose of canning and packing the meat which only days earlier had being roaming the plains freely and quite obliviously.

Town planners set to work on designing a neat functional town and soon shops and the odd hotel were being built to cater for the increase in trade. Special train tracks were laid down to carry citizens from all parts of the Bay Area to inspect this new town, many of whom marvelled at the then-hi-tech packing plants and Southern Pacific spur track that sent the meat off around the country. On the outside, business was booming, but it was a venture that was to ultimately fail. Within a mere twelve months, the packing plant had failed to cope with such a rapid expansion and subsequent heavy outgoings and was declared bankrupt in 1895. Ten years later an earthquake levelled the entire town and Rodeo's enterprise truly came to an abrupt end when its bricks were sold off for construction of newer, more successful towns and cities.

Today Rodeo is still small by any town's standards, its main street a dreary strip of boarded-up storefronts and regulation housing overshadowed by the industrial buildings that are still the beating heart of the area. It is, as Green Day frontman Billie Joe Armstrong would later describe: "a smudge on the map of California." As of the year 2000, the racial make-up of Rodeo was fifty per cent white, the other half a combination of black, African-American, native American, Asian, Hispanic, Latino etc; a third of its citizens under the age of eighteen. Geographically, Rodeo is hemmed in by the Bay and the larger cities that surround it. Things have changed little since that initial failed influx of investment in the latter years of the nineteenth century. An oil refinery, a lead smelting company and a lumber company provide work for thousands of local men, from Rodeo and beyond. The town failed to live up to its early economic promise but as Elaine Pond, Chamber of Commerce for Rodeo proudly states, "while Rodeo will never be a big city, for physical reasons, it would be hard to find a more pleasant community."

Interestingly, also in 2000, Animal Right's Group PETA petitioned Rodeo to change its name, reasoning that it evoked images of the blood sport after which it was named. Their alternative suggestion of 'Unity' and their offer of donating $20,000 worth of veggie burgers to local schools should the town comply found little favour with the citizens of Rodeo who rejected the group's ideas outright.

So ... a Californian town of tract homes, dime stores and diners, whose history is full of tales of both success and failure – of gold-hungry prospectors and idealistic industrialists, of sudden wealth and widespread poverty – whose stature is forever cast in shadow by the more cosmopolitan climes of San Francisco. Rodeo is, in many ways,

11

unremarkable. In fact it is typical of so many of the towns and cities that sprung up in the wake of the expansion of the American frontier and the boom-time days of the gold rush, the type of place that *Rolling Stone*'s Chris Mundy would later describe as "a town that flashes by in the time it takes to change the radio station." There are many more like it and their importance lies not in the Spanish street names or the refineries, but the spirit that lies within both its distant past and its near future. That desire to explore, expand, to change both the landscape and the way of thinking of the citizens who inhabit it. To make something out of nothing and building from the ground upwards, to *better* things for everyone. Rodeo and its many Californian counterparts is a great metaphor for one particular rock 'n' roll band who took what little they had and turned it into something quite magnificent, something that even plunging economies, earthquakes and the madcap schemes of demented town planners would struggle to destroy. A place where only one in a million will strike gold.

1972 was a good year for rock 'n' roll.

Rock music was shaking off its hippy hangover from the Sixties and getting harder and more excessive. Vietnam was still happening, Charles Manson and his followers had hacked the psychedelic hippy dream to pieces and the Rolling Stones had witnessed violent death at Altamont.

A long overdue social and cultural change was coming, whether America liked it or not, and it was the rock bands of the day who acted as the cat's eyes on this dark road into the unknown future.

The Stooges and MC5 had already pointed to a more psychotic, hard-edged sound just around the corner, an anti-social cacophony to challenge the boundaries of taste and convention. Albums released that year included future rock classics like Rolling Stones' *Exile On Main Street* and Alice Cooper's *School's Out,* glamorous pre-punk deviant masterpieces such as David Bowie's *Ziggy Stardust* and Lou Reed's *Transformer* and key hard rock/proto-metal albums like Black Sabbath's *Volume 4* and Deep Purple's *Machine Head.* Chuck Berry had his first and only number one hit 'My-Ding-A-Ling' and 'American Pie by Don McClean was the biggest selling single of the year.

In the wider world, President Richard Nixon became the first U.S. president to visit China and Moscow, before being disgraced when it was revealed he was behind the Watergate scandal in Washington DC later in the year; Arab terrorists murdered eleven Israeli athletes at the Olympic

Games in Munich; and *The Godfather* was the highest grossing movie of 1972.

Rock music, like politics, was in a persistent state of flux. The art and culture of the Sixties had failed to change the world in the multifarious ways it had promised – perhaps the Seventies would require more drastic measures. Peace and love had failed, what next? Hate and war?

Yep, things were changing alright.

It was into this cultural climate that Billie Joe Armstrong was born on February 17, 1972 in Rodeo, the youngest of six children. His oldest sibling, Alen, was twenty-two years older than him, and born into a whole different era. Their father Andy's collar was a blue as the vast Cali skies spanning off across the dustbowl and into America's heartland. He drove trucks for a living, while his wife Ollie, who gave birth to her youngest son at the age of forty, worked as a waitress filling coffee cups, serving racks of ribs and wiping down tables at a roadside barbeque joint, Rod's Hickory Pit, on Lincoln Road in nearby Vallejo. Then owned by Richard and Alison Cotton, Rod's Hickory Pit was formerly Terry's, Pinole's premier coffee shop since 1936.

In years to come, Ollie Armstrong's work place would double up as the venue for the debut performance by Billie Joe's first proper band, who, despite showing a keen ear for melody at an early stage, were more about raw energy and goofing off. Contrary to popular belief, Green Day's future frontman was never named William Joseph Armstrong – Ollie, originally from Oklahoma, was inspired by her beloved country-and-western to choose such a name for her youngest son.

Music was in Billie Joe Armstrong's blood from the time he learnt to read and write. The signs were there from the age of five when he occasionally sang in children's hospitals and old people's homes, a cute kid wheeled out to entertain Californian's immobile citizens. He was certainly a beautiful child blessed with wide eyes, a cherub-face and thick ringlets.

"Billie Joe was a good kid," remembers Richard Cotton, owner of Rod's speaking to *San Francisco Magazine*. "He'd sing and dance for the seniors in our banquet room. I told Ollie, 'I'm going to see this kid's name in lights one day …'"

The fact that he was never more happy than singing merrily along to songs made the young Billie Joe all the more charming. At the age of five – when the outside world of 1977 was reeling from the sound of the Sex Pistols and The Clash – young Billie Joe's *cuteability* led to him making his recording debut when he went into a local recording studio and sang a song called 'Looking For Love', written by a James J. Fiatarone and Marie Louise Fiatarone.

In the shape of punk to come, the song was subsequently released as a seven-inch single limited to 800 copies on the songwriters' own little label, Fiat Records. The B-side was a mock-interview entitled 'Meet Billie Joe', a five-second snippet of which can be heard at the beginning of Green Day's later *International Superhits* compilation: "Billie Joe, it's certainly exciting to meet you here at the recording studio right after you've just made your very first record, how does it feel?" gushes the female 'interviewer'.

"Hmmm ..." he wonders with a chipmunk-style chirpiness, as if he can already see thirty year of hi-jinks ahead of him, "wonderful!"

The single was released in a plain sleeve with a song book insert and a picture of the budding singer sporting his thick set of curls. Suddenly, by way of a lack of competition, Billie Joe was inadvertently one of the world's youngest solo artists! Everyone agreed it was a cool thing to do and 'Looking For Love' got plenty of spins on the Armstrong residence's turntable and made for a great Christmas gift to relatives.

It could all just as easily have ended there – which five-year-olds don't love to make a noise and be the centre of attention? The record was, after all, just one step up from any kid discovering the home stereo's microphone function for the first time.

But music *was* in Billie Joe's blood – and once in there that stuff is indelible. Looking back now, there seems a strange inevitability to the chain of events that led from singing along to the radio and his siblings' record collection, to writing his own compositions to performing them and releasing them as records all within a period of little over a decade. Music was there soundtracking Billie Joe's every moment – every tentative sip of beer, every girl kissed, every joint smoked. It was what got him out of the life he was leading and away from the neighbourhood from which he might never have otherwise left. But we're seeing all this with the benefit of hindsight, that neat device that is sadly not available to adolescents, in a time when a bit of perspective on life is most needed. At the age of ten no one knows what their life may bring; all you can do is hope and dream...

It wasn't just Billie Joe that loved his music. When he wasn't driving trucks, Andy Armstrong was a keen amateur jazz drummer. "He would go to bars, play, smoke pot with his friends – what people in jazz do," Billie Joe later explained. "I never really knew him too well."

As a counter to his father's love of jazz, Ollie Armstrong was more of country nut and certified "Elvis freak", as so many Americans were in the early Seventies, when the revitalized, self-styled 'King' was at his commercial peak. God-like country singer Hank Williams was also never off the stereo either. Being the youngest of six allowed Billie Joe to fill his rock quota by plundering the record collections of his elder siblings: "I've got a brother who's old enough to be my father. He listened to a lot of stuff like *Guess Who* by The Who. Because my mom was kind of an Elvis freak, the first album I ever bought was Elvis Presley's debut *The Sun Sessions*. I lucked out on that one. I had just seen one of his movies – *Double Trouble*, I think – and got it because he looked good on the cover. Even then, I wasn't into the jumpsuits though..." Soon, as he would get older, another of the Armstrong siblings, sister Anna, would be schooling her younger brother in more alternative music. It was an eclectic mix.

Aside from his early flirtation with a recording career, for the first ten years Billie Joe Armstrong's life was relatively normal. He attended school, he sang songs. He did kids' stuff. As the youngest of six he arguably got away with more than his eldest siblings, as many youngest children so often do, though he was far from spoiled or over-indulged.

Growing up in California in the Seventies and early Eighties was a time of classic rock radio, of emerging new wave bands, of *Sesame Street* and *Starsky & Hutch* and skateboards with the old polyurethane wheels. Fictional heroes came in the form of Luke Skywalker and Hans Solo (depending on whether you went for the plucky underdog or the cocky loudmouth), Christopher Reeve's *Superman*, or for the more sensitive kids, maybe Elliot from *ET*. The usual schoolyard antics prevailed – like the time two girls beat up Billie Joe in an attempt to get him to be their boyfriend (a sign of the adulation that was to follow years later, perhaps?). The usual schoolboy hi-jinx.

But in 1982, when Billie Joe was just ten years old, things changed forever in the Armstrong household when husband and father Andy passed away from cancer. Billie Joe suddenly found his family set-up changing at a time when an adolescent needs stability most. There was still parental love, of course, but from the dawn of his teenage years and the onset of puberty, Billie Joe, already bored and restless, had even less reason to obey authority.

"Our family changed a lot because my parents had been very kid-orientated and all of a sudden my mother withdrew and threw herself into waitressing," Anna Armstrong told Chris Mundy of *Rolling Stone* in 1995, in what remains to this day one of the finest articles on the band. "The family structure broke up. Then my mother remarried about a year or so afterward … I'd say we were as dysfunctional as any family with the death of a father, a stepfather who no one liked and almost losing our mother at the same time. We were a very physical family. There was a lot of fighting amongst the siblings, a lot of hitting. I don't know where the anger came from."

"I'm the epitome of a latchkey kid," affirmed Billie Joe in *Spin*. "By the time my Mom got around to raising me, she was like, 'You do what you want, I'm sick of being strict all the time ...'"

Although having never had the opportunity to get particularly close to his father – trucking, playing jazz and raising five other older kids before him put paid to that – Billie Joe's father did leave behind something for which he would no doubt be eternally grateful. Shortly before his death he bought his youngest son his first guitar, a 1956 Fender Stratocaster copy made by Fernandez – soon-to-be nicknamed 'Blue' – purchased from the member of a band called Big Bang Beat. This 'Strat' would become something of a trademark, ever-present in the crucial early years of Green Day and used later in front of crowds of tens of thousands, becoming increasingly battered and held together with strips of gaffer tape until it could be played no more (though he would later have several replicas made).

Billie Joe was lucky – by the early age of ten he was obsessed with music and had therefore found something worthwhile to occupy his time and his mind. It was the key to another universe – corny, but true. And so began an alternative education.

The discovery of music is a piecemeal process for any young potential fan. It's all about separating the wheat from the chaff and finding out about what moves you most. But good music always leads to further discoveries, usually through word of mouth, a passing reference or taking a chance in a bargain bin. The inquisitive fan moves laterally, taking it all in. Around the time he first picked up a guitar, Billie Joe made acquaintance with two brothers, Matt and Eric, who came from out of town every weekend to visit their estranged father, who lived across the street. Slightly older at a time when a year or two makes a crucial difference, the brothers were budding rockers happy to share their latest tapes with Billie Joe, who they recognised as one of them. Hell, that he liked music was enough. Most of the other kids were more interested in team sports, or TV. And so each week they would arrive with their latest discovery – Van Halen, Def Leppard or maybe Motley Crue's *Too Fast For Love*, released a couple of years earlier and a particular favourite alongside numerous other such rock and metal bands like Ozzy, AC/DC, Judas Priest – all the staple albums of any latterday wannabe rebel's collection.

It was enough to inspire Billie Joe into thinking of the songwriting process. The first song he wrote was on a piano and it was only afterwards that he realized it wasn't his song at all, but merely a subconscious re-write of Eighties-era Ozzy's 'Crazy Train'.

Soon Matt and Eric graduated to newer, leaner and somehow far more dangerous sounding music by the likes of TSOL, DOA from Canada and the Dead Kennedys, punk kingpins from down the road in San Francisco, a city that, if not geographically, then certainly metaphorically was a million miles away from the slow pace of life in Rodeo. Then there was the Sex Pistols, the daddies of punk, with their sneering, iconic singer John Lydon – the yardstick for all the punk frontmen to come.

"He was beautiful when he was in the Sex Pistols," said Billie. "That eye that wanders a little bit, and his voice. You can tell he just blatantly knows that he's smarter than you."

These newer bands sounded far faster and angrier than their hair metal contemporaries and instantly conveyed a sense of dissatisfaction with the world that was easy relate to. The message wasn't buried deep within the music or through lyrical abstractions, nor did it speak of a fantasy world of leather-clad chicks on the Sunset Strip; no, these messages were distilled down into soundbites and slogans to be sprayed on walls and leather jackets. It was something altogether more heartfelt and tangible. Maybe even something to believe in. The music was both anti-social and cheap but empowering and inspiring too, sometimes ugly and unlistenable, but just as likely to be melodic without ever being pop music. To the young wide-eyed fan still not yet in his teens who already loved Elvis and the melodies of Sixties genre transcendentalists like The Beatles and Stones, he was hooked. "I liked the rebellion and the style – those guys remind me of gangsters," said Billie. The music was called punk rock and Billie Joe Armstrong had been waiting all his life for it to come along. But the world had other ideas. Higher forces such as parents, teachers and the law were at work. Life kept getting in the way of living.

Fortunately, around about the time his father passed away and he tentatively embarked on mastering the basics of a guitar almost as big as himself, Billie Joe made a new friend one day in the school cafeteria.

Michael Ryan Pritchard was born ten weeks after Billie Joe, on May 4, 1972. His mother was a certified heroin addict separated from his father and consequently he was given up for adoption soon after birth. The maternal heroin dependence bestowed an unwanted legacy on Michael when he was born with an enlarged mitral valve in his heart that would be allied to the panic attacks and nervousness that he would suffer in later life (and which inspired, amongst others, 'Panic Song' on Green Day's *Insomniac* album) and that, during particularly stressful moments, caused extremely painful stabbing pains in the chest.

In the same year, in the nearby town of Willets, California, Frank Edwin Wright III was born on December 9, 1972. He enters the story a little later. Don't worry – he'll be sure to make his presence felt. You can't fail to miss him.

Mike's new home in Rodeo – his first proper home – was with his adoptive parents, the Dirnts, a Native American mother and a white father. This stability was short-lived when the couple split in 1979 citing irreconcilable differences. So Michael moved in with his father. Then, a while a later, with his mother. It was here, at a very early age, that Mike was said to have smoked his first joint with a friend. Far from being liberalism *in extremis*, life had become a nightmare scenario in which a child is forced to grow up far too soon. The stability seemingly needed to produce a well-rounded citizen was notable only by its absence and Mike too found himself living something of a transient, latch key existence.

"There were all sorts of things happening," he remembered in Chris Mundy's *Rolling Stone* piece. "When I was in fourth grade my mom stayed out all night, came home the next day with a guy, and he moved in. I'd never met the guy before, and all of a sudden he's my step-dad. We didn't get along for years. Later on, when I hit high school, my mom moved away from us, and me and my step-dad got real close. He instilled a lot in me. The one thing my family did give me is blue-collar morals."

Finally Mike moved back in with his adoptive mother and his sister

Myla, who in turn, first ran away at the age of thirteen and then again when their adoptive mother remarried. Tragically, in a pattern that seemed to be repeating itself, Mike's stepfather passed away when the bassist was only seventeen.

Given the circumstances of his upbringing, Mike – who by now was using the surname Dirnt – was developing into a likeable guy. Like Billie Joe, there was a distinct absence of a sole father figure throughout Mike's formative years. It was a tough time for the young pair. When others are worrying about the sprouting of their first pubic hairs or the errant nature of their changing voicebox, between them Mike and Billie Joe had been through adoption, the death of a parent, the acceptance of two step-fathers into their lives who they both respectively locked horns with, and all against a backdrop of low income, limited career options, pressures from parents and teachers, pressure from peers and the general mundanity of a small-town life. The prison system and rehab clinics are full of people with similar tales of chaotic upbringings. Not these two, however.

Mike was tall-ish for his age, skinny, energetic and had whippet-like features. Good looking in a rogue-ish, charming way. He was intelligent and articulate but not particularly academically motivated, and something of class comedian. By the time he found himself chatting to a smaller kid in his year at school sometime in 1983, a contemporary named Billie Joe, who he had seen around the corridors of Pinole but never actually spoken to, he recognised in his potential new friend a kindred spirit. Someone with whom he could sneer at the tedium of the education system and hang out with in opposition to the cliques and peer pressures of high school life. They also recognised in each other a similar latch key existence and sense of constant change at home. Perhaps most importantly though, the pair shared a similar sense of humour that was already ensuring each was relatively popular amongst their classmates, both seen as something of a likeable joker. Not a disruption, just ... funny. Smart-mouthed.

"It took a little while until Billie and I learned how to be friends," said Mike. "I think we were both a similar type of character, we both wanted to be the clown. But punk rock for me was always the way I wanted to be, it expressed something the way I thought it should be expressed. This was in the Eighties where American society was so competitive, where the meathead element was really encouraged – and nowhere does that kind of thing tend to express itself as clearly as it does in schools. And here was this music, this great music, that had nothing to do with that – nothing whatsoever. It really appealed to me."

The pair soon became obsessed with a key punk band, who Billie Joe had discovered at the age of nine when he chanced upon the recently-released film *Rock 'n' Rock High School* for the first time, starring four freaks in leather from Queens, New York: The Ramones.

"To me, what I saw was the perfect rock band," Billie said in 2001. "They had songs that just stuck in your head, just like a hammer they banged right into your brain. There's a real romance to the Ramones. Those lyrics. It wasn't just about being a meathead punk-rocker. If you think about every person who has been inspired by the Ramones, directly and indirectly, you're talking about half of what you hear on the radio today."

Mike and Billie Joe's love of music, coupled with the latter's rudimentary skills on the guitar was enough to persuade Mike that he wanted in. After messing about on a six-string he decided to go for the bass. The first song they wrote together was called 'Best Thing In Town'.

Like so many budding punk bassists – whether Sid Vicious, The Clash's Paul Simonon or Dee Dee Ramone – Dirnt learnt by playing along to his favourite artists, punk bands like Husker Du or The Replacements, introduced to him via Billie Joe, along with the usual teenage discoveries of the Dead Kennedys, Sex Pistols and so forth.

"I've always played," Mike said in *Bassist*. "I sit there and if I don't play my guitar for a day or two, I start freaking out and I get up in the middle of the night and I run to my instrument. Whenever I get really pissed or upset, that's been my outlet. The guitar has always been there for me – beat the shit out of it and you won't end up becoming some psycho-sniper."

Finances and family situations being what they were, the young Dirnt wasn't able to just ask his mother for the money to buy a guitar. Green Day have since pointed out that they barely had enough money to buy records and even if they had there were few outlets in which to purchase them. This was, after all, a small town, with little or no musical heritage. There's an anecdote about the time they met their heroes, melodic punk antecedents The Dickies, some time after Green Day's mainstream breakthrough album, *Dookie*, went big. Or at least, the Dickies assumed they were big fans given the constant press comparisons between the two bands until Mike confessed that he'd only recently heard them for the first time – he was far too poverty-stricken to have actually heard them in their late Seventies/early Eighties heyday.

"If you wanted to hear music in our town you had to play it," he told *Rip* magazine. "We didn't have a record store in town. We were little kids, and we had no way to get money – our parents were counting every dime, you know? So I started saving like crazy. It took me a while, but I learned to play guitar, and then I finally got one."

School was a drag. From the Ninth Grade, Billie and Mike went to nearby Pinole Valley High, along with 1700 other students.

Today, as then, the school's predominant focus is "on literacy, math and motivating students to take the testing program seriously. Pinole Valley recently instituted a new discipline and attendance policy that is showing positive results also," a mission statement that seems somehow at odds with the impression we have of two listless teenagers wandering the corridors listening to a host of new musical discoveries, killing time until they could get home and plug in. Suffice to say, attendance and excessive hours spent poring over the books did not rank high on their list of priorities – Billie Joe later claimed that had he not made it in music he would probably have become a swimming pool cleaner or TV repair man, neither of which call for an abundance of academic qualifications. Teenage life is inordinately complex and troublesome but an electric guitar is extremely simple. You turn it on and you hit it a bit. Keep hitting and sooner or later something good will occur.

As is often the way, a valuable source of musical input came from an older sibling, in this case Billie's sister, who turned him on to cool new underground bands like Minneapolis' The Replacements, whose ragged *Sorry Ma, Forgot To Take Out The Trash* album she bought and which he consequently scratched to pieces from over-use, much to her displeasure. At the age of thirteen, Billie was invited along by Anna to his first gig, fellow Minneapolis band Husker Du, who were one of the few worthwhile punk-influenced, alternative bands to gain wider critical appeal in the barren mid-Eighties. But at the last minute they were unable to get transport to and from the show and Billie Joe missed out on seeing the legends.

The bands that Billie – and by proxy, Mike – were discovering in their mid-teens were to have a lasting influence on them, many of whom they still name-check to this day. Not only bands like The Ramones, Minor

Threat and Dead Kennedys, but also those big rock bands of the early-to-mid Eighties, like Van Halen and Motley Crue, who stood diametrically opposed to the ethics, ideals and production bands of the punks, but are nothing less than walking gods when you're fourteen years old. Naturally, their interest in all things rock lead to the appropriate and numerous teenage sartorial *faux pas*.

"The first thirteen years of my life I was fashion disaster after fashion disaster," laughed Billie Joe. "I would wear third generation hand-me-downs, not even from my family, but from my friends. I had the same school shirt for three years in a row. I had a haircut once that made me look like Richard Marx. A mighty bad mullet."

Billie Joe's favourite song at the time was Generation X's youthful London street-fighting anthem 'Kiss Me Deadly', first released in 1980. "It embodied passion and rebellion," he said. "It was punk rock, but at the same time it was really sweet too. Generation X was the very first punk band I ever got into and that song was instrumental in me wanting to start a band."

They also spent many hours in Billie Joe's room making tapes and pretending to be radio DJs spinning their favourite songs. It was always music from a young age. Billie Joe in particular was a big fan of the British bands of the Sixties like The Who, who played with a kind of proto-punk fury and The Kinks, who seamlessly weaved together lasting melodies with evocative stories about their lives around them (and in doing so, inspired punk bands like The Clash, The Jam and Generation X). So Billie Joe was a young punk, but he was a melody junkie too. It was this combination of punk's raw energy and an ear for writing instantly memorable songs that were the two prevailing influences in the material that he began penning – and which he tried to bring to life in the band he and Mike decided to form.

Cool - *adjective 1. of or at a fairly low temperature. 2. keeping one from becoming too hot. 3. unfriendly or unenthusiastic. 4. free from anxiety or excitement: he kept a cool head. 5. (of jazz) restrained and relaxed. 6. fashionably attractive or impressive. 7. excellent. 8. used to emphasize a specified large amount of money: a cool 50 million quid.*

Frank Wright II flew helicopters in Vietnam.

When the conflict ended, he decided to move with his wife Linda, a housewife, and their two kids to the Mendocino mountains to experience a bit of seclusion and solitude and to live life without feeling like Armageddon was on their doorstep; a stress-free, back-to-the-land type existence. Wright moved his family near to the town of Willets up in the mountains where their closest neighbour was a mile away. Named after Hiram Willets, it was a small rural country north of Santa Rosa just off US Highway 101, a town rich in old West history set against a backdrop of rolling hills and picturesque ranches that, like Rodeo, was born out of the mid-19th century industrial boom when pioneering ranchers settled. Mendocino County is also considered hippy country, whose sense of seclusion and numerous beauty spots drew many people to relocate there from the larger cities in search of a classic Thoreau-csque agrarian lifestyle – mainstream drop-outs chasing an American idyll. Or perhaps these other people came because Mendocino is great weed-growing country, the mountains well known for playing host to numerous marijuana farms that famously manufactured product of an extremely high quality, and abundant enough to keep half of San Francisco high for months?

In relocating his family to Mendocino, Wright was pursuing a more relaxed lifestyle free of the many added worries that come with raising kids in a city. But one thing he possibly didn't consider was the boredom factor. Willets, California, offered little in the way of social interaction for his two kids, not least for his youngest child Frank Edwin Wright III, a naturally hyperactive kid with a seemingly limitless supply of energy and natural sense of mischievous – and a face to match. Perfect drummer material.

"It was mind-numbing," remembers Frank Wright III, better known as Green Day's future drummer Tre Cool. "I'd just walk around this huge mountain. It was complete wilderness."

Though the Wright's nearest neighbour was over a mile away, that neighbour turned out to be someone who would influence the young Frank, giving him not only a profession for life but a new name too. The neighbour was Lawrence Livermore, a local thirty-something punk rock fan-cum-fanzine writer and musician. Frank Wright II had helped build a number of houses in the area, including his own family home (complete with an out-house toilet) and Livermore's abode. Being in relatively close proximity and with little else to do, the eleven-year-old Frank Jr. would sometimes hang-out at Livermore's house listening to his cool record collection. It was here that he first played drums on a kit that belonged to a friend of Livermore's who had recently moved to

Brazil, abandoning the drum set in the process.

"I was like, 'Hey, let me try out the drums!'" he remembers in *Drummer*. "So immediately, they take away my cymbals because I was bashing and thrashing them. I had to play a lot of fast punk rock right away – that was the beginning of my drumming days."

So enthusiastic was Wright to hit things that Livermore locked the cymbals away in a cupboard and only returned them one at a time over the following weeks. The skinny kid was already making enough noise in his house without the full set.

When Livermore was looking for someone to play drums for his punk band, in which he played guitar, he asked Frank – less than half his age – if he wanted to jam with him. He asked another young local known only as 'Kain Kong' to play bass. He too had never played his instrument before. All three were to share vocal duties.

"I'd go over there on my bike, or walk over, and I'd practice with those guys," remembers Tre. "We'd play 'I Want To Love You But You Make Me Sick', 'Don't Cry For Me Nicaragua', 'My Mom Smokes Pot', 'Fuck Religion' and 'Typical American Fucked Up Kid'. From that moment on I was a punk rocker."

"One of the greatest (and some say, worst) legacies of the punk movement was the notion that anyone can be in a band," Livermore writes on the excellent www.lookoutrecords.com. "Even me, as it turned out. When I formed [that band] I quickly became the laughing stock of the remote mountain community ..." The Lookouts were punks and therefore quite undeterred. They already felt like outsiders anyway.

It was also around this time that Livermore jokingly bestowed upon Frank his new name, Tre Cool – as in *trés* (very) cool – that would stick with him to this day. Goofy, yes, but kind of appropriate. Here was a slight adolescent who was quickly mastering an instrument and able to socialise with adults on an equal level. With a squeaky all-American voice he was funny too, capable of doing scathing impressions and just generally bringing life and quick-witted humour to any situation. He has since legally changed his name by deed poll to Tre Cool.

The Lookouts began playing locally and making recordings. Like Billie Joe and Mike over in Rodeo, Tre was influenced by the best that punk rock had to offer and his musical education continued apace. He picked up tips by watching bands like Canadian punks No Means No: "We played a gig with them and I stood right behind him and watched him [the drummer] just go off. The guy's incredible. It was so tight and so powerful."

Young Tre soon also began to play regularly at school.

"I was in sixth grade and the teacher would come and pick me up every day to go and play with the High School band," he said in *Drummer*, "who I was playing with two years previous to going there because none of the High School-ers could play jazz. I was the only kid in town who could play jazz and she wanted some in the repertoire. So I was sitting there and I was only fourteen and there are these guys with moustaches sitting there, [saying] 'damn!', you know, with a cowbell or a tambourine, like, 'I want to play'. The same guys used to give me tonnes of shit and mess with me and stuff. It was, like, fuck off!"

In January 1987, when their drummer was still only fifteen, the Lookouts released their debut twelve-inch/cassette single, 'One Planet One People' on Larry's newly formed Lookout! label. On their debut the trio crammed twenty-two tracks into a little less than thirty minutes of music. Over the next two years they also went on to put out further records, including the eleven-track *Spy Rock Road* album, named after the road in which Livermore and Wright lived, and keeping the local theme going, the four-track 'Mendocino Homeland' single [Their later song 'Kick Me In The Head' (featured on Lookout!'s seminal 1992 *Can Of Pork* compilation) would also feature Billie Joe Armstrong on guitar].

The Lookouts were certainly an odd looking band, the first impression being they were three young kids – albeit one who had just had an accelerated and premature growth spurt – having fun, until people looked closer. Live, they were getting better, though not everyone agreed.

"The abuse wasn't limited to the verbal variety," remembers Livermore. "There was the matter of the legendary black eye I received when a local lunkhead tried to physically restrain us from playing at a town dance, a black eye I wore proudly at our first record release party at Gilman Street the next night."

Tre cool indeed.

The Lookouts' set at the time also included cover versions of the Rolling Stones' 'Last Time', Bob Dylan's 'Baby Blue', the Tre Cool-penned diatribe 'The Mushroom Is Exploding' and a cover version of short-lived post-Operation Ivy band Downfall's scene anthem 'North Berkeley'.

"There were a lot of $2 shows, $3 shows," Tre told *Kerrang!* magazine's Ian Winwood. "There were a lot of parties, a lot of warehouse gigs. I knew Dave Dictor the singer from MDC [Millions Of Dead Cops], and I used to crash in his room whenever he was on tour. The place was called the Rathouse. Everyone had a fanzine, everyone was in a band. My parents were either very brave or very stupid for letting me hang out with all these interesting, sexually diverse, drug-happy people."

The young drummer was certainly leading an existence of contradictions, a duel identity that he carried off with aplomb. On the one hand he was a precocious talented punk who was something of loveable mascot in the local scene, on the other his natural gift of the gab lead him to be elected class president by his peers – a position not traditionally reserved for hyperactive, quick-witted young punks.

There's one other well-known story from about this time that could only be corroborated by the select few. In later life Tre has claimed that he lost a testicle as a child in an unfortunate unicycle incident. Legend has it that he was riding it on a stage at school when he overshot and landed on the cycle itself, pushing a scrotum up inside him, rendering it somewhat useless. While the incident might explain a voice that sounds like it's perpetually stuck in that hormonal minefield of those teenage months when the male tone and pitch changes at will, it is also magnificently absurd. It might merely be born out of one too many tedious press interviews – an answer, perhaps, to an inquisitive journalist pondering the origins of his peculiar voice. But then again, this *is* Tre Cool, no ordinary man …

All good musical movements need an epicentre, whether physical or spiritual, and for the punk rock scene that emerged in the Nineties, it was 924 Gilman Street. That most of the major punk bands who emerged to cash-in on this resurgence missed out on the venue's glory days of 1987-1989 is irrelevant. Gilman became a by-word for punk rock credibility and a model for that do-it-yourself ethic intrinsic to the scene.

When, in 1986, *Maximum Rock 'n' Roll* magazine founder and editor Tim Yohannan took over 924 Gilman Street, it was practically out of necessity. There simply were few places in Berkeley-Oakland for punk bands to play and hang out unmolested. There had been the Minor Rock, The Twilight Zone and The Farm in San Francisco, but none catered exclusively for punk as a lifestyle and political choice. There was the Berkeley Square, but that was more a traditional rock club. Rock meant bands who sounded like Winger or Motley Crue. Most of the bigger touring punk bands would play San Francisco, which was accessible, but still meant a long bus ride into the city. At the time there was a divide between the hipper San Franciscans and the kids in East Bay, who they joked came from 'East Berlin' – the implication being that the East Bay was far grimmer and more culturally deprived than San Francisco. Which, let's face it, it was. But it was also for this reason that the punk fans in the East Bay decided to get organised.

The idea for opening an all-ages venue to cater for punk rock bands in Berkeley had been floating around for years. Gradually though people came together through a series of flyers and meetings. In April 1986 a venue was discovered at 924 Gilman Street, a relatively run-down industrial area located about a mile-and-a-half from the North Berkeley train station and four blocks from Highway 80. It had previously been a cane furniture shop and was now an empty space with dirty walls and a couple of basketball hoops. Perfect. A lease on the building was agreed upon.

For the building to be usable, the plumbing had to be replaced and wheelchair access made available. Renovation began, utilizing the labour of a number of punk kids who had a few skills and plenty of enthusiasm. The stage was in one corner of the room and a small make-shift bar erected nearby. After eight months of paying for rent and renovations and receiving the necessary permits from the surprisingly supportive Berkeley city council (though not that surprising, given its liberal history) 'The Gilman Street Project', as it was now known, passed health, safety and fire inspections and held its very first show on December 31, 1986.

Gilman was founded on simple, basic principles of equality and respect – things that seemed to be lacking within certain areas of music, or indeed the wider American society at large. So that meant no racism, sexism or homophobia – within the music or the clientele. There was also a 'no alcohol and drugs' policy due to licensing and legal stipulations though smoking was allowed, as the venue was technically categorized as a private members club (which brings to mind misleading images of Victorian gents puffing on after-dinner cigars in the drawing room ...). Everyone involved in Gilman, bar the security who themselves were also members of the punk scene, worked voluntarily [for no pay], the reason being that those who broke up fights and enforced the no drinking policy were getting the rough end of the deal. With no alcohol on the premises, paying customers could instead gorge themselves on Hansen's soda and candy bars.

Even today, two decades on, the venue is run democratically, where all ideas and suggestions have to be presented at a members' meeting. For example, if a newspaper is doing an article on the venue it must first be approved, then delegated out to a volunteer to liaise with the journalist and best represent the thoughts of the collective.

While the principles and political methodology behind Gilman ironically owed a lot to the communal approach of hippies in the Sixties, there were specific reasons for taking a stance over certain issues. The hardcore punk scene, lest we forget, had gone underground and was a place where fascism could fester, where violence could rear its ugly head in the pit and where a certain sense of self-policing was required to make sure each show didn't end in a riot and consequently give the press another reason to brand the punks as sub-human wastoids, as they had a few years earlier after shows by the likes of Dead Kennedys, The Germs and Black Flag, which saw riots and running battles with police in San Francisco and particularly LA.

Punk, for the most part, was a community and Gilman's aim was to reflect that in the way it was run, rather than its rhetoric.

Shows at the club only took place on Fridays, Saturdays and Sundays, with membership meetings taking place twice every month. Any card carrying member was invited, the idea being that the people who supported the club – the paying punters and the bands – were as much a part of it as those who opened it in the first place.

"A lot of the whole idea behind Gilman is the concept of having a community-type place where instead of saying *they* don't allow smoking in this room or whatever, and people go there saying *they*, meaning someone higher-up at the club or whatever, I'd like to hear people saying *we*," explained Jesse Michaels of Gilman Street band Operation Ivy on the exhaustive site, www.operationivy.com

Livermore agrees: "I saw so many kids who'd never had the nerve to try anything on their own before, who'd been rejected and abused by their families, who didn't have much of anything going for them, and who within the mini-world created at Gilman were able to break out of their desperation, to start bands, to start 'zines and record labels ... to make it a welcome place."

The music coming out of Gilman was different from a lot of the metal-leaning, macho hardcore of the day, with some of the regular bands opting to play a poppier brand of punk or throwing in some ska. This approach owed just as much to the punk and new wave bands of the late Seventies as it did the more brutal hardcore which followed.

Perhaps inevitably, given their love of punk and increasingly peripatetic lifestyle, Mike and Billie Joe were attracted to what was going on, after Bill's sister Anna first took him there in his mid-teens. Here was a place that could have been made for him and his ebullient pal. In allowing its regulars access to cool music, Gilman was soon playing host to bands inspired by what they had seen there. Equally as important, there were no hassles from cops, patronising bar-tenders requesting ID or any of that nonsense a thrill-seeking fourteen-year-old has to suffer. And not only that but it was in Berkeley. Not quite on the doorstep of Rodeo, but near enough.

They were sold, and the pair and their friends were soon regularly attending shows by popular local bands such as MDC and Gang Green but also by a host of others like Nasal Sex, Rabid Lassie, Sewer Trout and BO, all memorable for their names, if not for their contribution to world music.

Today Gilman Street has reached almost semi-mythical status and can now be mentioned in the same breath as key punk venues like CBGB's and Max's Kansas City in New York or The 100 Club and The Roxy in London. But it wasn't entirely unique. Punk in the Eighties was kept alive by similar such venues across the States, though few were as ideologically maintained as Gilman. As Dallas Denvey, singer with local band Sweet Baby explained: "Kids would say 'Is this anything like Gilman Street?' and we'd always tell them 'Hell, this is better!'"

The cold graffiti'd reality of it was that, as a small space it could only ever hold so many people – no more than a busy neighbourhood bar, or maybe one of LA's smaller rock clubs. Nevertheless, for a good while at least, being associated with Gilman was a fast-track to cult-dom. It was what was going on in and around the venue that struck a chord with the legions of fans of a type of music adrift from mainstream culture – and adrift from its own forefathers. Thanks to endless discussions played out in the underground fanzine world, Gilman came to represent punk's salvation in the late Eighties when a band was deemed a success if they sold in the thousands, rather than the millions as it would be ten years later. The option of 'selling out' had yet to raise its head – it simply didn't warrant any real contemplation.

"It was kind of neat when our van's transmission blew out and stuff," said Billie Joe of the venue's growing reputation. "It was cool that we were in a hole, because all we cared about was that we were really tight as a band and we got to play a lot of basements and rec halls and squats for beer, and kids would get together in the kitchens and the minute you mentioned Gilman Street or Lookout! you'd have this total connection."

But really Gilman's relevance lies in its legacy.

"Some nights there'd be a couple of hundred people there and you'd have a great gig to remember," said Billie Joe. "Some nights there'd be hardly anyone so you'd just have a great night hanging out with your friends, drinking beer. It really was a special time."

Perhaps more importantly to the myth, Gilman would soon practically have an in-house record label to document the sounds being created there week in and week out and the closest of ties with a magazine (*Maximum Rock 'n' Roll*) who could proselytise and chronicle what was going on in the East Bay on an international label. Rock music is full of such hot-beds of activity, whose word of mouth reputation grows off the back of some of its successful graduates or its place in a time gone by. Ever been to CBGB's? I have – it was and still is a shit-hole. But that's half the charm. It's what went on within those four walls that is important, not the faded décor and puddles of piss in the bathroom stalls, though the stench of Seventies punk is still thrillingly palpable.

And what went on in Gilman was a series of life-affirming – maybe even life-saving – shows that galvanised its participants into action. It gave them good memories of drinking and singing and dancing, of forming friendships and having a place in which to belong. Gilman may have been founded on the principal ideals of political dissent, equality and a sense of unbuttoned liberalism that's synonymous with Berkeley, yet primarily it was about the *fun*. This was, after all, essentially a punk rock youth club whose members averaged about fifteen-to-sixteen years of age, who cared less about personal politics and more about music and cutting loose amongst people far more tolerant to eccentricities than the usual cliques that Billie, Mike and many like them encountered in high school.

"I won a slam-dancing competition there!" Mike once joked. "The prize was a *Saturday Night Fever* album and the right to play guitar on stage with Sticky, this really terrible punk group. Gilman Street was my high school."

A high school quite unlike any other.

In a typical display of Gilman networking, it was during the spring of

1988 that two sets of friends just out of their teens came together to get their own thing going. Guitarist Tim 'Lint' Armstrong and bassist Matt McCall (real name Matt Freeman – 'McCall' was a joke name given to him by Lint in homage to TV cop show *The Equalizer*) had been friends since kindergarten in Albany, California, the former having already played in Berkeley ska band Basic Radio. They were typical working-class, Oakland street kids who loved their punk, hardcore, ska and reggae equally. Singer Jesse Michaels and drummer Dave Mello were also buddies. Michaels, whose father was a published author, was a sensitive young man with a strong social conscience who was writing lyrics for songs full of youthful idealism while commentating on the scene around him. He had previously played in local band, S.A.G., who later evolved into Chrimpshrine. Naming themselves Operation Ivy, the four friends started playing together, quickly amassing a set of hi-energy songs based around Lint's scratchy, skanky guitar and Jesse's raspy, heartfelt vocals that called for unity and positivity in a time when the scene was increasingly dominated by macho hardcore bands with thrash metal leanings or young exponents displaying a general apathetic artistic conservatism.

"Jesse Michaels could step onstage and take over a room just standing there," Billie Joe would later tell journalists. "He had charisma and a great sense of melody ..."

Operation Ivy played music you could dance to, a celebratory sound made by and for the kids. It possessed the same galvanised energy and bullshit-free outlook as great early Eighties hardcore bands like Minor Threat and 7 Seconds, but threw in reggae and ska-inspired bass lines to give an added edge of musicality. It wasn't the first time that a white punk band had dabbled in Jamaican music – British bands like The Clash and The Ruts had got there in the late-Seventies and the attendant Two-Tone Records scene had produced highly influential bands like The Specials and The Beat shortly afterwards – but this was more or less the first time it was done the American way, and with such gritty ferocity. Along with The Mighty Mighty Bosstones, who came out of the Boston bar scene and merged punk, hardcore and ska to similar effect, Operation Ivy went on to influence many of the ska-punk-skate bands of the Nineties, and heavily informed Lint and Matt's later band, Rancid.

But for the moment Operation Ivy were moving quickly. They played their first show – at Gilman, obviously – in April 1987, opening for thrash-punks Millions Of Dead Cops and Gang Green and found immediate favour among their peer group.

"When we play, the high energy of our music comes out the most clearly," said singer Jesse Michaels during an early Operation Ivy interview, defining the band's impact – and a suggestion of the bands who would follow in their wake. "It's not like a dramatic thing," he told *Maximum Rock 'n' Roll*, "we're not deliberately trying to look good, it's just direct communication of the vibe of our music. It depends a lot on the audience but generally we completely get into playing live, emotionally and physically ... taking music and playing it at a down-to-earth level which is not that common a thing. I think that is happening a lot more with some of the bands I've seen coming out lately. "

"I don't remember exactly how I met [Tim Armstrong]," writes Larry Livermore. "I went away for three months, and when I got back the first thing I heard was that there was this great new band at Gilman called Operation Ivy and that they were playing that night. I went inside and watched one of the most amazing shows I'd ever seen, and when Tim got off stage and asked me what I thought, I said, 'Let's make a record.'" [For more on Livermore and his label, see *www.lookoutrecords.com*]

The outcome was Op Ivy's first official recordings (they'd already had two songs from their first demo on *Maximum Rock 'n' Roll* compilation, *Turn It Around*) and a newly-formed record label, Lookout!, on which to release it. Lookout! grew out of a magazine of the same name that Larry Livermore founded in 1984. Primarily containing local news and political and environmental issues in and around Mendocino, *Lookout!* gradually started to run more pieces about the East Bay punk scene centred around the Gilman collective. Livermore would attend the club every week, either as fan, volunteer or with his band The Lookouts and by 1987 was so convinced by the new music that he was hearing, and the general sense of occasion of it all, that he and friend David Hayes decided that releasing records was the next logical step. Like so many punk labels before it, Lookout! was born out of its surroundings and created for little other reason than to document what was going on around them; an attempt to capture a moment in time on cheap perishable plastic.

In the first month of 1988, Livermore put out four EP releases in quick succession by Chrimpshrine, Isocracy, Corrupted Morals and the 'Hectic EP' by Operation Ivy, recorded two months earlier.

A combination of hardcore and ska played at lightning speed the 'Hectic' EP still stands up as an invigorating work, a short, sharp blur of hormonal energy; a record to rouse the rabble.

Upon its release the band embarked on a six week US tour and left a trail of ratty punk kid converts in their wake. So keen to avoid accusations of being anything other than the real deal, Operation Ivy recorded their debut album at Gilman Street shortly after the release of 'Hectic', but scrapped recordings when the acoustics in the high-ceilinged room proved not to work in their favour. Instead they went to a regular studio with engineer Kevin Army and recorded *Energy*, their one and only album and easily one of the finest punk records of modern times.

Energy crammed in anthem after anthem. It was a ragged record powered along by its own urgency — and all the better for it. In songs such as 'Bad Town', 'Vulnerability' and 'Jaded' there lay the same youthful zeal of hardcore bands like Minor Threat and Youth Brigade but updated into a scratchy ska-punk hybrid. Matt Freeman's melodic, reggae-inspired bass lines added a danceability that set the band apart from their punk peers, while Jesse Michael's lyrics consistently retained the prophetic edge of a street-smart kid with a head-full of ideas. Over the course of nineteen energised songs, Operation Ivy had created a sound as distinctive and invigorating as The Clash or The Specials and an album for their contemporaries to live by. The East Bay punk scene had its own 'White Riot', 'Ghost Town' and 'In My Eyes' rolled into one – and even better, no-one outside of the scene even knew about it.

"I hope we keep playing parties and we stay in touch with what's going on 'cause a lot of bands forget their roots and they start getting soft and selling out," said Lint (aka Tim) of their early ambitions on www.operationivy.com. "I hope maybe three years down the line that we still have our attitude that we have right now and that we still give our money back to Gilman. Wherever we play, I hope we don't lose that."

Operation Ivy were grass roots through and through. Their following was small, but their influence is still being felt today. Asked by *Maximum Rock 'n' Roll* what their immediate ambitions were, they said "a warm meal every day." It was all they could hope for. In its first year, *Energy* sold two thousand copies, a respectable amount for a band that formed only months before it was recorded. It was considered a definite success by Livermore and all concerned.

But despite being considered Gilman's house band, it had taken more than Operation Ivy and their followers to make a scene. Gilman was a breeding ground for other new young bands to play their first shows.

Bands like Isocracy, Chrimpshrine and Mr. T Experience, The Lookouts, Surrogate Brains, Blatz and countless others, all collectively attracting a small but enthusiastic following of local kids.

Kids like Billie Joe Armstrong.

The first time Billie Joe attempted to see Operation Ivy, at the age of fifteen, he was refused entry for being underage (not all venues were as welcoming to non-profitable, non-drinkers as Gilman). When one of the members of the band heard that a young fan wasn't allowed in, he came out and personally escorted him into the show. It was the courteous thing to do and a basic display of camaraderie and good manners; such minor incidents separate the punk scene from the wider world of mainstream rock and pop music with their quasi-religious overtones, where artists are placed on a pedestal, worshipped from afar and can act like a film diva on a bad day and be adored all the more. Remember, this was 1987, when punk was buried deep underground – no punk bands had hit the Top 40 for at least five years – and stars like Axl Rose or Vince Neil were about as cool as it got, and the biggest artists of the year were omnipresent untouchables like Madonna, Prince and Michael Jackson who seemingly existed only on celluloid and paper. Operation Ivy, like The Clash before them, made a point of treating their fans as equals – to do anything else would have been faking it anyway. At Gilman, the crowd was pretty much made up of performers, scenesters, fanzine writers or next year's bands taking notes from the back. To act like a rock star would have been anathema. Getting to not only meet your favourite band but to see first hand that they are just like you is a big thing and the night that Operation Ivy sneaked him into their show left an indelible impression on Billie Joe Armstrong. Not only was the music killer, but these guys were cool in the very best possible way. It was enough to convince him – as if he had needed convincing – that punk rock was a community where freaks, outcasts and outsiders were most welcome, and that it would be a helluva lot of fun to pursue his own band. Maybe one day they might even get to play Gilman. Imagine.

"The teenage experience of rock and roll is unique," remarks Jesse Michaels on www.operationivy.com, "and as much as I would like to, I don't think I will ever be as completely swept away as I was when I was sixteen and first hearing Minor Threat and The Bad Brains."

Though only selling a moderate amount of records, Operation Ivy had increasingly become the focus of the East Bay scene and as such were experiencing pressures. They were playing shows that they just weren't appearing to be enjoying and the performances sometimes suffered as a result. Not every gig was amazing as the history books might report.

"It just got too crazy," recalls Matt Freeman. "We started off as this little garage band, and then we got really popular, really quick. We had to start dealing with all sorts of crazy stuff. Before, if we showed up it was, 'Great, here they are', but later, if we didn't show up for some reason, it would be a tragedy ... I think the bigger you get the more pressures are put upon you. We were all young and just didn't want to do it like that anymore."

"We were playing this show in Fresno, and Larry came along," he recounted in *Goldmine* magazine. "I remember quite specifically him telling me, in the middle of a Californian desert, that Op Ivy was going to be one of those bands, like the Dead Kennedys, that would keep selling more records after we break up. I said, 'Whatever, Larry. I think you did too much acid in the hippie days, dude.' You've got to understand that back then it wasn't like it is now; major labels offering you millions of dollars, all these bands coming out of nowhere and getting contracts. When Larry was telling me that, I didn't believe him. But he's since proved me wrong ..."

By the time *Energy* was released, the united front of Operation Ivy had disintegrated amid disagreements when, in 1989, Jesse Michaels announced he didn't want to play in the band anymore. By the nature of the band, there was no question of them carrying on without their charismatic frontman and they played their last show on March 20, 1989, in front of a crowd rumoured to be pushing six hundred people in a three hundred capacity venue. True to their nature Operation Ivy actually played a less formal, more intimate show the following day at their friend Eggplant's house, marking the true chronological demise of the band. They'd played over 180 shows in a little over two years, many of them at impromptu parties. Perhaps because their music was so youth-orientated, like teenage acne or your first kiss, Operation Ivy were destined to be short-lived.

After Operation Ivy, Michaels went on to explore various spiritual and musical pursuits, including doing charity work in Nicaragua, before becoming a Zen Buddhist monk for a period in 1992 ("From this experience I learned the deep spiritual truth that it is cold as shit at four a.m. when you're wearing a silly robe," he writes).

Michaels returned to music with the rootsy-ska songwriting outlet Common Rider in the late Nineties (check out their excellent *Last Wave*

Rockers on Lookout!). Bassist MacCall briefly joined MDC. Despite playing for a while in Downfall (with Matt and drummer Dave Mello) and forming the Dance Hall Crashers (who went on to enjoy their own success without him), Tim Armstrong went through some tough personal times, subsequently well-documented in interviews and songs. Without the focus of Operation Ivy in his life, his drinking escalated and he'd ended up on the streets of Oakland, resorting to a stint staying in a Salvation Army shelter; the bottom of the social ladder. After Matt helped straighten out his childhood buddy by getting him into AA, the pair formed Rancid in December 1991 with Gilman Street regular Brett Reed on drums – and the rest is history.

But Operation Ivy prematurely splitting had done little to harm their sales. In fact, like the Sex Pistols before them, splitting up and leaving only one solid, unquestionable work behind undoubtedly worked in their favour. When a band no longer exists the true mythologizing can begin. By the time *Energy* was first released on CD, word had spread right around the world and sales picked up – as Matt Freeman puts it: "If after Op Ivy I'd have gone to some island or Antarctica or something, stayed there for five years, and then come back out, I probably would have been in shock."

I remember being loaned a copy of *Energy* in 1990 as a fourteen-year-old skateboarder. The music hit me and my friends immediately, a combination of all the things that had drawn us to punk in the first place: displacement, rebellion, energy and memorable choruses. You can see why by 1994 *Energy* was casually selling more copies each week than it had in its first year, with total sales figures now topping well over 500,000 worldwide. It was a great record that sold itself. With no advertising and little press beyond the fanzines like *Maximum Rock 'n' Roll* and *Flipside*, *Energy* somehow made it across the Atlantic and into the grubby hands of far-flung skate-punk scenes comprised of people like me and my grommet friends, always keen to hear the newest, rawest sounds. This was before skateboarding became truly commercial, before Tony Hawk and when Nirvana were an unknown garage band. Songs like 'Sound System', 'The Crowd' and future Green Day live favourite and album opener 'Knowledge' soundtracked a summer and spoke of another world, a scene thousands of miles away; it wasn't our world, but it was one in which we were interested.

To this day *Energy* is still one of my favourite and most listened to albums, yet I have never owned it on either CD or vinyl. All I have is one second-generation taped copy that's been played to death and passed on, or else broken down for a hundred teenage compilation tapes. Operation Ivy was a punk band in the traditional sense. Little did they know that their one album would directly inspire a local band and would change the way they thought about their music forever. A band that, for better or worse, would irrevocably divide the scene.

"How important were Operation Ivy to Lookout! and the whole East Bay scene?" ponders Livermore on the official website lookoutrecords.com. "I kind of doubt we'd even be here without them. Tim and Matt went on to form Rancid and gain even more fame, but they never forgot their roots … Operation Ivy came and went with the fleeting incandescence of a comet that will remain emblazoned forever on the consciousness of anyone who ever had the privilege of witnessing them in their glory. They stand, and undoubtedly always will, among the handful of bands that truly matter."

But all this was only just happening ...

In 1987 Billie Joe and Mike were now attending John Swett High in Crockett, a school whose catchment area also took in Rodeo. Numbering just over six hundred pupils, it was relatively small for a high school, though Billie Joe has since claimed that one of his classes had up to eighty pupils in it!

"We are extremely proud of our former students that have and continue to make large contributions to society as a whole," reports the John Swett High website, "including celebrities and athletes such as Super Bowl and Jets/Broncos Kicker Jim Turner, former Gold Rush Cheerleader and current Raiderette Shannon Burgess, action movie hero Aldo Ray (*Green Berets*), and rockers Billie Joe Armstrong and Mike Dirnt of the ground-breaking band, Green Day."

When not idling around on Tight Wad Hill, the hang-out overlooking John Swett's football pitch that later inspired the song of the same name, the pair decided to get semi-serious about their music and enlisted the services of a friend and fellow punk scenester, John Kiffmeyer, to play drums.

Kiffmeyer was a couple of years older than the cherub-cheeked Billie and his street-wise childhood pal and had already left home. A good-looking, fresh-faced guy, he had acquired the suitably cool/dumb nickname of Al Sobrante. The story goes that he fell while out running one day and somehow temporarily knocked himself out. When he awoke it was in front of a sign saying, 'Welcome to El Sobrante, California'. In his confusion he mis-read the sign as saying 'Welcome Al Sobrante, to California', and when he relayed the story a new name was taken on thereafter. The band likewise christened themselves Sweet Children: the tongue-in-cheek name was settled upon partly because Billie Joe had written a song of the same name, and partly as a sarcastic pre-emptive strike to would-be critics thinking of patronising the three fifteen-year-olds. Sweet Children? In their drainpipe trousers, battered sneakers and DIY haircuts, hardly.

Kiffmeyer fitted in well with the pair and over the course of the band's formative years certainly helped shape their sound. He was a smart, interesting guy with a similar sense of humour and a strong sense of punk rock suss. Perhaps more than the other band members, it was Kiffmeyer who instilled a work ethic into their earliest recordings, preferring to record quickly and cheaply like so many of the bands they were into. His interest in drumming was due in part to a few sessions on mutual friend Tre Cool's kit at home in his garage.

The songs that Billie Joe presented to the band at early rehearsals were clearly influenced by the poppier end of punk – Ramones, Buzzcocks, Dickies etc – and by similar lyrical themes, but without being an overt rip-off of anyone in particular. It was helped by the fact that their singer had a pretty distinctive voice, an expressive, nasally tone that blended perfectly with Mike's backing harmonies that recalled the surfy-sounds of early Beach Boys – only Sweet Children preferred to sofa surf rather than get their toes wet.

They also jammed their way through their fair share of cover versions, a combination of Seventies punk and Sixties Britbeat played at pared-down Ramones velocity, sprinkled with infectious harmonies and with plenty of pastiche hair metal licks and classic rock diversions thrown in for fun. As Billie later related, it was played on equipment they had 'liberated' from a contemporary: "There was this kid who lived on the other side of town, and we knew that he always left his side door unlocked, so one day, a friend and I walked in, and walked out with his PA system. He never did find out who did it …"

Sweet Children were heavily influenced by the bands that they had seen at Gilman and the wider punk community at large. In fact, by the time *Dookie* broke in 1994, Billie Joe would admit to having been to very few shows beyond Gilman or the ones that he himself had played. One key early show had been at the age of fourteen when he and a couple of friends saw local bands Bloodrage and Transgressor at the On Broadway in San Francisco: "It was when speed metal was happening in the Bay Area," he told *Rolling Stone*. "Me and my friends went. We had never seen slam dancing, and all of us sat on the side, but this group of skinheads ran by and dove on us. My first show, and I just got dove [sic] on...." That was about it. His live musical upbringing was pretty much confined to the many, many bands he saw at Gilman.

Sometime during 1987, Sweet Children played their first show in the side lounge at Rod's Hickory Pit to thirty friends and the odd curious patron wondering what all the noise was about. Much fun was had by all, though few suspected they had just witnessed a performance by one of the biggest bands of the coming decade. In the meantime, they'd gone down well enough – and Rod had sold enough racks of ribs from his infamous hickory pit, presumably – for them to be asked back for a second show.

By the time he was playing in his first band, home life for Mike had become near unbearable. He'd had enough of the disruptions, so when his real mother announced she was moving fifty miles away to Santa Rosa, Mike decided to stay behind. So at the tender age of fifteen he decided to move out.

"I took my mom aside and said 'This is how it is. You have so much shit going on in your life, so if once every semester you ask me if I've done my homework and jump all over my case, that's not right'," remembers Mike. "'Have I failed yet? No. And I'm going to graduate if you stay off my back. The one time in your life you choose to have morals, and it's going to fuck me up. Don't play mom once a year. It doesn't fucking cut it.'"

The first place Mike was welcomed was the Armstrong household and he moved into a spare room shortly afterwards. It was no free ride though and he took on work as a cook at a diner to meet his rent and board of $250 per month. He later did some work installing fibreglass in local houses. By night they rocked.

Never a permanent domestic arrangement, Mike moved out of the Armstrong's to live in a building with a group of fellow punks. Juggling school obligations, a part-time job and playing in the band was hard work, particularly without a parent around to supervise him or sign his work-related absentee slips. In his senior year Mike's questionable attendance – understandable given his home life situation – led to him dropping a grade point as his average slipped from the A's and B's he used to get, down to C's, D's and beyond. Mike was intelligent and hard working, but life was getting in the way of his education. It's a credit to his determination and maturity that this particular sixteen year old finally graduated from high school while living out on his own and working a part-time job.

Sweet Children gigged wherever they could for whoever would have them. Getting shows wasn't easy when they were all five years below the legal drinking limit. The regular gig circuit – the venues that make most of their money from alcohol sales – was more or less out of bounds. So they played everywhere: house parties, garages, at school. Anywhere with a power supply.

It was during one of these shows that the band first met Larry Livermore. Popular legend has it that Sweet Children 'auditioned' for Livermore at a show in remote Willits, when in fact the more prosaic truth was he just happened to be there at the same time and nothing as formal as a showcase for his local punk label actually took place. Billie had, however, previously written to Livermore in an attempt to draw attention to his band.

"The real story is that they came up to play a show with my band, the Lookouts," said Livermore on the excellent web resource, www.greenday.net. "This was in 1988, when Tre was still in the Lookouts, and John Kiffmeyer [aka Al Sobrante] was drumming. It wasn't actually a real show, more of a party for a bunch of kids that went to high school with Tre. But because the weather was bad, and there was some snow on the roads up in the mountains where the party was supposed to be, almost none of the kids showed up. Even the kid whose house it was didn't show up, so the other kids ended up breaking into the house and setting up a generator, because there wasn't any other electricity. So Sweet Children ended up playing for literally five kids, and yet they played as if they were The Beatles at Shea Stadium. I mean they played their hearts out, and I was thinking, 'I don't care whether anyone buys it or not, I'm putting out a record by this band.'"

This gig was typical of the punk rock scene throughout the late Eighties and on into the Nineties, before the success of two quite different bands would push the sound, lifestyle and commercialisation of punk into whole new territories. These two bands were Nirvana and Green Day and such changes were still half a decade away – for now the respective trio was still an unwashed band of small-town freaks getting high on a satisfying cocktail of alcohol, weed and their own embryonic music. "Three gigs a month would just about cover the beer," Billie Joe has said.

But for better or for worse – and without wishing to look back on it all with rose-tinted spectacles – the punk scene that Sweet Children were first involved in centred around a loose network of bands, fanzines, promoters, when the *struggle* was half of the fun. Teenagers featured heavily, whether putting on shows in their own homes or playing in the bands and buying the records; the major label record industry at large rarely, if ever, encroached on what they were doing in small pockets across the land, from Alaska to El Paso to Washington DC. That the three-hundred-capacity Gilman Street venue had swiftly gained a reverential international reputation was indicative of the punk rock tour circuit at the time – there wasn't one. Or at least, it was buried so far underground away from the standard mid-circuit American venues monopolized by a few large companies that it was only those in the know who ... er ... knew what was going on. You had to search the music out yourself because MTV or *Rolling Stone* certainly weren't covering it.

So bands booked their own shows and got on with it themselves. The downside was that many of these ultimately disappeared into obscurity, leaving behind the odd classic record and memories of many life-affirming shows. Where today punk bands can break big on their debut, pre-1991 (when alternative music was seized upon, with Nirvana et al) bands strived for survival rather than success. Yet in doing so – in doing music for the *right* reasons – some of these bands flourished and laid the foundation for the pop-punk bands of the Warped Tour generation of the Nineties – The Offspring and NOFX being prime examples. On their *10 Years Of Fucking Up* video collection, NOFX can be seen playing numerous shows in the mid-to-late Eighties, outdoors in backwoods towns thousands of miles away from their San Francisco base, to crowds in double figures *if they were lucky*. From the back of their battered transit, the enthusiastic teens can also be seen calculating that they've amassed a $100 profit "and a really great time!" for a gruelling six-week US tour. The point being, unlike many of their predecessors or descendants, the punks of the late Eighties were not motivated by money or fame. To have been so would have been quite foolish and wholly unrealistic. Again, the beer was often enough of an incentive.

Transplant Sweet Children in there and you have a similar scenario for the years which followed. There's a story about the time Livermore put the band on in Garberville, a small hippy-ish town in Northern California, on a bill that also included Bumblescrump, Screeching Weasel, the Lookouts and Mr. T Experience, when our three young heroes got so drunk they couldn't even hold their guitars the right way round, Mike puking seconds before going on stage, and Billie forgetting the words to most of his own songs – yet still everyone agreed the band had blown away the competition. Afterwards they were driven off by a friend and ended up outside Larry's house up in the mountains where they slept in the van, too scared by Larry's barking dogs to dare get out the van for a piss. A common occurrence in the early days – the van thing, that is. The scary dogs were few and far between.

But before they could qualify as seasoned road dogs, the still-green Sweet Children achieved their first major goal when they made the leap from audience members to performers at their first ever show at Gilman Street on November 26, 1988. The place was jammed and the local kids who'd shown the balls to get up on stage were well received – enough to warrant an return invitation, which they obliged with a show a few weeks later, on New Year's Day 1989. They played again on February 11, 1989 supporting Chrimpshrine at that band's last ever show, along with the Mr T. Experience and the Well-Hung Monks opening.

"When I first started playing, Chrimpshrine was a big influence on me," says Mike. "The bass player, Pete Rypins, is a good friend of mine. We still play together, and he's a much better bass player than I am. It's my favourite band to this day. I suggest you check out their record."

As their reputation began to spread – thanks in no small part to their association with some of the burgeoning scene's more respected bands – Sweet Children were booked to play more shows in and around the East Bay and beyond. Other bands playing Gilman in those first couple of months of 1989 included some of the most popular underground acts of the next couple of years, including NOFX, Melvins, No Means No, Soulside (soon to be Girls Against Boys), No Use For A Name, Instead, Bad Religion, Victims Family and Samiam – an inspiring bunch of bands for any budding musicians to observe from close quarters, on a regular basis. Against such competition, during their salad days Sweet Children were learning quickly. To compete they had to be *tight*, and it was during these first few months that the musicians honed their skills into what is now their trademark – warm harmonies, a note perfect-cohesion yet the ability to go off on musical tangents or into sarcastic cover versions if they felt like it.

Punk rock was known for being sloppy, ramshackle, aggressive and quite often tuneless, but Sweet Children were the antithesis of such a wilfully anti-muso stance. They could play fast and loud but they could *play* and write songs too; they made unprofessionalism seem quite professional and were already way poppier than most of their contemporaries, whose music, while energised, had limited appeal. However, this being Gilman, that in itself could be an asset. Few knew it at the time, but Sweet Children were harbouring musical ambitions that extended beyond the scope of Gilman's four walls (though, ironically, from which they have deviated little, even with today's multi-million selling model of the band).

On February 24, the trio returned to play their fourth show at Gilman in three months, second on a bill that included Sweet Baby, Short Dogs Grow, Samiam and openers The Judy Blooms.

"I remember it was packed and sweaty and everyone was *really* young," says rock photographer and *Kerrang!* US correspondent Lisa Johnson, who saw Sweet Children early on. "I remember Tim [Armstrong] was really adamant that we get there because he told me they were really good and he knew I'd love them … I couldn't even see the stage. I think it was a Sunday afternoon, and it was one of their first shows. There was such a magical hysteria in the room. I didn't really know what was going on. A few years later, I found out that that had been an early Green Day we'd seen. I've never forgotten that show."

When not hanging out at Gilman, the streets of Berkeley belonged to Billie Joe, Mike and Al. After Rodeo, the place was a cosmopolitan, adventure playground, a rich-kid-hippy paradise – a cool place to make friends. A cool place to come of age. The town had always been a haven for liberal thinkers, one of the more morally relaxed places in America, yet with a strong tradition of protest and political dissidence – a lot of the action centres around the progressive Berkeley college campus. The Free Speech Movement began there, as did most of the much-televised footage of Vietnam protests in the Sixties. Because of its liberal reputation, agreeable climate, high rates of tourism and close proximity to poverty-addled Oakland, Berkeley also has a disproportionate amount of homeless people. Such events and statistics have prompted some to label it the 'People's Republic of Berkeley' or, more entertainingly, 'Berzerkley'.

In an interesting aside, the citizens of Berkeley declared the place a 'Nuclear Free Zone' in 1986, despite the University of California playing a major part in the development of nuclear weapons. Even more bizarre, today's nuclear warheads were designed in a lab managed by UC Berkeley called the Lawrence Livermore National Laboratory!

Long days and nights were spent hanging out in Berzerkley. To pick up new records Billie, Mike and Al would head down to Mod Lang Records (named after a song by Big Star) on University Avenue. For pizza there was Café Mediterraneum on Telegraph Avenue or for a dose of fine coffee, one of three Peet's Coffee & Tea caffeine Meccas. For after-hours drinks there was The Mallard Club in Albany, a former hang-out of Billie Joe's dad, complete with saloon-style doors, moose antlers on the wall, Fifties leatherette banquettes, pool tables and toilets painted in day-glo colours, and a particular favourite of the singer. And to pick up free shit there was always the Lookout! office.

Like-wise, over in San Francisco the Lookouts' Tre Cool, who like Billie, Mike and Al, had his musical education on a stage as much as the moshpit, was discovering new sights and sounds of city life.

"I lived a three-and-a-half hour drive away from San Francisco so I'd come down to the city and stay for a week. We'd do a few shows, crash on the front couch, eat government cheese. I wasn't too interested in drinking or smoking or anything like that. I grew up in the woods, see, so the thing I got high on was people. My life was really about living dollar to dollar."

The slacker tag that was erroneously pinned to Green Day some years later was clearly misleading – in 1989 they were active and highly visible in the Bay Area. They were self-managed and self-funded by what little money they made playing shows – it was time to move things on. As any budding star will confirm, the music is only half of it – now some good old-fashioned hard work was required. Having already conquered Gilman – or at least become one of its most promising and popular debutantes – the next natural move was a sidestep onto Lookout!, the organisation aurally documenting the East Bay's new crude music. Having been won over by the band's live show and willingness to *work* – a key factor in any label's consideration of a group – Larry Livermore was the first to invest some money in the teens. Their popularity at Gilman was reason enough for the band to make their recording debut.

In early 1989 Sweet Children got busy. They went into a local studio and recorded four tracks. As debuts go, the '1000 Hours EP' was full of youthful zest and lovelorn teenage yearnings. Being in a studio offered few problems, the band simply laying the songs down as they would live and adding some overdubs.

Right from their first recordings, Sweet Children's sound was already *there* though. What's alarming listening to '1000 Hours' now is not the relatively cheap-sounding production (without huge recording budgets almost all punk bands of the time sounded rough and ready), but the ability of three school kids who have been lucky enough – or talented, or a bit of both – to find their own unique voice early on. It's something they've held onto ever since.

Aficionados could no doubt spot the reference points on '1000 Hours', but they are just that – reference points as opposed to rip-offs. A song such as 'Dry Ice' would have been perfectly at home on either their *Dookie* or *Warning* albums, released five and ten years respectively after this auspicious debut. Lead song and title track '1000 Hours' was a driving, fuzzed-up pop song with infectious harmonies, lyrically unsophisticated perhaps, but then so is most pop music about girls; it doesn't make it any less worthy.

Billie Joe later said that '1000 Hours' was the Sweet Children song he was least pleased with: "Not only was it not for a band to play or to play as a band, it's just the sappiest song about a girl, to the point where it's like a bad John Hughes movie!"

Sweet Children were undeniably teenagers, and relatively sensitive ones at that hearing the same recurring motifs of unrequited and unattainable love given electro-shock treatment by self-assured, amplified melodies. The other big surprise listening to '1000 Hours' today is just how similar songs such as 'Only Of You' and 'The One I Want' were to then-huge artists like Tiffany, whose 1988 pop hit 'I Think We're Alone Now' mixed up the same themes of teen confusion, alienation and lost love and sense of melody as Billie Joe's first released song. They'd no doubt argue otherwise, but even at this early stage, Sweet Children were as musically close to the teeny bop pop stars of their day as they were to ska boys Operation Ivy or the crushing metal of Bay-area band Neurosis. Strip away the guitars and bad dentistry and you have a pop band. One who won't jump through the appropriate hoops like the other performing pop seals, granted, but musically just as refined, if not socially.

'1000 Hours' was released in April 1989 on Lookout! As if to confuse future record collectors, the seven-inch single was released on various suitably punk rock-coloured formats – six hundred copies on green vinyl, two hundred on red, two hundred on purple, one hundred on clear vinyl, one hundred on yellow and blue.

The front cover simply had the band's logo and the name of the record in clean black letters on a green background, while the back pictured a youthful-looking band hanging-out, a skewed baseball cap keeping Billie's thick curls in place. Aside from the song titles, the only information given was: "Billy [sic]: Guitar, Hat", "Mike: Bass, Hair", and "John: Drums, Bus." (I vaguely remember a copy of this record passing through my hands as a punk-hungry collector and fan a year or so after its release, though as a perpetually-broke teenager, I may well have traded it for something far less significant, like some beer perhaps.)

Meanwhile, when '1000 Hours' returned from the pressing plant the band continued their typically punk rock, hands-on approach. "We used to go into the Lookout! office to help them fold all the sleeves for the seven-inch records," says Mike. "Yeah, and I remember thinking, 'Man, if putting the sleeves together is this hard, then I'm fucked if I want do the rest of the work.' That's when I realised that I probably wouldn't want to run my own label full-time."

Unleashed into the critical punk underground, '1000 Hours' was a relatively decent-seller for Lookout!, though more importantly it helped spread the word amongst a stagnant wider punk scene that had its fair share of smelly gutter punks and increasingly clichéd hardcore crews.

Sweet Children were a breath of fresh, sugary air into punk – lightweight by comparison to some of their peers, yes, but instantly likeable, and certainly part of a lineage of bands indebted to The Kinks/The Ramones/The Clash. For many they were the pop band it was OK to like – if they dared admit it. Even at such an early stage, Sweet Children were capable of dividing opinion between those who felt they shouldn't like the band because their music displayed little in the way of textbook nihilism or an overtly anti-social stance (always strong selling points to kids sold on the myth of punk as an obnoxious, low IQ medium) and those who allowed the music to hit them on a gut level. And as uplifting dynamic high-speed pop music, Sweet Children's growing catalogue already seemed like a cut above their rivals. They delivered every time.

They weren't doing anything new of course. Punk and pop have always made for harmonious bedfellows, especially in the late Seventies when the sound was smoothed out into New Wave. In the late Eighties, hardcore, skateboarding culture and ska were also stirred into the mix Stateside, where a wave of bands realized that mindless shouting only has limited appeal – and a limited shelf-life. Key bands in the development of what would become punk pop (or skate-punk) in the Nineties included Bad Religion, who layered their pissed off, politicised sound with the smoothest of harmonies and whose guitarist Brett Gurewitz founded key label Epitaph; Bad Religion's spiritual nephews NOFX and The Offspring – both still shoddy sounding, but road-worthy, bands; and scholarly godfathers the Descendents, who wrote almost surfy, Beach Boys-inspired boy songs about girls and food and being young(ish). A plethora of lesser known but equally influential melody junkies to merge in the mid-to-late Eighties included The Queers, Ben Weasel's Screeching Weasel, Dag Nasty, Mr. T Experience, post-Descendents band All, Samiam, The Muffs, Big Drill Car and Chrimpshrine who all contributed in the evolution of a sound that moved away from the Sex Pistols or Minor Threat towards something far more palatable. And that was just in America.

Around the same time in the UK, bands such as Snuff, Senseless Things, Leatherface, Mega City Four, Goober Patrol and China Drum were simultaneously starting to explore something similar (similar enough to soon be sharing stages with Green Day) with the same influences of Husker Du, Replacements, Ramones *et al* as their US cousins but with a decidedly English bent. The common ground was that all these bands were influenced by hardcore, but didn't want to be hardcore bands. They wanted to write songs that people could *sing*.

So when our trio released '1000 Hours' it was hardly a groundbreaking sound. It did however put them – and Berkeley – on the map. Anyone who could divide opinion in a scene possibly lacking in some true heroes was worth watching. With songs this good this early on, success in the punk world was looking like a distinct possibility.

The trio played their final show as Sweet Children on April 1 – a fitting day to say goodbye to an era – when they joined a Gilman benefit show bill with Samiam, Stikky, Squeable Squabble (I'm not making this up) and Square Meal. Perhaps it was this show that made the band realise that their chosen moniker was a little too close to that of the other Gilman bands, a little too dumb. And, given their rapid musical progression, a little too adolescent-sounding.

Either way, they felt they had outgrown the band name by which they were becoming increasingly known. Now, between recording '1000 Hours' and its release – before word spread any further – was as good a time as any for a reinvention.

Their new name was the relatively innocuous-sounding Green Day. It was inspired by an offhand remark made by the character of Ernie on children's educational favourite *Sesame Street*, and struck a chord with the band, who applied it to mean their own couch-bound smoking sessions. Soon 'green day' became an in-joke referring to those many idle hours spent slouching around stoned with friends, talking about everything and nothing, laughing at kid's TV until you drool and finally only stirring to seek out some much-needed sugar at the local 7-11.

Green Day. It summed up their agreeable lifestyle, though their increasingly busy lives didn't allow for a total descent into slackerdom and inertia. They were too young and energized – too punk – to become total stoner hippies. Billie Joe first wrote a song of the same name, Al wrote it on the back of his black leather jacket and pretty soon all three unanimously agreed upon their new name. It was unveiled on the cover of '1000 Hours', recorded as Sweet Children but released as Green Day.

"I think one of the main reasons was that there was already another band called Sweet Baby, and the guys thought the two names were too much alike," remembers Livermore, of the band's sudden name change. "They may have also thought that Sweet Children wasn't a good enough name, I don't know for sure. How did I feel? Well, I was just about to put out their first record and I went ballistic. I was like, 'Everybody knows you as Sweet Children. How am I supposed to sell a record by a band called Green Day?'"

March 20, 1989, was a momentous night in Gilman's short history and for the scene at large, though few quite realised the significance at the time. Operation Ivy, the biggest and most popular East Bay band, were bowing out. With their passing, the first wave of Gilman was over.

If a band is to be judged on its legacy rather than its sales – as most bands, punk or otherwise, should be – then Op Ivy succeeded. Their legacy was already surrounding them, respectfully snapping at their heels. Support for their final show came from the Lookouts, Chrimpshrine, Surrogate Brains and a familiar local band of teens playing their first show under a new name.

Green Day.

What's it mean, dude?
Beats me.

All eyes were on the headliners during that mixed emotional night of commiseration and celebration, but it was the support band Green Day who were to carry the torch of 924 Gilman Street so far that some at Gilman wouldn't want it back. Though they had yet to release an album and it would be a half-decade before the young trio would break big internationally, it was this night, perhaps more than any other, that marked a significant change in the punk scene. The godfathers of the scene – albeit still very young ones – had done their job and spawned a new breed to take their music out of the clubs, across the country and beyond. No longer would the scene be supported only by a few hundred kids and volunteers and written about in the pages of fanzines, their bands judged a success if they sold a thousand records. No longer would the only record labels involved be those run by fans on shoestring budgets.

The baton was passed on and Green Day ran with it.

Of course, sometimes things sound far more dramatic than they are. With the advantage of passing time, it's easy to splice together key events to turn cold facts into fantastic fairy tales. Green Day were, after all, still only seventeen-year-old nobodies whose small following was centred around the one venue. Life was good, if poverty-stricken. Their time was yet to come, their journey just beginning.

By 1989, Billie Joe had had enough of home life and decided to strike out on his own – or at least, after sleeping on couches, move in with his bass-playing partner-in-crime. The pair were completely ensconced in punk music and the attendant lifestyle. Life was for living and their time was devoted to drinking, smoking weed, writing songs, hanging out, making friends, seeing bands ... just being a part of something interesting. Billie was still attending school in the hope that he would graduate.

The building in which the pair were squatting was located in a desolate block at West 7th & Peralta, West Oakland, with the BART train noisily swishing overhead. It was a building later described by *Spin* magazine as "like discovering the slacker version of *New Jack City.*" Amenities were basic, but – so what? – so were their needs and, besides, rent was non-existent. By inhabiting a previously abandoned building, the punks were living below the law. Squatting is illegal and those who choose to do it are subverting the assumed tenet that everyone has to pay someone for a place to live – the most basic and necessary of human needs. I lived in a similar such squat in south London for four years and every day felt like sweet victory over the disorganised and corrupt local council who had squandered millions of pounds of residents' taxes and let the area go to seed; more importantly, it was the only way I could survive in the city at a time of extortionate rent costs. To work I needed somewhere to live, to find somewhere to live I needed somewhere to work – without squatting it would have been near-impossible to circumnavigate such a catch-22 situation. Some call squatters parasites of society, but, like parasites I'd also call them cunning and resourceful survivors. These two teenagers were just that.

"I've been fortunate to be part of the punk rock scene 'cause I see friends in Pinole and they're stuck in a rut," said Billie Joe. "An alternative lifestyle is a lot more fulfilling sometimes, just because you don't have money."

West 7th was to provide great inspiration for their new band. Billie wrote a wry new song called 'Welcome To Paradise' romanticizing the squalor of the place and those feelings when a young man strikes out on his own for the first time.

"When we met them, Mike and Billie were seventeen," said Ben Weasel, *Maximum Rock 'n' Roll* columnist and frontman with Lookout!-signed Screeching Weasel. "We were staying up in the mountains at Lawrence Livermore's house, and we were so disgusted by these guys. We thought they were the biggest idiots we had ever met. They were so drunk that they were puking, and they were constantly smoking pot. So the next time I saw them, I was pretty wary but they came up and were really nice and clear-headed."

It was also during this first year as Green Day that for the first – but not the last – time Mike and Billie Joe temporarily joined other bands. Billie briefly played guitar for Lookout! hardcore band Corrupted Morals and Mike took over vocal duties for the self-explanatory Crummy Musicians after the mother of the original singer allegedly refused to let her son go on tour. But they were short-lived side interests – more a case of helping out friends and jamming on people's tunes, than calculated career moves. They played another three shows at Gilman during the tail-end of 1989, as well as at many other venues besides.

Green Day was now their number one concern.

The pursuit of normality was out of the question.

On February 16, 1990, Billie Joe made an assertive career move and dropped out of high school the day before his eighteenth birthday.

"I fucking spent the worst years of my life in high school," he told *Rolling Stone*'s Alex Foege, a mere five years later. "It held me back from doing what I wanted to do. Nothing in it was interesting. Opinions are force-fed to you. You're forced to read – which is evil. You can't force someone to read. That's no way of dealing with people in society: 'do this or suffer the consequences.'"

Former teacher – and now Green Day fan – John Goar remembers Billie Joe well: "He used to sit in my math class on the third floor of the ancient, run-down brick building in the back of the room right next to the window. He had a perfect view of 'Tightwad Hill'. I don't remember if he was a good student or if he did his homework, but I do remember him as a good person. He got along with just about everyone – except perhaps [one teacher] – and he was pretty cool. Mature for his age. My biggest disappointment is that he once invited me to come and see Sweet Children but I didn't go. Now I'd kill to have seen that band!"

So while on paper the lyrics of Billie Joe may have read like the proclamations of an *idiot savant*, the frontman was neither stupid nor lazy – by the age of 22 he would have made his first million after six years of hard work on a minimal income. But out of this desire to abandon education in order pursue his own goals to better himself and move up in life – the epitome of the American Dream – came the more immediate stigma of being branded a drop-out, a loser, a *non-citizen*. Consequently the Green Day lyrical lexicon was packed with words to describe a lifestyle and statements of non-intent that so many fans have consequently been able to recognise as their own: 'loser', 'idiot', 'boredom'. Topics included masturbation, smoking weed, hanging out.

If it sounded flippant and tongue-in-cheek then it probably was, but Green Day's emerging musical tales of loserdom came from a real place of discontent and directly from the mindset of the frontman, a kind of deliberate dumbing down enforced by the apparent hopelessness of the present moment and the realisation that if you take life too seriously it might just kill you. The songs he was beginning to write might have sounded dumb but the feelings were all too real to teenagers the world over. The backdrop might differ from state to state and country to country, but the sense of alienation and agitation by which the entire Green Day canon was now being informed was timeless. Making sense of the confusion and then turning it to their own gain was what made them a punk rock band. It takes not a drooling idiot but something approaching an ironic genius to turn his lethargy into a full-time, money-making success. As Mike would later put it: "We work super hard not to have to work."

"I write a lot about being a loser because I was conditioned that way," said Billie. "I was brainwashed to think that I was nothing compared to these people, these so-called geniuses who were teaching me all that crap. So I was like 'Okay, I'll be my own art-form: being a fucking idiot, being a loser'. If that's what I was trained to think I am, then that's what I'm going to do, and I'm going to do it the best way I can. Now I'm 'losing' in a big way. But I still have nightmares about being behind in class."

From this background of opting out and ditching class for a sofa and a bag of weed, and later going so far as to write 'Stoopid' on his baseball shirt with an arrow pointing to his face, soon Billie Joe Armstrong would be inadvertently soundtracking a decade that practically prided itself on its political apathy and self-imposed torpor, the cusp of which they found themselves on at the dawn of the Nineties.

As if he needed it confirming, Billie Joe suffered one final cruel twist of irony at the hands of the establishment. On the day he left Pinole Valley for good he went to see his teacher to whom he had to hand a drop-out slip. The teacher looked at the slip, then looked at the student only four months from graduation and one day away from adulthood and asked with only the vaguest trace of curiosity: "Who are you?"

Just like in the song by Pete Townshend.

Over in Willets, Frank Wright was proving a popular pupil at school, an energetic practical joker and endless wise-cracker. He was intelligent too, but didn't always find it easy to sit still long enough. He too was bored with routine and eager to play more music at all costs. There was only so much an education could teach him and frustrated by his high school's traditional methods, he sat and passed a graduate equivalency exam at a local community college and also left high school forever.

After the relative success of '1000 Hours' – just getting a record released on Lookout! was a triumph in itself – Green Day went back into the studio. By the autumn of 1989 they were headlining Gilman, filling the battered size nine's vacated by Operation Ivy earlier in the summer. Gilman was thriving, bringing in relatively established punk bands such as the Dwarves, Shelter and Chumbawamba, who played Gilman that

September supported by former Crass member Eve Libertine, local favourites Neurosis and a new band out of Orange County who had a biochemist on vocals and a school janitor on guitar. They had gigged for a few years as Manic Subsidal but had recently changed their name to The Offspring and were beginning to build a small fanbase.

Encouraged by the band's debut, Larry Livermore signed Green Day to Lookout! to make an album. On December 29, 1989, the band went into Art of Ears Studio in San Francisco, set up their equipment and began recording at 4.30p.m. Mike and Billie recorded their vocal parts simultaneously to save time and money – something that would be unheard of for any of today's major label punk bands. They were at home in the studio. Their heroes were The Ramones, Buzzcocks, The Clash, all of whom recorded quickly, and it clearly showed as they applied the same sense of pared-down economy to their own debut.

By early afternoon the next day the bulk of the record was done. Guitar parts and harmonies were added, the record was mixed and by January 2, the dawning of a new decade, *39/Smooth* was finished. The total cost of studio time was $675 of Livermore's money –almost exactly the same exceedingly low amount it had cost Nirvana to record their debut album *Bleach* a few months earlier.

Before the release of the band's debut full-length, Livermore first released another single to test the water. The band returned to Art of Ears and recorded another four songs in a matter of hours. The result was the 'Slappy' single, another four-track, vinyl-only release. The lead track 'Paper Lanterns' was inspired by Billie Joe's first love, a girl called Jennifer. "The one that got away," as he later put it.

The song set a template of choppy chords, a jaunty, driving rhythm section and an instant chorus that attached itself like Velcro. It was a template that they would follow for most of their career. Similarly, like '1000 Hours' before it, 'Why Do You Want Him?' recalls the same adolescent yearning of Buzzcocks' Pete Shelley only transplanted into a Californian dialect. '409 In Your Coffeemaker' meanwhile, was allegedly a song about an incident in which Billie claims to have put some high-strength, all-purpose 409 cleaner into the coffeemaker of a teacher of his and Mike's. Or if they didn't actually do it then they had certainly thought about it …

As on their debut, they rounded off three of their own compositions with a cover, a laid-back and breezy version of Operation Ivy's Gilman Street favourite 'Knowledge'.

Of all the songs from Green Day's early days it's the one they consistently play live today, an always anarchic version with various audience members sitting in on guitar, bass and drums.

The cover for the EP featured a shot of a laconic-looking bulldog, who would later feature on many of the band's early T-shirts; again the single was released on a variety of coloured vinyl seven-inches, all art and lay-out done by Green Day's old pal and seasoned 'zine editor, Aaron Cometbus.

First released on green vinyl, 'Slappy' was one of thousands of punk rock seven-inch singles unleashed in 1990. Although limited and again only picking up reviews in fanzines, 'Slappy' extended Green Day's reputation further. Before e-mail and the internet, MP3's and CD burners the best way for a band of their nature to get known was word of mouth. The nature of punk fans – or most music fans in general, particularly those with more alternative or esoteric tastes – can often determine that for every limited, mail-order or imported single sold, another five or ten people might borrow, hear, steal or copy it. I know because as a fourteen-year-old in 1990, life was one continual record fair swap meet between me and my friends too poor to update our collections with new records – and Green Day records certainly featured regularly. Or maybe it was just that the same one or two copies of their records circulated more quickly than most.

Their approach to the marketing of music was different too. Labels had little or no money for big-budget advertising, so instead relied on a more feral approach and in doing so enabled the punk rock scene to be something of a level playing field. Most bands and labels sold so few records that, economically, there was a certain sense of equality. Bands were judged on their music and their shows, and the best ones generally won through in the end. The major difference now, in an era when punk rock is part of the mainstream music business, is that it is often bands with the biggest marketing budgets who triumph. Good Charlotte or the recently split Blink-182 are huge not (in my opinion) because they are the best so-called punk bands around but because they have been the most heavily marketed. Unlike Green Day, who have only ever been sold as a colourful, anarchic punk band – or, thanks to 2004's *American Idiot*, a politicized mainstream rock radio band – their followers have been sold as pouting pretty boys, rough-around-the-edges stud muffins capable of stealing a slice of the pop market pie.

So Green Day's second single certainly helped widen their reputation, but still only within underground circles. An album would leave a bigger impact. Over ten songs, *39/Smooth* managed to pin down a sound bubbling with energy, melodies and lyrical themes that struck a chord. It was punk rock with an urgent, economic approach, but it was a poppy jangle once again reminiscent of the same recurring reference points, Buzzcocks or Bob Mould's Husker Du. Songs such as 'Don't Leave Me' were barbed with barely suppressed shards of bitterness, but the music hopeful enough to uplift the listener. And at a time when punk rock was so often nothing more than a vocal-shredding display, on songs like 'I Was There', Billie Joe and Mike were harmonizing like John and Paul or The Kinks' Davies brothers. Close your eyes and you could almost picture the wiggling mop-tops.

The reasons for the choice of album title were somewhat random. While putting the finishing touches to the record they had been using the word 'smooth' a lot. Bands are prone to speaking in their own lingo or developing their own vocabularies and this word was one of them. They knew they wanted it in the title somewhere. Also around that time Billie's oldest brother Alen was celebrating his 39th birthday and jokingly happened to mention that it would be cool if such an occasion was marked somewhere in the album's name – after all, they might never make another one. And so *39/Smooth* was settled on. It sounded cool enough.

Green Day's debut was released in early 1990 on black and green twelve-inch vinyl and cassette and then on CD – still a burgeoning format – the following year. The ten tracks that comprised their debut once again combined their obvious love of the pop hooks of Sixties British bands and the regionalized intonation of British punks' strongest voices.

Like fellow East Bay boys Rancid, Green Day have, on occasion, been criticised for aping a little too closely the Cockney dialects – exaggerated vowels, clipped pronunciation – of the great bands of the Sixties, though it's likely these criticisms would have come from their own countrymen. Growing up listening to Operation Ivy, Rancid and Green Day, it was always apparent that these bands sounded distinctly American rather than directly aping the gruff tones of, say, Joe Strummer. Billie Joe and Tim Armstrong take the working-class spirit of Britain in the Sixties and Seventies and apply it to their own surroundings and blue-collar backgrounds; something far more progressive than they're given credit for.

No matter how close the economic situations, England and California are two very different places, whichever way you look at it. Listening to Green Day's music five thousand miles away from its original creation opened up – and continues to open up for a new generation of listeners – a whole new world where the reference points, lifestyle and dialect is different, but the themes, energy and general sense of urgency and dissatisfaction are much the same. Only a lazy critic would call Green Day a Who rip-off, likewise Rancid a Clash rip-off. "I sound like an Englishman impersonating an American impersonating an Englishman…" Billie once joked.

The album's artwork featured a black and white photograph of a girl in a floral dress and cowboy boots standing awkwardly in a cemetery beneath a blossom-laden tree, a design done by Jesse Michaels. Though effective enough, of all their albums it's probably the least *Green Day-looking* in that, save for the band's green logo, it was monochromatic and somewhat sombre in appearance. But then it was their debut and they were still finding their feet. Additional artwork inside was done by Aaron Cometbus, whose recognisable cartoony pen-and-ink style came to define the band's early works and nicely complemented the content within.

The year in which Green Day debuted, 1991, turned out to be a crucial one in the development of alternative music. Nirvana were a promising cult band playing music that referenced punk, hardcore, pop and metal. In January 1991 they released two relatively low-key and limited singles, 'Molly's Lips' on Sub Pop in the US and 'Sliver' in the UK. However, by the end of the year, Nirvana had enlisted new drummer Dave Grohl, released new single 'Smells Like Teen Spirit' and become, in the space of months, the biggest band on the planet. Suddenly the commercial appeal of noisy alternative music became apparent for the first time. 1991 also saw great releases in the US from Fugazi, Nation Of Ulysses, Hole, Pearl Jam, Rocket From The Crypt, Jawbox, Afghan Whigs, Helmet, Public Enemy – all punk rock in spirit, if not necessarily in sound.

But somehow the true punk bands – those unashamed to pigeonhole themselves derivatively as such – were not yet a concern. The music business was looking for the next Nirvana. Nirvana had long hair, heavy riffs and, to outsiders, a disposition as dreary as the weather in their hometown environs of Aberdeen in the Pacific North-West.

Green Day had short hair, pop riffs and, to outsiders, a joker's disposition as sunny and upbeat as the weather in their hometown environs of northern California. Clearly, they were two very different bands doing very different things.

When *39/Smooth* was released, bands such as Bad Religion, Pennywise, NOFX and The Offspring were all releasing records and gigging but yet were completely overlooked by the record companies, magazines and other media outlets. Alternative music and the way in which it was perceived was changing, but not *that* quickly. Green Day and the punks' true time was yet to come and for now they existed in a vacuum unaffected by traditional rock 'n' roll conceits.

The album was released and life carried on.

Short of funds, sometime during 1990 Billie and friend (and future Green Day member) Tre Cool briefly got jobs together selling newspaper subscriptions outside a Safeway supermarket on the somewhat genteel College Avenue in Rockridge, not far from UC Berkeley. A few hours into it they dumped the papers and spent the rest of the day smoking weed. They were fired after two days. For now, gainful employment was clearly not for them.

Billie and Mike returned to Pinole Valley High one final time though when they were offered an opening slot at the school's 'National Foods Day' concert, where foreign foods are sold, entertainment provided and, presumably, the cultural insight of the Californian students expanded ever-so-slightly for a few hours. Green Day played in the school's courtyard area (dubbed 'The Mall') and failed to impress the faculty members (who only showed their appreciation for the band that followed, Separate Ways) though some of the trio's contemporaries were a little more enthusiastic

Billie had a plan of sorts. It was a simple one: keep the band going. At all costs. While Mike and John were preoccupied with school and work, in spring 1990 the frontman concentrated on booking a forty-five date US tour for the band. He sent out copies of their recording with a letter and information about this fresh-faced band who had already made a name for themselves in the increasingly talked-about East Bay/Gilman scene. Gilman was both a microcosm of, and an ideal model *for* the less organised or more far-flung scenes and what was going on there has resonated across America. The coverage that the East Bay scene enjoyed was disproportionate to what was actually happening – in reality, one venue with a concrete ethos, a bunch of bands, a few hundred kids and a magazine to solidify the status of the scene. Whatever. Green Day used the East Bay coverage to their advantage and gained a little extra kudos because of their involvement.

So, by the time Mike had graduated from school, a total of forty-five dates had indeed been booked [no mean feat], and the very next day Green Day hit the road to show America how they did things back West. For the next three years the band would stay on tour for no less than seven months each year – an average of four shows per week, every week. *That* is how it's done.

They played anywhere and everywhere, improvising and adapting their itinerary along the way. Soon, they had played 48 of the 50 US states. Sometimes to 500 people, sometimes to just 50. But every time with the same energy and total commitment. Finances came by way of what money they had managed to scrape together for the tour and what little they got paid per show. A snapshot of the band's life and their brotherly bond around this time was detailed on the inlay of the 'Slappy EP': *"To raise spending money for the tour, Mike shucked clams, Billie Joe flipped pizzas, and John drove a diaper truck ..."*

There's a decent quality bootleg video of one of these early shows. In fact there are many, but the one filmed at The Paint Factory, a sizeable and suitable punk-looking club in Tampa, Florida, provides an insight into a typical early out-of-town punk rock show. It's dated 1989 though may well be 1990 given the audience's obvious familiarity with many of the band's songs, the impressive turnout of at least two or three hundred people, plus the fact that the band must have been on tour at the time (or faced a *long* drive home for the sake of one show).

Either way, it makes for interesting viewing today. Not because the band look alarmingly young or are either really terrible or mind-blowingly great (they're neither) but because they bear an uncanny resemblance to today's Green Day, who, save for a few extra lines around the eye, seems to be have been cryogenically frozen and transported here from this time.

The most outstanding thing about this glimpse into their past is just how poppy the band are – in 1989/1990 they sounded more janglier and turbo-charged than ever – rendering redundant any argument that the band have sold-out (definition: compromising your 'art' for financial gain) or softened their sound over the years. Displaying traces of puppy fat, Billie Joe sports cropped black hair and a Neurosis T-shirt. Mike sports bleached blond hair and jumps about all over the place. They dip into pastiche cover versions of other songs – in this case, Lynyrd Skynyrd's all-American 'Sweet Home Alabama'. Again, so little has changed.

The other notable point is the slight shock of seeing Al Sobrante in the band, who opens the show with a convoluted tale about getting a lift in someone's car earlier and could he please have his shoes back that he left in there! Aside from that it's business as usual. In fact, watching such bootleg films of early Green Day, there's an alarming similarity to the DIY punk and hardcore shows I was going to at the exact same time in community centres and other such hang-outs in northern England; it's a reminder that Green Day were neither mould-breakers or genre-makers. *They were just better than everyone else.* That and the fact that Gilman was not a one-off, but rather the most highly mythologized venue of its time. The accents might differ but the Paint Factory bootleg could have been filmed anywhere in the world.

It was out on the road during the band's first tour playing such gigs that Billie Joe met a girl in Minnesota called Adrienne Nestor, who he promptly fell for. When the tour would end, Billie's interest in Adrienne wouldn't and they embarked on a relationship that reached halfway across the States over the coming years and would be worked around touring and recording commitments for Billie and holding down a job for Adrienne.

"Al Sobrante was still in the band and I was one of only ten people at a Green Day gig and Billie and me ended up hitting if off," Adrienne remembers. "I had been working in this small town in Minnesota called Mankato as a manager for Pier 1 imports after I had graduated with a degree in sociology from Mankato State University and stayed there until Billie Joe convinced me to move out to Cali." At the age of eighteen, Billie had met his future wife and mother of his children, with whom he remains to this day.

Also along for the ride was the aforementioned Aaron Elliot, sometime member of Chrimpshrine and Pinhead Gunpowder friend and roadie, who would be with the band for their first five tours, a necessary facilitator during their toilet circuit days. Elliot also ran the popular punk fanzine, *Cometbus,* giving him his more known nickname of Aaron Cometbus.

Elliot was a true punk – the living embodiment of *Maximum Rock 'n' Roll's* young unwashed radical archetype. His collection of *Cometbus* writings later released in book form as *Despite Everything* provides a fine overview of the lifestyle of a Berkeley punk who *lives* it, rather than just puts on the uniform at the weekend. Full of tales of eating out of dumpsters, travelling the US, the challenges of poverty, musings on anarchism, punk collectives, mosh-pits, police thuggery and so on, it provides excellent context about what it meant to be a punk in the late Eighties and early Nineties and is a stark reminder just how much things have changed since then – how US punk went from being essentially working-class in the Eighties to middle-class in the Nineties [Ironically, Green Day were key to this shift. More of which later]. But in the meantime, Cometbus was a good person to have on tour with them. For now, in these less complicated times, he was one of them, going so far as occasionally standing in on drums when Sobrante wasn't around. He and Billie had also been known to occasionally play together in popular East Bay band Blatz.

What little income Green Day made from shows was soon gobbled up by pressing necessities such as petrol, food or equipment. In true punk style they subsidised their income with DIY merchandise when funds were particularly low.

"We used to go out and print merchandise over our guitar cases," said Dirnt. "People would bring along their own shorts, and we'd just charge them for the print. That's what kept us on the road and sold us a lot of independent albums."

While on tour in Minneapolis the trio went into a local studio and recorded four songs for an EP in the same manner in which they had recorded 'Slappy' – low-budget and quick, the punk rock way. "It was done cheap and fast and sounds crappy," was Larry Livermore's verdict, "and therefore many people think it is the oldest Green Day record, but it isn't." The record was called the 'Sweet Children' EP.

The 'fast and crappy' approach is apparent in the tinny, demo-like quality of the songs (later included as extra tracks on the re-release of *Kerplunk!),* though the songs were in possession of enough vim and vigour to make it a worthy enough release. Sharing a very similar intro to later hit 'Welcome To Paradise', 'Sweet Children' was something of a signature song, simple, effective with lyrics that conveyed the same sense of teen confusion as heard on their debut album.

'Best Thing In Town' and 'Strangeland' meanwhile were vital slices of fuzzed-up start-stop guitar pop, but nothing more; the dynamism is lost somewhere in the mix. The EP was rounded off with a cover version of The Who's windmilling, speaker-smashing anthem 'My Generation'. Lacking the power of the original, it still had a sunny, spontaneous appeal – like listening to a young band messing about through the rehearsal room wall.

In keeping with the impromptu nature of the single, 'Sweet Children' was released on Minneapolis's Skene! in late 1990, a label set up by Jeff Spiegel a couple of years earlier (and who over the course of the next eight years would go on to release other cool punk bands such as Jawbreaker and the Hard-Ons). Perhaps it was because of a connection to great Minneapolis bands like Husker Du and the Replacements – bands who irrevocably shaped Billie Joe Armstrong's songwriting skills – that Green Day opted to release on this up-and-coming label. The now much-sought after 'Sweet Children' single appeared on black, red and pink vinyl with different covers for each subsequent pressing – the first a black and white close-up photo of Mike's leg, the second a picture of a skuzzy VW Beetle, the third with the same picture on a red sleeve and so on.

Once again 'Sweet Children' was another well-received reputation-building release – and a curveball to the many later collectors who assumed it was the band's pre-Green Day debut. It wasn't.

In July 1990 The Lookouts played their final show. For a band of amateurs who had started by bashing away in isolation up the mountains they had done pretty good, performing at that semi-legendary final Operation Ivy show and their penultimate gig opening for Bad Religion being just two of their achievements. Plus, of course, there was the enduring Gilman Street/Lookout! association. The band also left behind a final four-track single 'IV', which was released posthumously in January 1991 and featured Billie Joe Armstrong on lead guitar and backing vocals.

"It wasn't so much that we were tired of the band or each other," says Livermore in the accompanying press release. "In fact we all felt as though we had finally hit our stride, and were capable of playing together as a pretty darn good band. But we were now living in three widely separate places and it was next to impossible to get together for shows or even practice, so we reluctantly called it quits."

Another member of the Gilman crew was thinking of moving on. In autumn 1990 Al Sobrante decided to quit Green Day in order to go to college full-time.

Though they had come of age together on this shared punk rock *rites de passage* and spent endless hours on top of each other in rehearsal rooms and tour vans, Sobrante's departure – or, rather, his method of departure – supposedly created some bad blood. Billie Joe apparently heard that their drummer wanted no more part in their steady rise through a third party, a mutual friend.

As they watched some of their peers and former classmates first graduate and then, like Master Sobrante, move away to college for a while, to Billie and Mike it might have seemed like the world was moving on without them – that without a drummer, perhaps their band would grind to a halt. It wasn't the case, though the pair have since admitted it's the closest Green Day have ever come to splitting. Conformity in the traditional sense just didn't really seem like an option for the pair. Music simply meant too much to them; it was no dalliance. Whatever the exact circumstances of his departure from the band, all credit must be given to Sobrante who had put in a good two or three years work with little in the way of financial reward. A little older than his band-mates, maybe he had merely been faced with decisions that, at eighteen years old, were arguably less significant to them.

What's lesser known is that Billie Joe's friend and future Green Day stalwart, Tre Cool, didn't immediately fill the space on the drum stool after Al Sobrante's departure. Instead, Dave EC, drummer for Filth and the Wynona Ryders, joined the band for a few weeks, but then left of his own accord. This new-look trio's brief union was amicable enough and although he appeared on none of the band's recorded output he did get a credit on their next album, *Kerplunk!*

The remaining pair already knew Tre Cool well, as has been documented. They were the same age, dug the same bands and shared all the same reference points. Tre liked to smoke weed and fool around and took little other than drumming seriously, at which point he was as serious as a heart attack. Green Day had already shared stages with Cool and moved in the same circles. All this would be a distinct advantage in breaking him in to the band. In November 1990 they asked him if he wanted to join their group. Cool accepted the invitation and Green Day – the Green Day we know and love today – was born. After leaving the band, Sobrante/Kiffmeyer went on to play in the Ne'erdowells, who later evolved into garagey punk Lookout! band the Hi-Fives.

"He's still getting paid from the first record," said Tre in 2004. "I think he fixes bicycles or something now. But he's a smart guy and he'll talk your ear off. He's a funny, interesting [guy]."

Rather fantastically, Sobrante did indeed fix bicycles. While a student he set up an impromptu service on campus at Humboldt State college – he is certainly smart and interesting, as these quotes from a rare interview on *www.outyourbackdoor.com* suggest: "The free bike repair started out because everyone was holding hands and lighting candles, singing 'Give Peace A Chance' on the day the Gulf War started [in 1991]. So I thought, 'I gotta do something to protest the war. What would be completely absurd? I know, I'll *fix bicycles for free!*' Bicycle repair, for me, is the closest I'm ever going to get to a spiritual experience. I used to harass the Christians when I did free bike repair ... they had these huge banners that would say, 'Victory In Jesus.' So I'd say 'Victory In Bicycles' on my banner. They'd say, 'Jesus Christ, The Prince Of Peace,' so I made one that said 'Al Sobrante, Prince Of Bike Repair.'" Magnificent.

Meanwhile back in Rodeo, the owners of Rod's Hickory Pit, Richard and Alice Cotton, had decided to sell the café shortly after Sweet Children had played their first shows there (though the two events were not connected!), and it had soon been turned into a Korean karaoke bar. Finally in 2003, in a development that seems to speak volumes about the evolution of town-planning in modern America – the notion that shoppers are essentially lazy and want everything in one, easy-to-drive-to place, all of which is more or less true – the venue that provided Rodeo with its one real bit of musical history and Green Day their first steps towards stardom would be torn down to make way for a strip mall. Gone was the down-home, time-honoured local hang-out, in its place a brand-spanking-new strip of generic stores set in such uniform surroundings that it looked like it could be lifted up and dropped down anywhere in the country.

What do you get if you cross – this isn't a joke by the way, so don't get too excited – Beavis, Butthead, *South Park's* Cartman, a quadruple shot of espresso and a bowl of weed? The answer: Tre Cool.

Upon joining the band, Tre's behaviour certainly made an impression on Billie Joe and Mike, who were hardly retiring puritans themselves. But Tre ... Tre would always go one further. He openly insulted people – including, on occasion, his band-mates – and somehow seemed to get away with it. He chatted and mimicked constantly, a hyperactive whirlwind of energy dryly firing out innuendos with an adolescent chuckle and a deviant's grin. It was not unknown for him to turn up at shows in a dress and full make-up. Drummers are famously a breed unto themselves anyway and even before he was famous – when he would at least have rock 'n' roll as an excuse – he displayed all the outward characteristics of an archetypal drummer: excessive energy, a prankster's approach to social situations – everything you would expect from the kind of drumming warrior whose greatest skill is hitting things with bits of wood in public. But he was damn funny with it too – his saving grace when he'd later take dicking about to new heights and find himself in endless scrapes around the world.

That he has always preferred to use the same drum kit as rock's most notoriously unhinged drummer, The Who's Keith Moon, suddenly makes even more sense. Nothing went beyond the boundaries of good taste in the pursuit of fun – things like famously 'milking' a dog when there was a shortage for his coffee in whatever house they happened to be staying in on tour. Tre Cool was doing what the likes of *Jackass, CKY* and *Dirty Sanchez* would later turn into a lucrative commercial venture for the pure hell of it. Acting the goat.

"I think Tre's behaviour is amazing," laughed Billie Joe. "He's totally out of control but he's also quite smart about it. He never gets his ass-kicked, because there's a kind of child-like innocence in his face. Mike is kind of a brutish-looking guy so if he did some of the things that Tre does, he would probably get in a fight. But people tend to look at Tre and think he's … mentally retarded or something!"

Years later Andy Doerschuk of *Drum* magazine spent an illuminating afternoon with Tre – "The king of Berkeley" – driving around in his late Sixties muscle car (complete with armour-plated undercarriage) to give an insight into the drummer's down-time.

"He requires constant input, diversity, stimulation – tons of stimulation, in fact, of every description," wrote the journalist. "Sidling up to us, a bunch of fraternity party boys in a Mazda recognize Tre, and begin hollering and gesturing excitedly. For the remainder of the afternoon, every corner we turn brings some new, startled Green Day spotter … Police cars sit on every corner. One merges into the lane behind us. Paranoia runs deep as Tre announces that his car is unregistered, so be cool. Oh great. We haven't even begun to discuss the spatial relationship between his bass drum beater and pedal board, and we could easily be on our way to jail within minutes."

Yes, Tre Cool fitted in just perfectly. You might even say he was the missing component to turn a good band into a great one. Above all else though, he was an excellent drummer – both metronomical and inventive, dashing out crazy drum-fills, hurling sticks and just generally adding a new angle to the band. He wasn't tucked away out of sight with the sole purpose of keeping the beat. If not physically, then spiritually, he was soon as upfront a presence in a Green Day show as either Billie or Mike.

Just how much Tre brought to the band would become apparent when they undertook their first US tour with him throughout 1991. The life of a touring band is quite like no other. The nearest comparison is that of a circus or old-time gypsy carnival pulling into town, setting up various tents and sideshows, selling its warcs, wowing (or incurring the wrath of) the locals, then departing by dawn. There is an air of mystique and romanticism surrounding these out-of-town strangers, forever just passing through to the next place.

But the life of a rock 'n' roll band, particularly a relatively unknown one, is also different in many ways. For starters, any plan, however vague, has to be adaptable for unseen circumstances – and there are *always* unseen circumstances. Vehicles for transport are, at best unpredictable. Payment is either low, scarce, or non-existent, many contracts cithcr verbal or agreed weeks ago by parties currently tucked up in bed thousands of miles away. Accordingly, any accommodation is a luxury. As is personal hygiene. Food is fast and functional, but alcohol flows. The day starts early, usually hungover, and everything that happens afterwards is geared towards a forty minute performance at some point in the next twelve to twenty hours. It ends drunk and late. A shower is nothing but a mirage. Equipment has to work every night or be either fixed and/or replaced somewhere along the way.

And that's all just the practicalities of a tour – the basic show-on-the-road type things. Stir in a variety of heightened emotions, themselves always subject to change depending on group dynamics, inter-band relationships and all-round morale, hostile audiences, overbearing promoters, jealous support bands, errant loved ones, unpredictable drummers, excitable girls and their knife-toting boyfriends, pituitary bouncers, comatose soundmen, 'former' fans, aggressive cops, the border patrol … the *weathe*r, and you're left with a lifestyle that only the pluckiest, most dedicated or socio-pathic would choose to live for extended periods of time.

Crucially, unlike other occupations that require huge amounts of travelling and living out of a suitcase – salesman, truck driver – touring in a band is not about the lone individual but the collective group effort. You can't just turn around and go home. You stay and rock.

Despite so much potential adversity, life on tour is strangely addictive, an eye-opening, horizon-expanding but nevertheless bubble-like existence. Being young undoubtedly helps and evidently fuelled by raw adrenaline and teen restlessness all along, thankfully Green Day were at an advantage; that tank never ran dry. On tour all the usual mundane responsibilities of rent and bills or setting the alarm clock go out the window – you're living on wits and raw instinct alone. At this level you're answerable to no-one but you and your trusty road dogs. You can drink whenever you like. People are paying to see you – some of them might even want to fuck you. You have just livened up their dull existence and as you ride off into the sunset in your trusty metal Trojan horse to a select few people, for one night only, you are *cool as fuck*.

This then was Green Day's life throughout 1991 as the word on *39/Smooth* spread and they found themselves playing increasingly far flung places – more often than not, fan's houses, skate parks and VFW (Veterans of Foreign Wars) community halls.

One night, after a show in New Orleans, the band returned to the van to find that it had been broken into and the bag containing their money had been stolen, along with most of their possessions. Accompanying them on the tour were two friends, John, and the appropriately-named Road Dog, who took turns driving as well as helping load gear, sell merchandise etc. Dejected, the band and their entourage left New Orleans to drive through the night straight to their next destination of Auburn, Alabama, where they arrived in the small hours with no money and no change of clothes.

Auburn is a college town and word went around that the band were playing a show in the kitchen and living room of a rented house on the town's Stamford Avenue that night. When they arrived they were met with donations of clothes and money, and found such generosity of a few dozen students and punk rockers at such a low-point in the tour completely humbling. The show earned them enough money for food and petrol to take them to the next show in Birmingham, Alabama, where they played another living room and made enough to get them to the next show. Repeat the formula until untold success, madness or death comes knocking …

It was while on their first tour of duty with Tre on the drum stool that

Green Day were allegedly approached by a record label other than Lookout! – the ominously-named, but well-established IRS Records, established by Miles Copeland, brother of The Police's drummer Stewart Copeland. As the sometime home to punk and new wave bands such as Buzzcocks, The Go-Go's, Magazine, The Damned and also an early champion of REM, most young artists would have jumped at the chance to be on roster with such credible acts. But, with an impressive amount of foresight from Mike and some self-restraint on the band's part, they declined. At that show in Birmingham, Alabama, Mike was overheard explaining to people that if they signed a contract with IRS they'd be touring in a tour bus and staying in hotels – as opposed to a van and on people's floors. They were, he reasoned, still more or less kids and all that other stuff could wait until later. They may have spent the majority of their waking hours acting like dorks, but there were wise heads on Green Day's young shoulders.

"Mike's pretty smart, huh?" said Tre. "We always wanted to experience music from every aspect. I mean, we've played living rooms, squats and places like that so many times. It's better to regret something you have done than something you haven't done."

A quick digression on the subject of style: right from the beginning Green Day looked like any other down-at-the-heel punk kids, but always naturally stylish with it. Their every day street clothes and stage gear were one and the same – a combination of thrift store garments often decorated or accessorised or just plain threadbare: battered baseball sneakers, vests, leather jackets, work pants, trucker's shirts. Whether deliberate or not, Green Day's style was defiantly blue-collar. They wore the cast-offs of the working-class. Such a natural, non-contrived look certainly helped endear them to their small, growing fan base in the US and Europe, being as it was an easy look to recreate. Like the Seventies punks before them, Green Day's look was born out of poverty, imagination and a basic desire to stand out from the identikit of the high street stores. Fifteen years on, from Melrose Place to Oxford Street, it's somewhat ironic that many of the same shops now sell genuine 'punk' clothes at inflated prices – ripped up designer tat for weekend rebels and clueless fashion victims alike.

Likewise, their haircuts were also distinctly DIY as all three had been cutting and dying at will from their mid-teens. Ever since Richard Hell had taken a pair of scissors to his own hair in the mid-Seventies and

Johnny Rotten had dyed his an uneasy shade of green while an art student, it had been the look of choice for punks. Cheap (free, even) and confrontational – anti-social at a base level. For many of the critics of Green Day, the haircuts were to become the first reference point and sometimes all they needed to know about the band: *oh, they're punks, they must sound like this, then* ...

Again, it's an anti-style that has been co-opted and bastardised for the sake of fashion – everyone from kid's TV presenters to sportsmen to bankers to boy bands can get away with sporting a quasi-punk cut. Whether cropped, spiked or feathered, either way its gradual acceptance on the High Street has rendered it a completely acceptable look. You can't help ponder over the degree to which Green Day are to be thanked/blamed for this co-option of a once controversial, confrontational look – how a haircut that once evoked violence can now breed acceptance.

That said, aside from Billie growing his bog-brush crop into an ill-advised clutch of dreads that he would sport in the band's first promotional photographs sent out to the press to publicise their major label debut, their choice of clothes is an overall style they've deviated little from in fifteen years. The very first time I would encounter Mike Dirnt – already a millionaire at that point – the first thing he would say was how he had just haggled over a pair of garish, dog-tooth patterned trousers priced at $10. The clothes of modern day Green Day might be more durable and possibly more expensive, but they still look like scruffy-ass rockers whichever way you look at it. You can take the boy out of punk but you can't take the punk out of the boy ...

When they entered a studio for the first time with Tre Cool, Green Day's frontman had been busy writing a new set of songs, some of which had been refined on a nightly basis across the States, while others came fresh from his four-track home recorder. Once again they opted to record in the familiar surroundings of San Francisco's Art of Ears studio, primarily because it was cheap. Thanks to the small-time success of *39/Smooth,* the recording budget had more than doubled to the still relatively minuscule $2000.

Billie Joe had a strong set of songs – a mixture of their now-familiar punk pop surges and more mid-placed introspective songs such as the touching 'Christie Road', along with the Tre Cool-penned dumb country joke piece, 'Dominated Love Slave'. Lyrically too, the frontman had crafted a form of youthful street poetry. He was able to tackle complicated subjects such as love, alienation and disappointment in an accessible and empathetic manner in songs which may sound inordinately simple, yet contain a sense of style and intelligence.

So it was with some disappointment that the band rejected the initial demo recordings of the album and decided to re-record the songs in order to truly do them justice. Nevertheless, they weren't overly precious. Unlike some bands they had neither the time, money nor inclination to indulge themselves musically. Recordings were split between two short sessions in May and September of 1991 with producer/engineer Andy Ernst at the helm – a total of four days in all. Less is more. Bang it out. Move on.

There was a reason for sticking to a schedule.

By the time the album – now known as *Kerplunk!,* in homage to the children's game of the same name – was being sent off to the pressing plant, the band were packing their bags in preparation of their first trip abroad. Europe was beckoning …

With their hard-earned savings, in autumn 1991 Green Day bought economy transatlantic tickets and flew to Europe. On the flight over they smoked – "How many bands can claim they toured Europe back when you could still smoke on the plane?" Mike Dirnt laughed in 2005.

Each band member was still only nineteen.

It was to be a hard slog, and true to early Green Day form, many of the shows were in unconventional off-the-beaten track venues, most of them booked by an American friend living in the UK. If they were lucky they would get paid. Touring in such a manner is about the roughest, but ultimately most rewarding way for a band to operate. It is also educational and for the first time beyond their native land the band experienced punk, the European way. They met new bands of similar stature and sound, they made many friends and developed an air of professionalism in their performance. Rolling into a new town each night in which they would play with local opening bands and attempt to break any cultural or language barriers, often by getting supremely drunk, for once the trio were the cool kids. They were the touring Americans, adaptable and with an appetite for revelling in the seedy glamour of the fleapits of Europe, lighting musical fires that over the years would slowly engulf the continent.

The entire European tour was self-funded, the band saving up their modest royalty cheques from their Lookout! releases and any US touring profits to pay for basic necessities such as air-fare and van hire. They played 64 shows in three months, using equipment borrowed from other bands every single night.

"We snuck copies of our records over by hand to sell," recalls Mike. "To get our own T-shirts made we had to sneak over the photo negative and get a screen made in Germany so we could print them as and when we needed to. Then we had our amp heads, which were hell-heavy to carry. Mine lasted a week and Billie's a total of one day. In Denmark if they like you they throw beer at you, so that was very much it. Our instruments were toast." "What was cool was that it wasn't even my amp!" laughs Billie. "It was Lawrence Livermore's!"

"It really brought us together as a band, because we were headlining shows and most people hadn't heard of us," adds Tre. "But there'd always be a few hip people who would have our stuff, so they'd tell all their friends to come. There would be anywhere between 50 and 500 people in places like Germany, Poland and Spain. I'd prefer to tour Europe any day than the States."

"There are so many Americans over in Europe these days – I think there should be a rule that any American band that goes to Europe or the UK has to have toured the United States at least twice because they're a bunch of little spoiled rotten brats," Mike told me. "They come over here [to Europe] and people give them lots of beer and food and money and shit like that ... I mean, I remember we once played in Denmark, in a squat to about six people, and afterwards they came over and said, 'Here is all of our money, we had to go into our house fund to get it,' and we were, like, 'No, keep your money, just give us some food or a little bit of gas and that's fine.' They expected us to want all their money, and it was really sweet of them, but we're not your average American band. We're not shitheads."

If you need to know the difference between Green Day or Good Charlotte – or why Green Day are a punk band and Good Charlotte are not – then it's right there. The former made their name by playing squats, bars and community halls for chump change; the latter made it big partly by presenting their own MTV show.

It was an action-packed, incident-filled tour funded by whatever they made from shows and what money Lookout! could give them. Their few releases to date were limited-pressings which were hard to find in the US and nigh on impossible to buy in the shops in Europe (copies were only available by mail order from the US), so Green Day's first tour was on a shoestring budget out of necessity. They simply hadn't made enough from record sales nor could they command sufficient fees to afford a comfortable on-the-road existence. If they were lucky, at some shows, like the one they played at Stoke Wheatsheaf, they would get paid above their guarantee of £100 (that night they received £130 because the turn-out was unexpected), whereas at others they might only get some beer or some communal chilli – again, if they were lucky.

So, it was the hard way or not at all. But it mattered little because it was primarily a fun experience, the trio's own low-budget version of the American college kid's tradition of 'doing' Europe on their summer vacations, only unlike the students taking a crash course in culture before heading back to re-immerse themselves in American life, Green Day would return again and again. On October 31, they found themselves playing in Denmark on Halloween to "a crowd of Vikings going completely ape-shit. Drunk, crusty people from Denmark were actually having sex onstage."

Afterwards a friend of the promoter offered to put them up in his flat, where he promised to introduce them to his friend 'Sleepy'. Billie takes up the rest of the story: "We show up, and he had a small apartment … all of a sudden, the guy wheels in this big glass jar about waist-high and announces, 'This is my friend Sleepy.' There was a head in formaldehyde inside. And he's, like, 'My friend stole this for my birthday.' It looked like they got it from some laboratory."

"The skin was peeled away and it was labelled in Danish," remembered Tre. "Heck, creepy! He left it on the floor and we slept next to it. That was a great Halloween." "Whereas I had to go in the hallway because I've got a phobia against sleeping next to random body parts …" said Billie Joe.

In Spain they shared a bill with Brit psychobilly band The Meteors (veterans even back then), who threatened to kick Mike's ass if he so much as scratched their amp.

"It really gelled us up as a band too," Tre recalled. "We got so good at our instruments, from playing that way. I had drummers threatening to kick my ass if I moved anything on their kit. And these are retarded fucking set ups that are like drums over here and shit over here and things at weird angles. This rockabilly dude with muscles is going to kill me if I touched anything. In Poland there was no distortion…"

Mike: "We had to drive ten miles to find a distortion pedal …"

"I plugged into a stereo system that night," said Billie. "I plugged in my guitar – and I know a lot of garage bands these days would think this is really cool – but the noise was a *per-ling*, the cleanest sound you ever heard. And I was trying to communicate with these guys who had plugged me in the noise I wanted, so I made the noise of a distorted guitar with my mouth, and they ran out and come back two hours later with the one distortion pedal in the whole town. I plug it in and it sounds like a duck farting. But we played and it was a great show…"

It was during their stay in Spain that Billie Joe seemed to be decidedly under the weather, no doubt brought on by a combination of travel, exhaustion and hard work. He explained that he'd turned vegetarian and had lost a lot of weight as a result. Their relentless work-rate is something that not even Green Day's harshest critics can deny or ignore and, inevitably, it can take its toll.

The band headed to Germany, the country in which they played the most shows on the tour. German audiences may have a reputation as being a nation of bad metal or Europop lovers, but it was also home to a thriving punk scene quick to take in American bands before they'd even broke back home. Similar bands such as Bad Religion and NOFX built huge followings there in the early Nineties, playing to large festival crowds when they were still playing clubs in the US. But to reach that stage there was also a lot of hostile, cynical audiences to convert in the most unconventional of surroundings.

"We played squats in Germany for months," Billie Joe told journalist Ian Winwood in February 2005. "And there were five bands on the bill, four of which sounded like Napalm Death. And then there was us. We were only supposed to do about fifty shows, but the woman doing the booking asked us if we wanted to play some more? We were so exhausted we were practically hallucinating, and so we said, 'Sure! We can't think of anything dumber! Let's keep going!'"

"We were playing a squat and one of our friends, Sean, came up to the woman who was doing the door and said, jokingly, 'What would you do if I pulled out all the money that's in your pot, there?'" laughed Billie. "And she just pulled out a .45 gun, pointed it at him and said, calmly, 'I would shoot you.'"

"Those Germans were packing, man," said Tre. "All these squats would have rooms with ski masks and slings and buckets of rocks and bricks and things, in case the squatters had to go to war with the police or the Nazi skins or whoever. It was fucking gnarly, man."

In mid-December 1991 the band arrived in the UK, beginning with a show in London at a now-defunct venue called The Rails, situated beneath some railway arches. The band shared the bill with one of the UK's leading underground anarcho 'peace punk' bands, Thatcher On Acid, before heading off to play such places as Leeds Cockpit, The Attic in Dublin and the Rumble Club in Tunbridge Wells. Green Day got on with Thatcher On Acid well enough to hang out with them a few years later when the Brit punks journeyed to the States to play, amongst other places, Gilman.

Buoyed by the welcoming nature of their new UK punk friends, much madness ensued – like the time in Belfast when Tre took a shit slap-bang in the centre of the Botanic Gardens' bowling green.

"As far as Europe was concerned, Britain was the only place that was actually excited to see us," said Tre. "We toured with some really tight bands. I think, as music fans, we were slightly intimidated going to the UK because it was, like, 'Oh shit! The Beatles, Zeppelin ...'"

"The show at the Leeds Cockpit stands out as being one of the best shows we did early on," Billie Joe remembers. "I think we played for, like, three hours or something. We played every possible song we could think of and every bad cover version we knew. Even early on, we were always able to adapt to any atmosphere, in front of any amount of people. And even when we got big we've never suffered from arena-itis."

As with the rest of their European jaunt, in the UK Green Day found themselves playing – usually headlining – bills with an assortment of similar lower-rung punk bands. They played with the equally as irreverent East Anglian pop punkers Goober Patrol (whose albums *Truck Off!* and *Dutch Ovens* were toilet-humoured pre-cursors to *Dookie*) and the cool hardcore band Jailcell Recipes, both respected acts with strong cult followings within the UK punk underground. Others such as Angus Bagpipe and Couch Potato have been lost in the mists of recent rock history. One band they bonded with – and stayed in touch with over the years – were London-based punks Wat Tyler, a quartet who took their name from the English peasant who led a revolution in the fourteenth century. Wat Tyler were known for their satirical songs and regularly played shows with fellow skuzzy, tongue-in-cheek Brit boys Snuff. Drummer Sean (who also ran record label Rugger Bugger) famously hit the UK tabloids when the band produced their own version of Madonna's art-wank book *Sex*, entitled *Sexless*, which featured the bearded man naked in various poses. Unsurprisingly, with so much in common, Wat Tyler and Green Day got on famously.

December 17, 1991 was the day the band first received finished copies of their sophomore album. They were in Southampton for a show with Wigan boys Jailcell, so they made an impromptu decision that the show would also double as *Kerplunk!'s* album release party. They were a long way from the East Bay that had spawned it and Lookout!, who had, of course financed it, but why the hell not? They needed little excuse to break open the beers with the new English friends they were making in each town they played. The Southampton party set included a number of choice *Kerplunk*! cuts, including the album's 'big' songs 'Welcome To Paradise', 'Christie Road' and '2000 Light Years Away', all at that point unknown to those few fans who only had ever-circulating copies of *39/Smooth* and a couple of singles to go on.

"It was great," remembers Billie Joe. "For some reason we had a bunch of weird clothes that we kept finding in these different towns that we would play, and which we were wearing. It was a great show, though I did fall off the stage."

Christmas abroad was an occasion that called for another celebration, Green Day-style, when the band decided to stage an impromptu and improvised version of the nativity scene for their show at The Cricketers in Wigan, organized by local punk/skate store, Alan's.

"We were playing with Jailcell Recipes and because it was Christmas every band decided to do something special," Billie Joe told me. "They came out dressed up as the Sex Pistols, I think another band came out as Kiss, and for our thing we decided to do the Nativity scene in its entirety. Tre was the Virgin Mary, Mike was the anorexic Santa Claus narrator and I was the schizophrenic three wise men. Our friend Aidan was a mid-wife and our friend Sean was Jesus because he had really long hair."

"The whole thing was, we'd been through the entire scene, Jesus had been born and I came out saying 'It is I, Santa Claus, that is the true meaning of Christmas!'," laughs Mike. "Jesus came out and said the same thing, then fucking Sean, the big guy from Wat Tyler, came out with a beer dressed as the Easter Bunny. He ran around knocking everyone's beers out of their hands, shouting 'straight edge!' at them. Tre was up on a table with his legs spread out giving birth to Sean, who was under the table with a plastic carrier bag that was full of a bunch of ketchup, tomato soup and rice pudding, which we then threw on the audience. Some of it landed on this poor guy wearing glasses. Some people were eating it. We thought it was fucking funny."

"It was a bad idea that just got worse," chuckles Billie. "It was kind of the finale of the night – silly string and beer everywhere. I don't think we fully recovered from that, because by the time we actually played people had seen it all."

The party then moved back down south to a show at TJ's in Newport, Wales, where they played the venue's annual punk rock Christmas party with Knucklehead and Midway Still, a show compered by then-Membranes frontman, writer and all-round punk ace face, John Robb.

"From 1987 to 1994 when no-one cared about punk rock, people like Simon at Rockaway Records in Newport and the promoters at TJ's were putting together all these great punk bills and keeping the scene alive," says John. "So you would always make the effort to see the opening band on the bill. At that time Green Day were just another one of them – a first-on-the-bill American band some of us had vaguely heard of. I seem to remember introducing myself to them as the compere and they were, like, 'What the fuck is a *compere*?' But they were great that night, really tight, and people were into them – I'd imagine that at that time Green Day probably sold more records in Newport than anywhere else in the world.

"It's a punk rock place, is TJ's," he adds. "A year later Kurt Cobain got engaged to Courtney Love there. But even so it's really weird seeing Green Day go from fourth on the bill at a scruffy punk rock dive like that to playing to 28,000 in Manchester. It's like a dream come true, isn't it? It's proof that it *can* be done." A live version of 'At The Library' from this show made it onto an *S&M* fanzine compilation album alongside the likes of Jon Spencer, Girls Against Boys and Huggy Bear.

John Robb also relates a story about what happened after the raucous Newport show. Once again, Green Day had been offered some floor space at a friend of the promoter's house in Newport, where his children were quietly sleeping upstairs. Like excitable school friends having a sleepover – which is essentially what they were doing, only in a total stranger's house five thousand miles away from their own – and still drunk and buzzing from the show the trio were making a bit of a racket. When they still hadn't settled down despite his protests, their host came downstairs, took a samurai sword down from the wall and threatened to chop them up if they didn't shut up *right now*.

Sixty seconds later the house was finally silent.

The next day – Christmas Eve – saw the sheepish trio drive on to Bath where they spent a sub-zero Christmas Day with the members of Knucklehead.

"It was awesome," Mike remembered a decade on. "On Christmas Eve we were racing around Bath with Billie in a shopping cart, stealing Christmas trees off people's porches. Way off the hook. Then the next morning I made these huge veggie-omelettes for everyone, really good ones with everything from hash browns to brussel sprouts in them. Each one took twenty minutes to make – we only had one pan between us …"

Green Day's time in the UK was the start of a healthy relationship with the country that they would keep returning to. They liked the beer, the curry houses, the multi-culturalism of the bigger cities. And they liked the people. But the band's new found popularity and cultural awakenings weren't just confined to the UK. By the end of their first European tour they had seen more of the continent than many more established bands get to. It was an exhausting trip, whose organic approach was evident in the dose of head-lice Billie Joe brought back with him.

But it was also a tour whose rewards the band are still reaping the benefits from to this day. They'd been bitten by the worldwide road bug and in three months had built up a solid grass-roots fan base that would serve them well for years to come.

All of which was just as well, because given the success and good times had by all on that first tour, they were going to be spending a hell of a lot of time out there over the next decade.

Kerplunk
intr.v. - to fall with a sound like that of a heavy object falling rapidly into water; n. - a kerplunking sound or movement; a children's game involving plastic cocktail sticks.

Green Day's second album seemed somehow sharper than its predecessor. The nervous energy was still there in abundance, but the songs were stronger and more diverse, no doubt inspired and refined by life on the road in Europe and a defter approach to songwriting by Billie Joe.

From the opening clash of a cymbal, opener '2000 Light Years Away' pounded along like one long chorus, pausing only briefly for bass-line breakdown in the middle, before Billie Joe brought the song back in again. The tempo didn't let up there. As with The Ramones there was an almost formulaic Green Day familiarity to songs such as 'One For The

Razorbacks' and the squat life tale of 'Welcome To Paradise' and almost sing-song hopeful quality to Billie Joe's neurosis.

The song 'Who Wrote Holden Caulfield?' aligned itself with one of literature's great dysfunctional teen American anti-heroes from JD Salinger's timeless *Catcher In The Rye*. "My teachers tried to force me to read it in high school, so naturally I didn't," explained Billie Joe. "I did finally read it later and, ironically, rebellion is what it's about. This guy tries to fit but can never quite do it. Finally he just celebrates his uniqueness by rebelling and getting kicked out of high school and going on this crazy adventure. I could identify with that ..."

"The song [is] about trying to [be] motivated to do something because your elders tell you to get motivated. So then you get frustrated and you think that you should do something but you end up doing nothing."

Another standout track was the emotive 'Christie Road', a commentary on street life set to chugging mid-paced guitars and with a redemptive coda. Billie Joe encapsulated the spirit of Oakland as only a resident can, in what sounds like a sequel to the "dear mother ..." letter-writing tone of 'Welcome To Paradise'. Other songs included the aforementioned 'Dominated Love Slave', a tongue-in-cheek track featuring Tre on vocals, singing in an affected bumpkin twang about sado-masochism and the use of power tools.

On January 17, 1992, Green Day's second album *Kerplunk!* was released by Lookout! on CD, vinyl and cassette. It was easily their best recorded work so far and initial reactions were positive from label, fans and press alike. Mainly though, *Kerplunk!* was resigned to the usual coverage in magazines such as *Flipside, Maximum Rock 'n' Roll* and the odd larger publication with the foresight to recognise an emerging class act.

Those aware of the band already almost universally agreed that *Kerplunk!* was a vast improvement on the highly likeable but ultimately more one-dimensional *39/Smooth*. The pen and ink drawing of a teenage girl toting a gun on the cover tied in with the album's liner notes, a tale entitled 'My Adventure With Green Day' written by Pinole Valley High School pupil 'Laurie L', (a thinly disguised reference to label boss Larry Livermore). The story tied in with the album's themes of disenchantment and alienation as explored in *Catcher In The Rye*, though its suitably over-the-top tone is clearly only ever a parody of over-excited fandom. Told in the gushing terms of a teenage girl, Laurie wins a 'Dream Date With Green Day' competition and decides to kill her parents rather than miss the show. As she hits the road in search of her idols, many references of the Green Day world are scattered throughout – like Telegraph Avenue, "where the scummy people hang out". It all comes to a head when Laurie is arrested by the police seconds before the band hit the stage. "Everyone's got two parents but there's only one Green Day!" she concludes.

Though they didn't know it at the time, as the band's final independent release, their 'Thanks' list fittingly also read like a 'who's who' of the East Bay scene and beyond, though the album itself was dedicated to the memory of 'Gravy'.

Gravy was Mike's late cat.

By early 1992, when *Kerplunk!* was released, Green Day were still broke and relatively unknown. For stretches at a time Billie Joe stored all his personal stuff at his mother's house in Pinole and when not out playing shows he spent his spare time driving around and staying at friend's houses. Mike and Tre lived similarly transient existences – perfect training for the months and years of living out of suitcases for the next decade. And a new record meant a new desire – a necessity – to tour once again.

Home for Green Day's next US jaunt was a former mobile library that Tre's father bought in Phoenix. He ripped out the interiors and installed bunks, equipments racks and the odd attempt at a home comfort and also, for a while at least, became their new designated driver.

"I watched them go from a bunch of kids to a group of musicians with a work ethic," says Frank Wright II. "On their first tour or two, it was more like a party than anything else. I still scratch my head and say, 'How in the hell did they make it?' They used to practice in my living room ... you hear it coming together, but you don't expect people are going to go out and buy it."

Shows stretched across the states from Sproul Plaza back in Berkeley in the West through Illinois to New Jersey in the East. Life was still far from luxurious and the band were still roughing it. Playing a show in Hollywood, they stayed on the floor of a former *Flipside* writer's house for the weekend – a typical night on the road.

There are various bootleg videos available that capture Green Day playing such shows to increasingly growing audiences singing along to their songs, as opposed to the crowds of the early days who, not knowing any recorded material, tended to just get off on the energy of it all. But they were still in the clubs. Being one of the freshest and biggest new punk bands around was about as good as it could get. Or so they thought.

So Green Day were still a low-visibility band. Yet over the course of 1992 and 1993, thanks to endless touring, *Kerplunk!* disseminated. With little in the way of advertising, in the months that followed its release the album was passed on from friend to friend around the world. Before the internet and before downloads, Green Day tapped into the punk rock word-of-mouth subculture in which bands are discovered through recommendation or association with other bands; for me – and thousands of others – it was the fact that they shared a label with Operation Ivy. Songs from *Kerplunk!* made it onto mix tapes. In the UK it was reviewed almost solely in fanzines, though *NME* writer (and future head of Fierce Panda records) Simon Williams had pinpointed the band as ones to watch, and providers of a much-needed welcome break from the glut of tortured sounds coming out of Seattle: "a storming-but-soothing antidotal cream to smear on the current rash of grunge merchants."

But it was never heard on the radio.

I was sixteen when I first heard *Kerplunk!* after a friend of mine, Mark, had made me a copy. Sixteen seemed like a good time to discover Green Day. Their simple song structures recalled The Ramones and a hundred other punk bands I'd already discovered, while their lyrics were broad enough to speak to a generation of teenagers and adolescents whose main objective is to mock everyone and everything around them – there's nothing quite as powerful as a teenager's disdain for the world. Plus they sang about drinking, sex, drugs, boredom, punk rock – all the things with which I hoped to occupy my time. In amongst the metal fans, shaven-headed hardcore boys, old school punks and indie kids who I associated with, Green Day seemed to strike a chord (well, three actually) where few others had in such a manner. Only the occasional band like the Sex Pistols or Metallica had infiltrated the tribes and found favour amongst staunchly snobbish music fans like Green Day did.

The friend who introduced me to their music, Mark, was a couple of years younger than most of us and was a troubled kid. I knew that his home and school life was tough enough and that he'd been in many scrapes as a teenager. He was a big playful kid, eager to impress and never shy in letting the truth get in the way of a good story. I always associate Mark with *Kerplunk!* because he not only introduced me to the band but because he seemed like an archetypal Green Day fan. I remember the album on his stereo as we sat in his bedroom, wasted after a night of over-indulgences. I remember the album being one of the first on the car stereo when I learnt to drive a few months later. I remember thinking, this band is singing about Mark's life. This band is singing about 'the alienated' the world over.

Mark dabbled in drugs like we all did, but couldn't seem to get it together at school, a less rough and altogether more prestigious school than the one me and my friends attended some three miles away. He got into squabbles, the odd fight, was caught truanting – nothing drastic, but enough to warrant more concern from his parents and teachers. We knew Mark was just a lost kid whose friendship with us – a relatively responsible bunch despite everything – kept him grounded in some ways. If he was being a bullshitter we told him so.

But then one day during the 1992-1993 school year, when drinking, girls and music were the only things that mattered, he did something that surprised everyone – except us. He came first in a poetry competition at school and won some sort of award. His work was published in the local paper and Mark was the toast of his teachers who finally believed they had unearthed a previously hidden great talent; they knew they could get through to this likeable, listless teenager in a Gorilla Biscuits T-shirt in the end. The next time we saw Mark he was beaming with pride at his achievements, and we congratulated him accordingly.

The next week we got talking to another friend who went to Mark's school. Apparently the poem with which he had won a regional poetry competition was entitled 'Welcome To Paradise' – he had copied the lyrics to a Green Day song out word for word and submitted them as his own; plagiarism of the highest order. Naturally, we found the hoodwinking of his peers and the entire administration of his snobby school hilarious, and were quite unsurprised. In fact, we applauded this punk rock-flavoured deception – given that most bands rip-off other bands that have gone before in one way or another, what did it matter? If Green Day hadn't been on the brink of massive international success and weren't currently enjoying a swelling underground fan base the world over Mark would have got away with it and things might have turned out differently. But they were and he was rumbled when some other kids in the school that had also got into the band via *Kerplunk!* pointed out the similarities to a song by this then-relatively unknown band from across the water. The award was immediately retracted, the prize withdrawn, his parents alerted. In going for glory and in trying to please his parents and teachers he had wound up in more trouble. The following year

I moved to college and gradually lost contact with Mark.

Then the next thing I heard he was dead. Details were shady, but apparently he had choked on his own vomit while intoxicated. We were shocked. He was still a teenager.

Why does all this matter? Because Mark was a Green Day fan and band and person are inextricably linked forever in my mind. He was the every day kid they were writing for and about – for a few action-packed teenage months, maybe a year or two when the world feels like its yours and for the first time you realise that there are others out there like you, he was one of them and they were one of us. And it matters because without Mark, the bullshitting, troublesome highly loveable teenager, I wouldn't be here writing this today. Call it a personal tribute if you like. I don't know, perhaps Mark just represents lost youth the world over and is part of a wider culture that spawned Green Day and to whom they are singing today. If you like the band I think you'll see the connection.

Kerplunk! had Billie Joe Armstrong's personality stamped all over it. It also signalled a new-found creative confidence for the frontman who was now writing more songs than Green Day needed. The band had always had a relaxed approach to playing music with other people and during time off throughout 1991-1992, Billie had been playing with some Berkeley associates in their new band, Pinhead Gunpowder.

The band was a group of punk fans playing together for the hell of it, a loose arrangement that was all the better for its casual approach. The original idea came from former Chrimpshrine drummer Aaron Cometbus, who had attempted to form a band while living in Arcata, California (Green Day had dropped him off there while on tour and he had yet to return) using various musicians when all his closer friends were away touring with their proper bands. The band name was also his, a reference to a type of particularly potent green tea sold at the local co-op store.

When Cometbus moved back to Berkeley, he kept the songs and the band name and set about turning it into something cohesive. By virtue of his ties with the scene it became a post-Gilman supergroup of sorts. Joining Billie Joe on guitar and Aaron on drums was Mike Kersh from Fuel on guitar and Bill Schnieder from Monsula on bass, two well-respected Bay Area bands who, for a time, were as popular amongst their peers as Green Day. In 1994 the quartet would be joined by future

Green Day touring guitarist Jason White.

Songwriting sessions had dated back to early 1990 in local home-cum-rehearsal hang out House-O-Toast after the members' other bands had finished playing for the day. They never intended to be a band as such, but instead placed the emphasis on writing songs for a possible release at some point. No stress, no pressures – just a garage band having fun.

"A band of people who were always at the same shows, always dancing, always hanging out," writes Cometbus in Pinhead Gunpowder's official biography for Lookout!, "dedicated enough to put all their energies into a band, but so busy with other projects and travels that we knew Pinhead Gunpowder could only be part time, once or twice a year for a few months at a time. And that's the way it's been ever since. It's funny because we barely knew each other when we started, and though we don't really hang out at the same places or go to the same shows anymore, we're much closer now."

Though shows were few and far between, Pinhead Gunpowder's first recording was their contribution 'Benicia By The Bay' on Lookout!'s *Can Of Pork* compilation in January 1992, alongside popular East Bay bands such as The Lookouts, Downfall, Spitboy and Fifteen. That month also saw the release of Pinhead's four-track debut EP, 'Fahiza', produced by Kevin Seconds of anthemic Eighties hardcore band 7 Seconds. Pinhead Gunpowder have been releasing albums and singles of their frenetic punk every three years or so since, the chief irony being that the band who never set out to be a band have outlasted so many more who *did* and at the time of writing have now been in existence in one form or another for close to fifteen years.

In late 1992, Billie Joe also played one show as guitarist with new trio Rancid. Whether it was done to help out friend Tim Armstrong (Rancid's second guitarist and ex-UK Sub Lars Frederickson had yet to join) or, most unlikely, a tentative step towards joining the post-Operation Ivy band semi-permanently, it resolutely remained a one-off and Billie Joe went back to concentrating on Green Day full-time.

In August 1992 at a show at Gilman, Green Day previewed a couple of new songs, 'Longview' and 'Better Not Come Around', soon to be given slightly different lyrics and retitled 'When I Come Around'. To the three hundred fervent fans crammed into the venue, it sounded like their best material yet (a bootleg single from this show was released the following year). Clearly, a change was in the air – and, as it happened, the hair.

A major development came when Green Day took on two managers to handle the band's business, which was becoming both lucrative and complicated. "A bunch of small shows would get cancelled and we'd end up playing medium-sized, slimy club bars," explained Billie Joe. "Without representation we'd get fucked out of our money. At the smaller clubs people would turn up who didn't understand those places and things would get really violent."

Increasingly shows in over-subscribed venues were being cancelled. At the same time, living out of Tre's father's van was taking its toll, especially as they were commanding decent fees in sold-out clubs. Having had a *laissez-faire* attitude to management in the past, the trio realised the necessity of having an organisation other than a label behind them, particularly to handle the day-to-day, nuts-and-bolts business.

They met with Cahnman Management, a company run by two attorneys, Elliot Cahn and Jeff Saltzman. The duo had previously managed Primus, Melvins and Mudhoney and impressed the band enough to take them on as their managers.

This growing ambition to break out of the secular punk scene was backed up by Larry Livermore. "We don't have the ability to get them on MTV, or to be on all commercial radio stations or into every record store in the land," he commented in 1994. "Depending on your beliefs, that might be an advantage or a drawback. But undoubtedly a large factor in Green Day choosing the path they did was the fact they wanted to do these things."

Cahn and Saltzman immediately set to work spreading the word about Green Day in a whole new way. They started approaching the major record labels, tempting them with a band who had sold over fifty thousand albums on raw talent alone. This wasn't a world of fanzine interviews and communal chilli; this was the realm of lawyers and labels' long expense account lunches. The band left them to it and carried on with life as abnormal.

1992-1993 were, to many, Green Day's glory years. Not because they were any better then, but because each show they played and each new song that Billie Joe penned was a realisation of their potential. There was little external pressure, yet they were increasingly becoming one of the most popular underground bands in the world, known amongst the sussed punk initiates, albeit photo-shoots and tedious interviews were not yet an every day occurrence. Everything was exciting the sky was the limit.

As élitist and crass as it sounds, a band on the up is always more appealing than a band who has 'made it'. When a band goes big, everyone knows about them and you find your own personal tastes suddenly overlapping with people's whose record collections would probably horrify you – with people who would have sneered at your grubby little punk tastes a year earlier. Such is the way of the pop lottery. One year they're playing to five hundred people, the next fifty thousand. Of course, true fans should like a band for their music and all that goes with it, but sometimes it's hard having clueless gimps tell you about the great new band they've discovered. Comfort yourself with the knowledge that you'll always be cooler than them. Never let go of that sense of snobbery and discrimination – and if your heroes start pandering to the gimps, then let it go.

And anyone lucky enough to catch Green Day between the releases of *Kerplunk!* and forthcoming third album *Dookie* saw a band teetering on the brink of something. They saw a band capable of filling arenas, but still in a club environment, playing with an almost telepathic confidence.

"The first time I saw them was before *Dookie* came out, sometime in '92 or '93," says Mark Hoppus of Blink-182, arguably the first band to enjoy their own multi-million success on the back of Green Day. "They were playing in a club called Soma in San Diego. I remember it was funny because all the talk was that Green Day were gonna be signed to a major label, and back then there were lots of arguments as to whether people should sign to major labels. Billie Joe was onstage and he said, 'Hey everyone, make sure you clap really loud because the executives from the label are trying to decide whether they want to sign us or not tonight, so let them know what you think'. He was making a joke out of it which was pretty cool."

I too remember quite vividly a drunken teenage night in 1993 when the main point of discussion was whether Green Day were going to sign a highly lucrative deal with one of the big labels, and whether that would signal 'the end' of the band. It almost seems absurd now, given the amount of insipid pop-punk bands currently on the payroll of the big labels, but it really did feel like a major change was in the air. It wasn't the end of the world, but it was *weird.* If the record industry was discovering the commercial potential of bands like Green Day, then who else was next, and what were the implications? And who was buying the next round? (we weren't *that* bothered by one of our bands being taken away from us – Nirvana had got there first). Yet it was a talking point that sticks in my mind to this day. Only twelve months earlier a half dozen of us had been passing round the same copy of *Kerplunk!* in amongst swapping records by Bad Brains and Operation Ivy, Nations Of Ulysses and Born Against and all those other cool bands those people still hung up on Nirvana or Pearl Jam just didn't know about. The year before that we had been part of the thirty or so people who had seen NOFX play in a community centre and spent the day hanging out with them, just because we could. Because they weren't rock stars. And now their younger contemporaries and recent support band were being courted for millions of dollars. *What the fuck?*

What the fuck indeed.

In spring 1993, Green Day were living together in the basement of a large ramshackle student-dominated Victorian house at 2243 Ashby Street, just down the block from the pristine entrance to the esteemed University Of Berkeley (it's the college that features in the Dustin Hoffman movie *The Graduate*). The same basement would later be used to film the video for Green Day's 'Long View' the following year.

The house on Ashby served as a base for Green Day as they began to receive an increasing amount of calls from the major record labels of America. Regardless of musical tastes and preferences, the larger labels are nothing but efficiently-run businesses, motivated predominantly by profit. Once word had got out that this just-out-their-teens cult trio had now sold a total of 60,000 copies of their two cheaply-recorded independent releases and were filling clubs right across the country, it was music to their ears. It was all they needed to hear. Despite exterior appearances suggesting otherwise, the music business is run by lawyers and accountants. These suits may not have understood the meaning or cultural relevance of Green Day, but they certainly understood the figures.

"The record company guys would come to see us rehearse in the basement and their wives would go shopping on Telegraph Avenue," said Tre. "And when we went on tour we would come back to discover these crusty punks had squatted our place, and every single thing we owned was gone. All of our records, all our stuff. And my love letters ended up on the internet ..."

Having seen the figures, a number of record labels were very interested in Green Day. For these people, punk ethics didn't enter into it. Profit was the main motivation and it was clear to many than Green Day were one of the hottest bands around, practically reeking of still-untapped potential.

A parade of record company representatives passed through Berkeley, meeting the band and watching them play. It was confusing and overwhelming and a little bit ridiculous, but it was also mildly exciting. The band took full advantage of the open cheque books and generous expense accounts available to those out to woo them. One major label was ruled out of the picture after their A&R man turned up in a limousine and, according to the band, seemed nervous about the neighbourhood as he repeatedly checked his (clearly expensive) watch.

"Warners, Geffen, Sony and everybody's mother wanted to sign us," said Tre, "but we held off for quite a long time. Why? Because David Geffen's money was paying for us to go to Disneyland. We kind of milked them. We wanted to hold out until we got complete artistic control. We wanted to be the bosses and not let somebody else tell us what to do. Of course, the first offer is bullshit, the second slightly less, the third still kind of sucks …we thought 'Fuck this, it's our lives.' It's like getting married or something."

It's easy to see the major label A&R men as slightly outdated vultures who move *en masse* towards their latest prey, but there's a reason these labels discover and break so many great new artists. They have the good sense to employ young people who know what's going on – and what sells. Often the A&R men come from punk or alternative backgrounds themselves, or are at least in touch with what's going on at a street level. Rob Cavallo of Reprise Records, a subsidiary label of the vast Warners empire, was one of them, a young enthusiastic talent spotter-cum-producer.

Cavallo's father had been a club owner and band manager, counting Prince as one of his clients, and his son was introduced to music and the business behind it from a young age. Rob had been a keen guitarist and was experimenting with recording techniques from an early age. After school he worked as an assistant engineer before his father introduced him to contacts at Warners/Reprise, who offered him a job assisting their head of A&R, Michael Ostin. It was while developing new bands for Reprise that a colleague asked him to produce another new-ish signing, The Muffs. Shortly afterwards he received a Green Day demo from Cahn and Saltzman.

Cavallo would later go on to produce Ash, Goo Goo Dolls, L7, Alanis

Morissette, Jawbreaker, Chris Isaak and numerous film soundtrack albums, before becoming Senior Vice President at Reprise.

But it was his involvement on The Muffs' self-titled debut, released in May of that year, that piqued Green Day's interest. The LA quartet had previously released records on Sub Pop and Sympathy For The Record Industry, before being signed. Lead by singer Kim Shattuck, The Muffs played post-Ramones three-chord, beefed-up melodic punk given a Seventies rock sheen – exactly the type of music Green Day were into.

When Cavallo visited Green Day in Berkeley he reportedly turned up with his guitar and joined them jamming some tunes together. Clearly he spoke their language. They went out for ice cream and drove up into the Berkeley Hills, where Cavallo presented a convincing argument as to why they should sign with him.

"He's from LA and stuff," Billie commented shortly afterwards to the eminent journalist Gina Arnold. "But he's married and thinking about having kids and that makes him seem like more of a genuine person, whereas a lot of those fuckers just seem like hipsters. Some of them just seemed to want to get laid, to tell you the truth."

"I'll never forget when Green Day said 'We're going to be a great band,'" says Cavallo to Bud Scoppa on www.taxi.com. "And they knew it. 'We're going to be a great band no matter what Reprise does for us.' They already could draw 1,000 kids in a good ten or twelve cities across this country, and they'd already played Europe. These kids were 21 years old. They knew what it took to be successful in the music business. They never had jobs. They made their living being a band by the time they were aged 16 or 17. They were like, 'We think we need the help of Reprise to realise our potential; however, we are fully confident that we are going to do it on our own anyway. So you're going to take the record that we make and you're going to send it to radio stations for us. So when they hear it, they're going to like it and they're going to want to play it.'"

After much deliberation, Green Day signed to Warners/Reprise in April 1993 for an initial deal of five albums, with the plan that Cavallo would producer their major label debut. The band also stipulated that Lookout! would continue to own the rights to their two albums, the idea being that the indie label's tireless support would continue to be rewarded even if Green Day were no longer with them – a move that has since justifiably paid handsome dividends to Livermore and Co over the past ten years. The first thing Billie Joe did with his money was pay rent on his basement for a year. At last, he had a place to call home – even if he wasn't going to be there.

It was, symbolically at least, the end of an era for Green Day. They played two more shows at Gilman, their 'official' final show in the venue in September 1993 and a later unadvertised one using an assumed name, sharing the stage with a band called Brent's TV. Because the show hadn't been advertised as featuring Green Day, only 150 people were in attendance – one of them being Larry Livermore: "Almost everyone knew each other and knew the words to all the songs by both bands. So we were all dancing and singing along together, and it was warm and festive and family-like, but there was also this bitter-sweet feeling that came from knowing that things would never be like this again, that this was the last time we'd all be together this way."

The punk rock party as it had once been was now over. Green Day's *rites de passage* through the punk ranks was nearly complete. Call it an impending loss-of-innocence, call it a seismic shift in both economics and rock 'n' roll culture. Call it the selling out of an ideal if you wish – but at least have the argument ready to back up the point. Soon people on the scene would be talking about little else.

Despite losing their biggest selling – and still most promising band – Livermore and Lookout! had little reason to be bitter. By the end of 1993 they had racked up sales of 100,000 Green Day albums. Pretty good going. *Pretty unexpected*. Twelve months later they'd double that to 200,000 and by the close of 1995 the combined sales of *39/Smooth* and *Kerplunk!* would have increased five-fold to the staggering one million mark.

Things were changing in ways that no-one – not Green Day, not Lookout!, not *Maximum Rock 'n' Roll*, not even any of the speculative records labels – could ever have truly predicted.

By the time Billie Joe would finally return to Gilman as a paying punter in December 1994, the punk purist's perception towards him had shifted somewhat.

"I ran into an old friend of mine," remembered Billie Joe and all he could say was 'Wow, what the fuck are *you* doing here?'"

PART II: THE MIDDLE

It meant 'baby shit'.

No hidden meaning, no subliminal message, no grand statement.

Baby shit – the smelliest there is.

Had they known they were releasing one of the biggest albums of the decade, a genuine musical phenomenon, it's unlikely Green Day would have named it *Dookie.*

Or maybe they *especially* would have named it as such.

"If you can say the word 'dookie' you can keep in touch with the child within," said Mike Dirnt in the official Warners band biog. "I've always thought that's part of our success – we're immature."

The lyrics that comprised Green Day's third album were written by Billie Joe Armstrong in the basement of 2243 Ashby, surrounded by clothes, bits of equipment, empty beers cans and a bong for weed. He wasn't living in complete squalor, but he was living punk. Income came by way of royalties from their Lookout! albums, shows (though touring is a good way *not* to get rich) and increasing merchandise sales.

And yet here he was, twenty-two years old, with his same blue Fender Strat covered in stickers of obscure punk bands and the sweat and blood of hundreds of shows, sitting in Fantasy Studios in his home-town (near enough), with his friends, working with a producer they liked and trusted and a sizeable budget to pay for it all. Sweet.

Fantasy studio was a laid-back place with a healthy pedigree of bands ranging from Credence Clearwater Revival to Sonny Rollins to Aerosmith (and, after Green Day, punk bands such as Rancid and Jawbreaker.)

For once, the band weren't constrained by time and money. After initial demos had been recorded, they spent a total of five weeks laying down more songs than were needed.

"I feel really blessed that I got to make that record with them," producer Rob Cavallo said in an interview about his career to date. "Right from getting the drum sound, everything seemed to click. We always knew it. Every time we had a take that was the right take, it was like Tre would throw his sticks and you would always hear them click hitting the floor – and then we would take a break."

Once again, drugs played a supporting role in the creative process –

this time it was psychedelics. As Mike later proudly recalled, the opening bass line to 'Longview', one of the album's key tracks, was written by him during a drug session-cum-rehearsal.

"When Billie gave me a shuffle beat for 'Longview' I was flying on acid so hard," he told *Rolling Stone*. "I was laying up against the wall with my bass lying on my lap. It just came to me. I said, 'Bill, check this out. Isn't that the wackiest thing you've ever heard?' Later, it took me a long time to be able to play it, but it made sense when I was on drugs." Maybe it was because their economical approach in the studio on their first albums had paid off so well that Green Day showed no signs of slowing things down just because they were working on a big budget. Or perhaps they were aware that much of the money spent ultimately comes off their own profits. Either way, as ever the trio continued to be quick and focused. All Billie's lead vocals was done in two days, amounting to 16 or 17 songs. Many were done in single takes.

With the album completed, Green Day were invited to play a clutch of dates during the summer with Bad Religion on their 'Recipe For Hate' tour. After a hiatus in the late Eighties, this socially-aware LA quintet were back on form with their album *Against The Grain*, released the previous year, and over a decade since they had formed had reaffirmed themselves as Godfathers of the new breed. In fact, in 1993 Bad Religion were probably the biggest active punk band around and although their followers would go on to reap greater commercial rewards, they were arguably the first US band to mix punk and hardcore energy with big guitars, melodies and singer Greg Graffin's rich harmonies. Green Day were later given credit for instigating a pop-punk uprising, but Bad Religion had done it first. What Green Day added was *colour*. Their guitarist Brett Gurewitz was also founder of Epitaph Records, on its way to becoming the independent label success story of the decade.

As an aside, years later in the late Nineties, Bad Religion decided to tour with the now-huge punk bands who they had given a break early in their careers, subsequently expressing disappointment in an interview saying that Green Day and others like them failed to return the favour. "Greg [Graffin, Bad Religion's lead singer] and I talked for a long time," said bassist Jay Bentley. "We talked with these people – Billie Joe and Dexter Holland [of the Offspring] – about taking us out on the road with them when we went on tour, and both of them said no. We were quick to remind them, 'Look, we took you guys out on the road all the time.'"

Apparently both Billie Joe and Holland said that they respected Bad Religion too much to let the group open for them – something Bentley said was "horse shit" on www.livedaily.com.

As part of this punk rock groundswell, 1993 also saw the return of Operation Ivy's Tim Armstrong and Matt Freeman with new band Rancid, who released a debut single, 'Radio Radio Radio' on Fat Wreck, the label run by NOFX frontman Fat Mike Burkett. Still one of Rancid's finest moment, the lead track was an emotive punk song about days gone by and the salvation to be found in music during a tough upbringing. E ffectively combining the grittiness and speed of Operation Ivy (and before them first and second wave British punk rock), with the poppy choruses associated with Green Day, the song covered sentiments that applied to a lot of those people in the Berkeley punk scene who had grown up in broken homes, poverty or with alcoholic parents; the two Armstrongs, Tim and Billie Joe, co-wrote the song together in a beautiful display of post-Gilman band symbiosis. As with Green Day, Rancid's time was about to come ... any second now.

On January 11, 1994, *Dookie* was released to an unsuspecting public. Copies had been sent out to the press a couple of months earlier, complete with a semi-fictionalised biography by band associate and Gilman regular Ben Weasel, and the reaction had been positive.

It was a good time to release an upbeat rock record.

The rock industry as a whole was enjoying decent record sales. As with all economies and fashions, the popularity of the genre perpetually follows an ebb and flow pattern as reliable as the tide itself. Sometimes when certain big artists break, for a while at least their specific genres such as chart pop, dance or hip-hop become the prevailing styles capable of producing the biggest sellers and being the preferred listening on the world's stereos – in recent times everyone from the Spice Girls to Oasis and The Darkness have inspired renewed interest in manufactured pop, laddish guitar rock and classic rock respectively.

Thanks to Nirvana and the post-Sub Pop explosion of bands, in the early Nineties rock music was very much back on the agenda. Compared to a decade earlier when America was rocking to new wave bands, boring balladeers and synth pop, the early Nineties was awash with surly young men and women making a noise. Of course, not all of it was good. In fact, as soon as Nirvana were tagged 'grunge' and the first articles discussing 'grunge fashion' began to appear in broadsheet newspapers and lifestyle mags post-'Smells Like Teen Spirit', the music dissipated into something else and all sorts of awful bands crawled out of the woodwork in the name of grunge or 'alt-rock' circa 1993-1994.

While the first grunge bands were all about power and volume with no small amounts of black humour thrown in (I defy anyone to disagree that, for a large part of their seven year career, Nirvana were essentially a playful, *fun* band), the ones who followed picked up more on the bleakness and nihilism of the music. Grunge became a lifestyle choice whose essence was increasingly being distorted, diluted and mythologized in articles and movies. Cool, true grunge bands like Tad, Mudhoney and Screaming Trees were overlooked in favour of endless tedious (yet radio-friendly) rock-lite bands like Bush, Silverchair, Candlebox, Live, Moist and Matchbox Twenty, who all gained record contracts and varied degrees of commercial success on the back of grunge, most of them fronted by 'enigmatic' poster boys riddled by the pain of modern life, and usually blessed with a voice that sounded like Kurt's. Yuk. Little wonder he was feeling under the weather.

"All of a sudden you had Guns N' Roses and the Seattle bands saying, 'We want to reflect our punk-rock roots'," Rob Cavallo told *Spin* magazine. "But Green Day were the ones who broke punk."

The big screen successes of the time also seemed to reflect a vapidity at the heart of American youth culture – either schmaltz like *Forrest Gump*, the latest Jim Carrey Tourettes routine or the ultra-ironic *Beavis & Butthead,* who satirized their own square-eyed audience so adroitly that most of them missed the message and it barely even mattered.

Out in the real world, the music tied in with a general malaise among large sections of American youth and post-adolescents, a feeling of apathy and selfishness as a reaction to God-less times. These were sentiments that formed the basis for an article by writer Douglas Coupland, exploring what he determined as the 'Generation X', the latest demographic within the shifting parameters and beliefs of a culture in flux. The article was soon expanded into a book that would soon seize the zeitgeist of the early Nineties, when, for a while at least certain areas of music, literature and film seemed to coalesce into a body of work that encapsulated the feeling of America's young, intelligent and restless – witness films like Richard Linklater's *Slacker* and *Dazed & Confused*, Gus Van Sant's *My Own Private Idaho* or books such as Elizabeth Wurtzel's *Prozac Nation* or Bret Easton Ellis' *Less Than Zero*.

But it was Coupland's *Generation X* that provided the media with a handy tag for this apathetic culture of disenfranchised, disillusioned 'slackers' – people who were anti-the-American-Dream. Sub-titled *"Tales for an accelerated culture"*, *Generation X* is described in the book *Cult Fiction* as "featuring a group of detached, white, twenty-something Americans, dispossessed of all but the merest motivation and living with a double dose of irony in the soul. This was the book that launched a thousand think-tanks and commercial strategies."

Some would slot Green Day into this demographic, but the difference was they had a strong work ethic – a desire to better themselves – that dictated that boredom and slothfulness were fine, but inactivity, inertia and lack of ambition were not. Billie Joe had once written an article back in 1989 called 'how to be a couch potato' for his friend Eggplant's fanzine, *Absolutely Zippo*, in which he outlined root beer, pizza and TV as the essential ingredients for a good day's loafing, but it was likely written between tours, recording or jamming with another band. Green Day weren't slackers, they merely did what they wanted to do. Besides, by the early Nineties 'Generation X' seemed to belong to the middle-class and Green Day, as we know, are resolutely working-class. The slackers were the kid brothers and sisters of the Yuppies of the mid-Eighties – they rejected their recent past yet had no better suggestions, living by a watered-down, dead-end version of nihilism. Or some would say laziness. Green Day, a band who were simultaneously branded part of this culture, yet helped destroy it with three chords and an irreverent quip, had fought too hard so far to risk going back to the couch yet. Besides, the other difference was many Gen X-ers were no doubt financed by parents who could afford such an indulgence.

"I fucking hate college students, to tell you the truth because they've been able to go to school, get an education, live in the dorms, and get a free ride from their parents," spat Billie Joe. "I'm also envious, because I never had that opportunity to learn. I wrote a song called 'Brat' about waiting for your parents to die so you can get your inheritance ... which my son will probably be singing one day himself."

In April 1994, slacker/Gen-X culture reached a zenith when Nirvana frontman Kurt Cobain, the biggest and most believable 'reluctant rock star' of his time, took a shotgun and killed himself at his home in Seattle. For a while at least the world of music stopped turning and fans of music globally entered a period of mourning. As with all suicides, the death of Kurt was undeniably tragic, heart-breaking and pointless, the act of a man whose exact reasons for taking his own life would go with him to the grave. He left behind a wife, a young daughter and a highly successful band. But the wider implications were seismic and as the story of the biggest rock star death of the decade broke, everyone had opinions on why he did it. Given that Cobain was an unwitting and unwilling frontman for all things 'slacker' and was considered the leader of such a generation of disaffected Prozac-poppers, the outright crippling effects of his depression brought on by the pressures of fame, as well as family life and heroin addiction didn't seem like enough of an explanation. Right from the start, Nirvana's music was over-wrought, pained, angry, the sound of outsiders at odds with the world – should we have been surprised when their songwriter took such sentiments to their most extreme conclusion? Like Green Day, Nirvana were consistently accused of selling themselves out. In killing himself, Kurt perhaps proved that he cared so much about what he did that he didn't want to live in a world where he would forever be disappointing people, or where he himself would feel like a fraud. Perhaps he'd just had enough and felt that, between the juxtaposition of his many new-found roles – as hero/villain, rock star/father, smalltown boy/multi-millionaire earner – ultimately no one could help him. Perhaps he was aware that the realisation of ambitions doesn't necessarily equate with happiness. It was a dilemma that few people would ever be able to truly relate to, but the tight-knit members of Green Day were three of them.

"*Maximum Rock 'n' Roll*, who have never liked us, just don't understand," Mike told me. "Can you imagine what it feels like to pick up that magazine, something you totally respect, and read all these fucking opinions on you?" said Billie Joe. "Of course you're gonna be manic-depressive. Because you're either totally high or someone's totally shooting you down, thinking that you're a total dick. A fucking god or a fucking asshole. If they [the media] think that in any way major labels are partly responsible for the reason Kurt Cobain blew his face off, I think they were partly responsible for that too."

"Putting him on a pedestal," added Mike. "If you want to be a regular guy, all of a sudden people just assume that you're an asshole 'cause you're rich or something, or they love you for it, you know? You can't be modest and play music. He died for my sins ... so I could sign to a major label?"

Perhaps the last word on the whole media-tagged Generation X debacle should be left to Tre Cool: "Their first album was great!"

"D-U-M-B / Everyone's accusing me…"
'Pinhead' by The Ramones

So in these times of dark clouds and rock 'n' roll suicides along came a record with a cartoon sleeve, fast little catchy songs rarely over three minutes in length and a title that was child-like slang for excrement: *Dookie*. For fans of the band, the beauty of it was that despite the jump to a big label, Green Day was still Green Day, the songs much the same as those on their Lookout! releases though with a more polished production. So once those familiar with Green Day – whether fans or foes alike – had got over the shock that absolutely nothing had changed, what remained was a self-contained album to devour.

From self-explanatory album opener 'Burnout', all the usual Billie Joe themes of isolation, inertia and boredom are in place, and arguably more refined so that *Dookie* works as a cohesive slice of adolescent angst.

"I wrote that song when I was stoned on the way home from Laytonville," Billie Joe later said. "It was kind of like all I do is smoke pot and do nothing. I'm a fucking burnout and an idiot. I'm a fucking idiot anyway, but sometimes you feel like an idiot times ten when you're stoned."

The first three songs on *Dookie* passed by in such a quick blur that it was more like listening to three different choruses in succession, before the grandiose rock ending of 'Chump' gave way to a double-whammy of 'Longview', with its misleadingly gentle bassline introduction, and a re-recorded version of *Kerplunk*!'s 'Welcome To Paradise', a song too good to confine to the band's indie punk past just yet.

Dookie was to become such a success because it was the realisation of the band's lifestyle, ideas, opinions and concerns and by extension, those of their many young listeners. It was a sign of the times; early Nineties journalism of the soul and a cultural marker for years to come.

The songs were simple and true to the band's experience. 'Coming Clean' considered the minefield that is teenage sexuality so effectively it could only have been written by someone unsure of his own persuasion. It was the first time Billie had raised the issues of his own confusion and how sexuality is not always easily defined (more of which later).

"Kids will always stop to think about the facts of the possibilities of not knowing what their sexuality is all about," Billie bravely explained in the biography that accompanied the album's release. "'Am

I homosexual? Am I bisexual? Am I heterosexual? Am I no-sexual? Or am I just plain sexual?' People don't know what the fuck they are. I still struggle with that too – it's part of adolescence and growing up."

Elsewhere, 'Pulling Teeth' was inspired by a very real incident that took place between Mike and his then-girlfriend Anastasia around the time of *Kerplunk!* The band were staying at a friend's house when Mike and Anastasia started a pillow fight with one another. In his excitement, the ever-energetic and occasionally accident prone bassist ran around a corner and hit his head hard on a low ceiling beam. To compound the situation he fell backwards and broke both his elbows and was carted off to hospital in ambulance when Billie and Tre had finally stopped laughing and realised he might actually be hurt.

It was the end of a farcical night, subsequently relived through Billie's self-explanatory lyrics. The title was believed to be inspired by Metallica's 'Anesthesia Pulling Teeth', because of the closeness to Mike's girlfriend's name.

Dookie also included a hidden track, 'All By Myself' tagged onto the end as an unlisted bonus song. Recorded on a four-track at a party somewhere, it featured another vocal display from Tre, this time sounding like a Jim Henson character while musing on those two key Green Day themes – masturbation and loneliness.

For the album cover, the band commissioned artist Richie Bucher, whose work on a seven-inch by a band called Raooul Billie had admired and who had been playing in East Bay for a number of years. Bucher came up with a colourful and chaotic cartoon image depicting a microcosm of chaos – people fighting in the street as dogs hurl shit at them from the sidelines, a sky full of dropping bombs marked 'dookie', a Bad Year blimp hovering overhead and a plethora of other hidden details. AC/DC's Angus Young makes an appearance solo-ing on a roof top, while the blimp's banner marked 'Eat at Chef Wong's' is a reference is to a T-shirt worn in *Punk* magazine founder John Holstrom's illustration for The Ramones *Rocket To Russia* release.

In an interview with VH1 in 2002, Billie explained the concept behind the artwork: "I wanted it to represent the East Bay and where we come from, because there's a lot of artists in the East Bay scene that are just as important as the music. There's pieces of us buried on the album cover. There's one guy with his camera up in the air taking a picture with a beard. He's this guy Murray [Bowles] that's been around the scene for a long time. He took pictures of bands every weekend at Gilman's. The robed character that looks like Ozzy Osbourne is the woman on the cover of the first Ozzy album. The graffiti reading 'Twisted Dog Sisters' refers to these two girls from Berkeley, punk rock girls that have been around for years. I think the guy saying 'The fritter, fat boy' was a reference to a local cop. There's a ton of weird little references and inside jokes all over that record."

The back cover was a photograph of *Sesame Street* character Ernie making merry in a mosh-pit – certain copies of which were released with him omitted after talk of a lawsuit.

To say that *Dookie* was something of an antidote to the general damaged psyche of rock music is an understatement – it felt like the first burst of colour in an otherwise monochrome landscape. I'm over-dramatizing here of course, but you see the point. Green Day were deliberately dumb and loud and funny when aloofness was all that the rock stars of the day strived for.

'Longview' was *Dookie*'s lead single, also released in January. If one Green Day song epitomized what they – and soon the new breed of punk bands – were about then it was this. Dripping in cynicism, Billie Joe's lyrics could have been speaking for America's yawning, channel-hopping, seen-it-all-before youth. It was the sound of a generation mesmerized by TV, numbed by weed, bored by politics, resentful of having to work the nine-to-five just to survive. The key lines in the song were a blunt antithesis of Buzzcocks' frenzied meat-beating anthem 'Orgasm Addict' and the choruses were the sound of a God-less, sex-less post-teen torpor. Crucially though, Green Day were singing about a familiar way of life rather than living it entirely, a contrast recognized in songs that shifted from the laconic apathy of the verses to the rousing big rock burst of the choruses.

The video, depicting the band playing in cramped conditions and Billie Joe trashing the place, was shot in the basement flat at Green Day HQ on Telegraph, then home to Billie, Tre, Tre's girlfriend, a roadie-cum-merchandise friend called Ben, another friend called Tad and a couple of others; a typical punk hang out, basically. The video was quickly picked upon by MTV who put it on heavy rotation and soon after the single was playlisted on radio stations across the country.

"I love seeing that video because it reminds me of what I saw when I first went down there," said Rob Cavallo. "It's exactly what I saw. We played some guitars and got stoned – where the camera is in the video is where I was sitting when I was first there."

A month later 'Longview' topped the *Billboard* Modern Rock

Tracks chart – one of the few of any significance – and the band were up and away. With *Dookie*, Green Day struck gold. It was their own pan-handled nugget hewn from a half decade of scuzz and grime.

As if to mark their rising stock, Billie Joe became the first member of the band to marry when he and Adrienne tied the knot in a swift ceremony in July, right before things got *really* hectic.

Their marriage was somewhat unconventional. Both Billie and Adrienne were nervous so knocked back the beers beforehand, had a five-minute service that, as atheists, combined pieces of Catholic, Jewish and Protestant marriage ceremonies, before the happy couple departed to the nearby Claremont Hotel in Berkeley where they proceeded to 'honeymoon'.

The very next day Billie Joe's new wife revealed she had been feeling somewhat different recently so they stopped off at a Safeway on the drive back home and picked up a pregnancy test. A few minutes later the twenty-two year old newly-weds found out that they were about to become parents.

If 1994 was the apex of grunge (or nadir, depending on your view), the year when the genre that was once considered subterranean and mildly subversive was accepted in the wider arena of mainstream American rock music, then the Lollapalooza festival reflected the preferred listening tastes of the day. Perhaps the most significant moment of that year's travelling rock festival-cum-alternative culture carnival (which had been started in 1991 by Jane's Addiction's colourful frontman Perry Farrell), was the absence of scheduled headliners Nirvana. The band was no more and left a gaping hole which was filled by Smashing Pumpkins; symbolically, the corrosive punk-inspired rock of Nirvana being replaced by the Pumpkins meant a lot. Though loosely fitting into the same niche, the band were polar opposites and there had been no love lost between Cobain and Pumpkins leader, Billy Corgan. To compound matters, Cobain's widow had been appearing at various dates to talk to crowds about the death of Kurt in time allotted to her by Corgan. Suddenly the playfulness of early Nirvana, Mudhoney and Co seemed a million miles away. The word was: *grunge kills.*

The supporting bill for Lollapalooza 1994 contained bankable acts such as the Beastie Boys, Cypress Hill, L7 and Nick Cave & The Bad Seeds and interesting alt-rock band such as The Breeders, The Flaming Lips and Guided By Voices. And, providing a much-needed splash of colour and injection of youthful energy, Green Day, who joined the tour in New York for its second month, replacing opening band Boredoms.

In six months Green Day had gone from being an underground band, to being one of MTV's most-played acts to now being included on the Lollapalooza bill – on the main stage no less – merely cementing their new-found status as members of America's ruling élite. They had, to many, 'arrived'.

"It was a very chaotic time for us," remembers Mike. "It was weird, because we were the opening act. We had just come back from Europe, and at that point we had sold more albums than anyone else on the tour. The staff would get mad at us because people were rushing the stage. It was a catch-22. It took the other bands a while to warm up to us, but once they did, it was cool. They realized we weren't dicks. It was fun and I enjoyed it, but – to quote Les Claypool [of Primus] – it was a travelling barbecue. The day after the show it looked like some white-trash carnival came through town. But we reacted well with the crowd. Billie would hop offstage and run all the way to the very back of the amphitheatre."

"It was cool because we only had to play thirty minutes," laughs Billie Joe, "then we could go back drinking while the other bands played. There was no pressure."

The trio's Lollapalooza appearances seemed to capture the changing zeitgeist perfectly. With grunge still in mourning it was left to Green Day to remind, in the simplest terms, how liberating three chords and a guitar can be – that perhaps rock music is about celebration as much as commiseration. And, as we know, every Green Day performance is a celebration. The tide was turning. And *Dookie* kept on selling.

Green Day's rapid ascension took another large leap when they were invited to play at Woodstock 2 the following week, as a late addition. In a few short months *Dookie* had sold ten times the amount of either of its predecessors and Green Day, perhaps more than anyone, captured the imagination and the airwaves that summer. Who better then, for the cultural event of the year – hopefully the decade – than the most popular new band of the time (even if they were playing Lollapalooza simultaneously).

But, of course Woodstock 2 wasn't quite the epoch-making, generation-defining event that the first festival had been in 1969. How could it be? A happy accidental mixture of timing, drugs, music, political dissidence came over one long weekend in the gathering of

America's tribes. Woodstock was the domain of the hippies but it also came to represent America's many disenchanted, a place to cast aside prejudices, get naked and boogie your way to enlightenment. In the years and months that followed the first festival, Charles Manson, unresolved conflicts in Vietnam and Nixon's Watergate scandal all served to remind that Woodstock, the zenith of counterculture, had been a blip – albeit a sizeable one – on mainstream right wing America's radar. A reminder that it takes more than peace and love to overthrow a government in a time when hate and war reigns. Nevertheless, in the cultural history books, Woodstock is still seen by many as equally significant as the moon landing for a generation's finest – Jimi Hendrix, Janis Joplin, Grateful Dead, The Who, Sly & The Family Stone – gathered at 'Woodstock Music & Arts Fair: an Aquarian Exposition' to throw a once-in-a-lifetime party for up to half a million people. Psychedelic rock music, protest folk and ass-shaking funk were all given equal space. Entrance was free to everyone (though accidental – the exterior fences weren't completed in time). And the crucial thing about once-in-a-lifetime events is they can't be repeated, only replicated.

The generation whom the organizers of Woodstock 2 were aiming at were very different to their parents. And even if they did share many of the same liberal beliefs, the economic landscape was very different, as was the way in which youth culture was sold back to its youth. Now corporate America was involved and the vibes were very different.

"The first Woodstock organizers wanted to make money just a much as they did on the Woodstock '94, but they had the hippy schtick going on, whereas this time around it was more blatant," Billie Joe told me during an interview. "Despite the scale of it though it was just another gig for us really, another day on the calendar to fill. We were asked 'Do you want to play in front of three hundred thousand people?' and we said, 'Sure, why not?' I mean, we played right before Peter Gabriel, and then I think Slash [performing with Bad Company's Paul Rodgers] played after us. There's no plan of action or preparation for playing on a bill with people like that!"

When Green Day arrived at Woodstock in upstate New York on August 11 it had been raining continuously and the collective spirit of the vast crowd – estimated to be anywhere between 350,000 and 500,000 people – was somewhat dampened and defeated. The ground had been churned up and looked more like a World War I battle field while basic necessities such as food and water were being sold at inflated prices to the captive customers. Peter Gabriel's WOMAD probably didn't help tempers. Billed as one group, they were actually a succession of individual world music artists whose set(s) seemed never-ending. When Gabriel tried to coerce the crowd into a singalong, they were happy to oblige by chanting Green Day's name throughout the rest of his set.

"I remember that I had just bought a new pair of Converse," Billie Joe recalled. "It was raining that day and I really didn't want to mess them up so soon. So I was being really careful where I walked. I was trying to avoid the puddles and the mud."

The image of the singer daintily picking his way around the puddles backstage is an enduring, if ironic, one. When the band hit the stage the crowd seemed to stretch for miles. Things went *off.* "It was absolute insanity," remembers Mike. "Looking out there, I can't begin to tell you what it looked like."

After the bad weather, below-par bands and the total absence of the original festival's spirit, here, finally, was a chance to have a bit of *fun* – the one thing that seemed lacking from Woodstock Mk 2. As the band played a *Dookie*-heavy set, the crowd moshed and surged, pogo-ed and slammed in the mud, heavy clots of it being heaved into the air or stagewards, something that appealed to the band's shared sense of punk rock mischievousness. If they were going to play this corporate hippy-turned-yuppie nonsense then they'd make sure it was memorable for all concerned. Billie Joe caught the first clod and shoved it in his mouth.

More mud reigned down from the crowd and happy chaos ensued for all but the security who were freaking out. Maybe if they'd been brought up punk they'd have seen that it was just good clean (well, not clean) fun – a sign of appreciation from the crowd as much as anything. Some of Green Day's road crew moved onto the stage to start throwing mud back, as did Wavy Gravy, the stage's compere and enduring totem for the original Woodstock.

To compound the moment, Billie removed his trousers and pants and took in the wonderful sight of thousands of new converts going ape shit.

In a move to get closer to the band, some fans started climbing over the safety barriers and onto the stage as the set collapsed into farce, with Mike performing mud slides and a semi-naked Billie entertaining the crowd. One kid hugged the singer and ran off, only to be chased by Billie Joe and brought back to sing a few lines of the song in his place. Mistaking him for a member of the crowd, one security guard tackled Mike hard, slamming him down onto a monitor and knocking some of his teeth out.

"I was trying to say to this guy, 'I'm in the band, you fucking asshole!'" said Mike. "I had to go to the dentist to get my mouth fixed up. It was bad, I can tell you."

The band and crew decided the best move would be to get the hell out of there. Though no-one had been hurt, there had, in the eyes of the law, arguably just been a riot; something the cops and the authorities don't like.

"I remember on the way in we were offered a ride in a helicopter but I didn't want to go in one," recalled Billie Joe. "I don't feel safe with the idea of getting in a helicopter because, if you look at it, there's no scientific reason as to why it can fly [actually, there is – the author]. But after the show we needed to get out of there in such a hurry that I had to get in the helicopter, there was no choice. So that part of the plan didn't really work out for me."

"It was amazing!" was Tre's take on it. "I look back on it now and it still makes me smile – all that mud, that chaos and trouble. The thing that made the day for me was that I did get to ride in a helicopter. I know Mike and Billie didn't want to, but my dad used to fly them in Vietnam so, for me, everything worked out fine."

In the aftermath of such a career-defining performance, not everyone saw the band in such a favourable light. Amongst the odd now-expected 'sell-out' criticisms from the punk police and the general wrath of the authorities, the band received "a hate letter" from one Mrs. Armstrong of Rodeo, California.

"She said I was disrespectful and indecent," Billie Joe told *Rolling Stone* the following January, "and that if my father was alive, he would be ashamed of me. She couldn't believe I pulled my pants down and got in a fight onstage. Everything's fine now, but her letter was just unreal. She was not happy with my performance at all. She even talked shit about my wife, and said how she's supposed to be my loving wife, but she's never even come over and visited. It was pretty brutal."

The tour rolled on.

Things became ever-more surreal.

The trio spent the best part of the year on tour, playing to bigger crowds the majority of whom had been turned onto Green Day thanks to radio and MTV singles 'Welcome To Paradise', 'Longview' and, probably most recognizable of all, the blistering new single, 'Basket Case' released in August.

If people only know Green Day for one song today then it remains 'Basket Case', whose wry lyrics seemed to inadvertently tap into the brain-dead subconscious of 'Generation X'. In the space of three minutes Billie Joe expresses selfish indulgence, self-deprecation and sluggish stoned flippancy, as well as telling of visits to a shrink and a whore for advice on his seeping sense of psychosis, all told in the simplest of terms.

The video for the song took the idea one step further, depicting the blank-eyed, drooling trio on a psychiatric hospital ward who come to life from their wheelchairs and gurneys to rip through the song in suitably upbeat style, before being led back to their beds and their medication. You might say it was a literal interpretation of the song.

The summer of 1994 was a strange and thrilling time – like beginning again, but on a whole different level, in altogether unfamiliar surroundings. August alone saw them wind their way though Florida and Louisiana, before playing a handful of shows in Texas, then California, up to Washington State, back down to California for two more shows, then a flight back east to New York for the 1994 MTV Video Music Awards at the Metropolitan City Opera House (where 'Longview' was nominated in the 'Best Group Video' and 'Best Alternative Video' categories – what's the difference? – and the band put up for a 'Best Newcomer' award, though they lost out to Aerosmith, Nirvana and Counting Crows respectively), then up to Massachusetts for a show the next night, across to Ohio …well, you get the picture. A different state every day, crossing invisible borders and boundaries, stepping in and out of large sports halls, each the same as the last – only bigger, and rowdier. On and on. Show after show, drink after drink. Good times.

Less than a month after their career-defining performance at Woodstock, Green Day found themselves in trouble once again. In September they played at a free show arranged by a Boston radio station which attracted an unprecedented 100,000 people. Clearly, the organizers had underestimated the popularity of Green Day. Security was provided by police and state troopers and – unbelievably – a fifteen-man security team of inmates from the local prison. Within minutes of hitting the stage, the crowd had surged forward and knocked over safety barriers and pandemonium broke out. Concerned that the entire lighting rig was going to come down, the promoter pulled the plug, which hardly mattered. The crowd rioted harder and the bedlam spread onto the streets of downtown Boston. All hell broke loose – that night the local news reported sixty arrests and dozens of injuries.

"The police were getting beat up and stuff," said Tre. "They were tear-gassing the crowd and all these things." The band were whisked away for their own safety, where they watched from a distance while signing autographs for the prisoners. You couldn't make it up.

"Next thing they're announcing 'Green Day has left the building! Green Day has left the building', it was fucking funny," added the drummer. "The thing is, not one of them fucked off. They all went back to jail the next day!"

After a summer of highs and even-highers, of mud-fights and magazine covers, Green Day were coasting all the way to the bank. *Dookie* was selling thousands of copies per week and the band had stepped up onto the cow-shed circuit of middle America. They could go anywhere and command crowds of thousands.

They had visited Europe once that year in the spring when Rob Cavallo had flown in to spend some time with the band in Spain and record some live material for future use as B-sides, as he had at a show in Florida the previous month: "I could already see that their show was changing as they got mature. I thought 'Nine months from now, this show is going to be a different show.' I thought it was really important to document one of those early sessions before they became massive. Cavallo had also stuck around to help the band record a BBC Radio session at London's Maida Vale studios.

When they returned to Europe again in the autumn for their second tour of the year, the difference in reaction was obvious. When they *then* went straight back to the US for another tour, their appearance at Woodstock had been on rotation on MTV and was already passing into the annals of rock history as a seminal moment, a mud-flecked riot of fun that seemed to represent the arrival of American's new breed.

The band were adhering to a policy that door prices be kept affordably low – a practice perpetuated by few huge bands, with Fugazi and Pearl Jam being noticeable big-name exceptions – with a ceiling price of $20. Some shows, even in 1994, cost as little as $5 to get into. The band's many official T-shirts costs a maximum of $10.

"We lost thousands of dollars on that tour," said Mike. "Something like $15,000. Doesn't sound like a lot, but I guess it is ..."

By the autumn, Green Day had jumped from jam-packed clubs to large arenas and the expense of touring suddenly seemed less of a worry – the plan had worked and *Dookie* was paying dividends.

For their latest US tour the band personally invited Germany's biggest punk band Die Toten Hosen (who an unknown Green Day had opened for in front of ten to fifteen thousand people each night on the German leg of an earlier European tour) and rising punk-popsters Pansy Division to open for them each night. A three-piece from San Francisco, on first glance Pansy Division seemed like just another decent melodic punk-pop band to come out of the area. But unlike 99.9% of all-male rock bands, Pansy Division were openly homosexual and had an arsenal of great gay love songs to back it up – their latest album *Deflowered* featured songs such as 'Groovy Underwear' and 'Beer Can Boy', the latter about a man blessed with girth rather than length in the trouser department – and a cover of Buzzcock Pete Shelley's androgynous anthem 'Homosapien'. The band were leading figureheads in a burgeoning movement dubbed 'queercore', a group of bands lumped together due to their sexual preferences and by virtue of the fact that guitar music had been strangely bereft of gay performers (or, rather, performers who publicly acknowledged their sexuality).

Pansy Division's power lay in their groundbreaking ability to infiltrate the frustratingly hetero rock world, convert the masses to their poppy punk ways then casually reveal themselves to be attracted to men – a move guaranteed to rankle down in the testosterone-driven mosh pit. The band's place on the tour also indirectly resulted in wider discussion about Green Day's frontman's own thoughts on sexuality.

"I think Green Day's popularity is one reason they invited us to open for them," said Pansy Division's lead singer Jon Ginoli. "Now that they're more mainstream, they have elements in their audience they'd rather not have and having us along lets them tweak that part of the audience. They're able to get under their skin and irritate them, saying, 'If you're going to see us, you've gotta see this!'"

Each night Pansy Division's performance to crowds unfamiliar with their material prompted certain audience members to give them the finger (oh, the irony…) and throw things at them.

"The funny thing was watching some of these guys in the audience when Pansy Division opened," remembered Billie Joe, who soon took to stopping Green Day's performance mid-set to berate the less-than-tolerant factions of his own fan base and inform them that Pansy Division were the future of rock 'n' roll. "They were out there flexing their muscles and acting real macho, not really realizing that Pansy

Division is gay. Then Chris Freeman, Pansy's bass player, would stop in the middle of a song and say, 'So, have you guys figured out we're a bunch of fags yet?' I think Pansy Division is the kind of band that changes people's lives. They're catchy, educational, and they're honest about their sexuality."

In a revealing interview with Judy Wieder of *The Advocate*, Billie Joe was admirably candid in discussing his own mixed sexual feelings and bisexual tendencies – a brave move for anyone, not least the most prominent figure in punk rock, a scene evidently still capable of harbouring its own set of prejudices.

"I think I've always been bisexual," he explained "I mean, it's something I've always been interested in. I think everybody kind of fantasizes about the same sex. I think people are born bisexual, and it's just that our parents and society kind of veer us off into this feeling of 'Oh, I can't'. They say it's taboo. It's ingrained in our heads that it's bad when it's not bad at all. It's a very beautiful thing."

When asked whether he ever acted on these feelings, Billie Joe was equally candid. "I think mostly it's been kept in my head. I've never really had a relationship with a man, but it is something that comes up as a struggle in me ... especially when I was about 16 or 17. In high school people think you have to be macho and people get attacked just because someone insinuates something about their sexuality. I think that's gruesome."

Aside from expressing admiration for outwardly gay performers such as Melissa Etheridge and the terminally lower-case kd lang to obscure bands like the White Trash Debutantes, Billie Joe also revealed that a gay uncle to whom he was close had recently contracted full-blown AIDS, a broad and divisive subject he felt would be extremely difficult for him to broach in his music.

"I don't feel educated enough, but I certainly could write about losing someone who's close to me. I'm more the type of person who would write about how ignorant and stupid people are about something like AIDS," he said in *The Advocate*.

Green Day's most successful US tour yet peaked with a sell-out at New York's 16,000 seater Nassau Coliseum in a matter of minutes – a massive feat. "Someone said to me, fifteen thousand people at this arena – everything you ever dreamed of'," said Mike. "I turned to him and said 'Correction. It's everything *I never* dreamed of.'"

A momentous year ended with one more show, this time at Madison

Square Gardens sponsored by Z-100 radio station for the benefit of AIDS charities. On a mixed bill that also included Bon Jovi, Weezer, Sheryl Crow and Pansy Division, Billie Joe once again got naked – by now an increasingly regular appearance, often off-set by his fetching pair of skimpy leopard print briefs.

"I'm just exhausted," panted a fully-clothed Billie Joe at the close of 1994. "Totally. We've outdone ourselves in a serious way. I have insomnia problems anyway, so it's hard for me to sleep. That's the main thing I'm looking forward to: I'll probably sleep for the rest of the year."

The insomnia that Billie had been experiencing amidst the chaos of *Dookie* was to prove to be a prime influence on the band's next work. More of which after this interlude.

Eleven years after he had formed the company, Brett Gurewitz's Epitaph Records was experiencing financial challenges. In 1992 he could count emerging punk bands such as NOFX, Down By Law and Pennywise and curios such as all-girl skuzzy punk/metal band L7 on his roster, yet had not achieved the sales to carry his expenditure. Against the sounds of bands such as Nirvana and Pearl Jam, three-chord punk just wasn't competing. The overbearing mood in rock music – the rock music that got played on the radio anyway – was of doomy introspection and a sense of hopelessness at odds with NOFX's barbed wits and songs about sexually transmitted diseases or Pennywise's spirited fists-in-the-air melodic hardcore. Punk was still for the select few.

"In 1992 I was in very real danger of losing everything," says Gurewitz. "I can't remember how much I had to drum up, but it was hundreds of thousands of dollars."

While Gurewitz's own band Bad Religion were finally beginning to make a healthy living, they were consequently the label's biggest sellers (averaging a healthy 100,000 copies per release); nevertheless they were a separate entity from the label they had spawned. Also the guitarist's own position in the band was becoming increasingly unsustainable, for two main reasons. Firstly, Gurewitz's then-unknown struggles with heroin addiction was impinging on his business acumen and musical input. Secondly, after years in the wilderness, in 1993 Bad Religion were offered, and decided to accept, a major label recording contract with Atlantic Records. Few could truly begrudge the financial stability that such a deal facilitated, but as head of one of punk's most vital independent labels, Gurewitz recognised the importance of staying independent in a scene where political integrity is the chief currency.

Though he played on the band's major label debut (1994's *Stranger Than Fiction*) he wasn't comfortable with his position and announced his departure from the band shortly afterwards. In a smart move they replaced him with former Minor Threat/Dag Nasty guitarist Brian Baker, therefore maintaining a certain level of credibility. Bad Religion went on to enjoy their greatest success in the mid-Nineties, helped in no small part by the fact that, like The Ramones before them, they have two songs – fast and faster. But they are a good two songs. If you like one record you generally like them all.

But Gurewitz had other concerns. In Epitaph's darkest financial hours, he received the mixes of a forthcoming album by another Californian band on his roster, Orange County's The Offspring. Their first for the label, *Ignition* had sold reasonably well – around 45,000 copies – and the band had been to Europe for the first time, as tour support to NOFX, playing in clubs averaging 500-1000 people per night – way more than The Offspring could pull at their own hometown shows. But expectations weren't particularly high for the new album, entitled *Smash*, that Gurewitz slipped into his car stereo driving home from the office one day.

"I couldn't believe what I was hearing," he says. "I didn't drive straight home that day. I drove round and round the block, just listening to the music. Two songs in particular grabbed my attention, 'Come Out And Play' and 'Low Self Esteem'. I had all these thoughts flying through my head as I was driving around. And when I did finally get home I walked into the house and said to my then-wife Maggie, 'Hi honey, we're going to be rich!' She said, 'That's nice dear – dinner's ready!'"

Gurewitz's intuition was right. 'Come Out And Play' was plugged to radio stations as *Smash*'s lead track and quickly pounced upon by influential LA station KROQ who put the song on rotation – a decision aided by the band themselves inundating the station with calls to ask who this hot new band was.

MTV followed suit, broadcasting the band's low-budget video. Then things took off. Released in April, *Smash* started selling and didn't stop – so much so that Epitaph struggled to meet the demands of the endless stream of vans pulling up to their warehouse to collect fresh stock for the shops. It was also exporting in vast quantities to Europe where the single was taking off amid much talk of a new punk renaissance.

Endearingly, the band were still holding down their jobs – guitarist Noodles only finally relinquishing his janitor's job when the school year ended and a European tour beckoned.

The Offspring's *Smash* was an overnight (as much as struggling for a decade can be considered overnight ...), off-the-page success matched only in sales and a similar surprise factor by Green Day's *Dookie*. By the close of 1994, between them these seven punk rock fans had achieved collective sales of 24 million albums, approximately 23.8 million of which had been in the previous twelve months or less. Based in some ways on the success of one album alone, Epitaph was now the most successful independent record label in the world, a modern day success to rival past mighty independent labels such as Stax or Motown.

Punk's second coming had truly arrived.

"Billie Joe Must Die"
Graffiti on the wall of 924 Gilman Street, circa 1994.

For every upside there has to be a down. That's the balance of the universe. It's a natural trade-off felt all the more strongly by those who live a life of extremes. Extremes of poverty and wealth. Of anonymity and worldwide fame. Of friends and foes.

For every resurrection a crucifixion ...

Sometime during 1994, that piece of graffiti appeared on the wall of Gilman Street. This in itself was unremarkable – after all, the place was a flea-pit strewn with scribbles and flyers, a metaphorical building of mirrors reflecting back the views and feelings of its inhabitants. But this piece of graffiti seemed particularly poignant. In a mere four words it encapsulated the punk rock dilemma of the Nineties succinctly. *Billie Joe must die.*

The question remained, not who would write such a thing – tens of thousands of old school punkers would happily admit to coining this insight – but why must Billie Joe, a likeable young man who for a time was the toast of the fertile East Bay punk rock scene, respected amongst his peers who he himself had looked up to in the first place, have to die? His band Green Day had packed out Gilman every time they'd gigged there and had certainly played a pivotal role in making this small club a worldwide name.

And therein lay the problem.

Just as that popular toilet read *The Holy Bible* has been re-written, misinterpreted and twisted to justify man's own actions, by the Nineties punk rock had also become a pliable concept. It meant different things to different people – and that was OK. The music itself had splintered into all sorts of sub-genres such as straight-forward pop punk, ska-punk or old school gutter punk. In the late Seventies/early Eighties it had also spawned the more brutal sounds of hardcore, which itself had also organically divided into various cliques and factions – whether the hard-line, clean-living no-drink-and-drugs stance of the straight-edge scene, to the more metal-minded bands and on to the cerebral post-hardcore and emotional (emo) hardcore scenes. Then there was grunge, a sound and look which pretty lay much equidistant from Seventies rock/proto-metal bands like Black Sabbath, the rudimentary hardcore punk of bands like Black Flag and the pop suss and devotion to melody of The Beatles and their many successors.

With all these style and sounds and ways of doing things all coming under the umbrella of 'punk' and taking place on a world scale in localized scenes, it can be a bloody minefield out there if you don't stick to the rules.

Rules? This is punk we're talking about here, where rules are about as welcome as hippies …

"Right before *Dookie* came out, I was really at odds with myself," says Billie Joe. "I was like, man, do I really want to live like this? A lot of the time I was thinking about suicide, how it's so easy to kill yourself, but so hard to stay alive. [Prior to meeting Adrienne] I was in a break-up with my then-girlfriend, a total, raving punk rocker who didn't approve of being on a major label. She moved down to Ecuador, saying she couldn't live in with McDonald's and such. It was fucking me up pretty bad."

By the time Green Day had watched *Dookie* shoot up the charts, punk had become a massive tangle of opinions that fell into two opposing schools of thought: those who believed that punk was something organic and exclusive that should never be a part of mainstream life and could work alongside or within the 'establishment' – therefore, no signing to the pro-globalization major record companies, some of whom involved themselves in various other shady business deals such as the financing of arms and weapons (as certain record companies have done in the past) and various other non-PC pursuits, no eating at corporate chains as epitomized by McDonalds, no wearing of clothes made by companies who utilised sweatshop work forces, no airplay on those broadcasters who were already homogenizing, co-opting or just outright pillaging youth culture MTV, no talking to lame magazines out to misrepresent or use bands for their own gain – the list goes on. It was punk rock as an ethical stance as debated and played out in the pages of punk bible *Maximum Rock 'n' Roll*, and down at Gilman, a venue now renowned for being something of a model for other punk venues, promoters, bands and fans the world over, and therefore a microcosm of the worldwide scene.

Then there was the other camp of punk rocker who just didn't give a fuck either way. They just got off on the music, the beer, the drugs, whatever.

And the beauty of it all was that, so long as it didn't turn to violence these two schools of thought could co-exist in the same scene, the same mosh-pit – sometimes even the same band.

But wishing death on someone for their own lifestyle choices?

It wasn't the first time punk rock had turned on its own either. In May 1994, in the days of *Dookie* and Kurt Cobain's death, former Dead Kennedys frontman Jello Biafra found this out at Gilman when he was attacked by a group of outraged punks at a show featuring, appropriately, a band called Society Gone Mad. Few people had retained as much local punk credibility as Biafra, which made the incident all the more sickening. A prankster, sometime Green Party politician, anti-censorship spokesman and tireless campaigner against the corporate predators of the world – not to mention writer of some of the greatest music made in modern times – Biafra had stockpiled enough Brownie points to elevate him to a high status within the scene. However, for reasons never fully understood, others disagreed, jeering 'sell-out' and 'rich rock star!' at him prior to a beating outside Gilman that left him with head and leg injuries.

So what were, in essence, the sick actions of a handful of drunk buffoons nevertheless represented the standpoint taken by the various punks who had thrived on the scene's élitism, unmolested by the outside world. If Gilman and the East Bay was a microcosm of punk, then ill winds were certainly blowing through.

It was this same sense of disappointment at seeing one of *their* bands appearing on MTV, David Letterman or Woodstock in the type of clothes they themselves lost jobs over or got shit for wearing that prompted someone – probably either a bitter aging punk or an underage newcomer, given the venue's demographic – to scrawl *Billie Joe must die*. Not Bono or Madonna or even members of Nirvana, who themselves changed rock music for better *and* worse by signing to a major in 1991, but one of *them*. The kid who grew up here, who came of age on that stage over there. The guy who never diluted and compromised a single note of his music for his success, yet was still considered a sell-out of such monumental proportions he deserved a lynching by the 924 precinct of pubescents. Hang 'em high with a neck tie from the lamp-posts of Berkeley and let God sort 'em out. This was, after all, former cowboy country ...

With the success of *Dookie*, various grass-roots organisations like Gilman and Lookout! suddenly and unexpectedly found themselves having to question and reaffirm their own ethical ideologies. They may have received unwanted attention from outlets who had previously ignored them, but such high-profile exposure did bring some benefits to the scene. Speaking a couple of years after the album broke, Lookout!'s then-publicist (and former member of respected riot grrl band Bratmobile) Molly Neuman explained punk life post-*Dookie* to journalist Gina Arnold for her definitive chronicle, *Kiss This*. "On the whole it's helped us more than it's hurt. We've probably sold twenty times as many copies of every record. But there are complications and problems that go along with that ... all of a sudden you have to deal with bands saying 'you have all this money, give it to us.'"

"One question we get asked a lot now is 'How much money do you make?'" affirmed Mike in the *Dookie* aftermath. "When I was younger I asked that question to my mom's friend. My mom took me and slapped me in the face and said 'Do not ask that question! It's none of your business.' Sure, we make money. We make plenty of money. And it's a peace of mind for me to know that I've bought my mom a house, and that my little sisters don't have to live in a trailer any more."

"The fucked up thing about being famous and having money is that if you complain about something, people are like, 'What the fuck are you complaining about?" said Billie Joe, sometime during what would have been his first year as a millionaire. "'You don't have to work a real job. You don't have to worry about money or a place to live.' I feel like I don't have anyone to vent my frustrations to because they won't understand."

"The funniest thing about fame is family reunions, like, 'Hey, it's the zillionaire! How about lending me a hunn'erd thousand dollars?'" Tre told me. "'Fuck off!' It's funny though – like I give away hundreds of

Welcome to Paradise: a dreadlocked Billie Joe and Co. pose for
a prototype edition of MTV's *Cribs*, late 1992.

Pre-*Dookie* Green Day, pictured with a bag of baby shit, 1993.

Woodstock II, 1994, joined on-stage by half of a field.

The 1997 New York in-store signing where events got a little out of hand.

Pinhead Gunpowder performing in San Francisco, 2001.

With Rancid's Tim Armstrong backstage
at Irving Plaza in New York City, May, 2003.

Classic Green Day.

Mike tries desperately to swat a stage-diving fly.

Tre took the producer's advice to 'hit the bass drum harder', too literally.

Life in Green Day had begun to become a chore.
Tre with Miss USA and Miss Teen USA.

Punk rock hits the The 47th Annual Grammy Awards, the Staples
Center, Los Angeles, February 13, 2005.

Back on the road – the start of yet another world tour, kicking off at the
University of Miami's Convention Center, March 15, 2005.

The Network in San Francisco, November, 2003.

Green Day: punk rock gods?

thousand of dollars on the street every day ..."

High-profile and widely distributed fanzine *Maximum Rock 'n' Roll* had always prided itself on its punk rock exclusivity, on only covering bands on independent labels, and always regardless of stature. And just because one of their bands had 'made it' didn't mean they were about to change that tack. Though when it came to Green Day, *MRR* were at least consistent. The band had received coverage from the magazine during the Lookout! years, though even then not without some degree of division between readers, some of whom had always viewed Green Day as being too poppy (they'd clearly never heard The Ramones, The Dickies or Buzzcocks – or if they had, couldn't appreciate the irony) and would happily write in to say so. But when their popularity found a wider audience, the magazine was quick to nail its colours to the mast: *Maximum Rock 'n' Roll's* allegiance was with the underground and no band was bigger than the scene itself. So, just as the Sex Pistols had seen their early contingent of art school fans abandon them when the band went overground in 1977-1978, so too Green Day saw one set of fans departing and another arriving. Of course, it wasn't that black and white.

On signing to Warners, Green Day had not altered, softened or compromised their sound one iota so no-one could accuse them of selling out artistically. I know, because if *Dookie* had sounded like it was influenced by Nirvana or Pearl Jam, or whoever else was big in 1993-94, then I for one would not have been interested, for that would have been a sign that the band were under the thumb of their paymasters. The disapproval by certain magazines and sections of fans was just an unavoidable part of being a successful band. Fact.

Billie Joe once said, "I've never waved a flag for punk rock in my life." And this, perhaps, was where the wrath of the underground lay. In singing about and being a very visible part of a punk rock scene – in wearing punk clothes and dyed hair and extolling the virtues of the lifestyle – Green Day *were* flying the flag for punk rock. Being on Lookout! made them punk rock. Being one of Gilman's most popular bands made them punk. But by the time *Dookie* broke, many saw such denials as a betrayal. Green Day, many said, had used the close-knit network of the underground punk scene for their own gains, exploited it, and now moved on. Green Day, it seemed, couldn't win. That the band were rumoured to have donated money to Gilman made little difference (though this is unconfirmed, as the trio decline to speak about it in interviews for fear of appearing overly philanthropic).

"People in the punk community don't like the fact Green Day have attracted this huge audience with a lot of boneheads, but it's still a good album," said Ben Weasel, whose band supported Green Day that autumn. "If you liked them before, but don't like this album, then it's for political reasons, not musical reasons."

"We sell out every show we play," shrugged Tre Cool, when I asked him about such accusations. "Besides, everything is for sale in this world."

"People who call us sell-outs are being moderately politically correct," added Mike. "To counter that accusation you would have to sit in your room, you'd never work and you'd never play a show for money, ever. Selling out to me is compromising my musical intentions and my musical intentions are to play music and not work for some asshole at some job that I really don't want to do. I'm going to do whatever *I* want to do. And what I do is play bass. Fuck it."

Either way, by the close of 1994 it was too late to go back. Like grunge three years earlier, punk rock was not only in the pages of *Rolling Stone* and *Spin*, but also teen mags and broadsheet newspapers. The thrift store look that the band – and so many others – sported and which was born out of relative poverty, was suddenly 'fashion', kids rushed out to buy hair dye or gas station attendant shorts and jackets just like the ones Billie Joe favoured. Gilman was the subject of numerous articles. What previously existed in a relative cultural vacuum was suddenly pounced upon by the media who had cottoned on to a whole subculture they were previously unaware of. It was clear that punk was changing into something else – what by the close of Nineties would be categorised as 'mall-punk': affluent middle-class kids flirting with the imagery while exploring the genre's music no further than the latest Blink-182 or Sum 41 record.

And for that, argued the punk police, *Billie Joe must die*.

Perhaps though it was the man in question who best defined what punk was – and what it was fast becoming in his wake: "A guy walks up to me and asks 'What's punk?'," said Billie Joe from the stage one night. "So I kick over a garbage can and say, 'That's punk!' So he kicks over the garbage can and says, 'That's punk?', and I say, 'No, that's *trendy*.'"

Meanwhile back in the real world, where most people don't spend too much thought about ideologies and ethics, where it's every man for himself and the devil may care, things in the Green Day camp were

114

changing. After five years of living in a bubble of recording, touring and partying they were becoming almost well … dare we say it, adult?

Yes, we do. Though no rock star is truly adult – not when there are people around you to lavish enough attention to keep you in a perpetual state of pampered adolescence. Thankfully, Green Day found a decent grounding in their private relationships. At the start of the year, their latest single from *Dookie*, 'When I Come Around' was taking up residency on the American airwaves and had soon climbed to the number one spot in the modern rock charts (US singles charts being based upon radio and TV airplay), where it would stay for seven weeks. In March 1995 in a rare break from touring and recording duties, Tre married his girlfriend Lisea Lyons. That same month Billie and Adrienne became parents when they gave birth to a son Joseph Marciano Armstrong in March (the names were believed to be inspired by two American heroes – Joey Ramone and boxer Rocky Marciano). Later in the year Tre and his new wife had a daughter, Ramona.

The image of these young men who, only months earlier had been instigating mud fights and baring their arses for all the world to see, now settling down into family life was a confusing one, though creatively, would have little effect on Green Day as a band – they weren't about to start writing sentimental slush, as some rock stars are prone to do.

They did however throw themselves into the lives of domesticity and parenthood before the inevitable pull of the now highly-lucrative Green Day machine took them back out there again.

"Being a parent means being totally selfless whereas being in a band or rock 'n' roll scene usually means you're self-absorbed," Billie Joe told me. "It keeps you grounded, and it keeps you on that fine line between being totally cool with everything and totally insane, which is what you need, especially to write good songs."

The first half of 1995 was spent with their families and writing new material. Temporarily away from the spotlight, Billie Joe elected to do no press interviews until the new record was out, which provided a welcome nine-month break from the usual round of promotions. It didn't matter – *Dookie* was still selling by the bucketload.

A blast from the past compounded Billie's Joe's increasingly iconic status when Wat Tyler, with whom Green Day had bonded back in 1991, released a single on Lookout! called 'I Wanna Be Billie Joe', with a picture of Billie on the cover in his pants and on the back, Sean from the band wearing only underwear and a tie ("I think I still have a copy of it at home somewhere ..." a bemused Billie Joe told me).

But by June 1995 it was action stations again when work on Green Day's fourth album began in earnest.

"My name's Bill and sometimes I like to take bunch of speed and stay up all night talking shit and grinding my teeth ..."

50,000 people roar in approval with a deafening, drunken laugh.

It's August 1995 and I'm standing in a field off my nut on some very cheap and nasty amphetamine.

Actually, rewind a minute. I'm in a portaloo, retching and gagging and heaving and stretching, simultaneously trying to expel what feels like a hard lump of fossilised matter from within my bowels (to no avail), while simultaneously tooting up the last of the speed to get into the general spirit of the occasion that a Saturday night commands. 'When in Rome ...' has been the prevailing thought for the evening.

Over on the main stage Green Day are doing their thing, and in this over-heated plastic shit box I'm missing the action.

I've also lost my friends and I'm wearing badly-applied eyeliner. This can mean only one thing: I'm at a festival.

But where? Judging by the overpriced food and the watery lager, I'm fairly certain I'm in England.

A quick check of my wrist: oh yes, the Reading festival, an entire three days devoted to British bands whose one-word names seem to speak volumes about their musical ambitions (Reef, Gene etc) and American rock's biggest players (Soundgarden, Hole, Smashing Pumpkins and a debuting Foo Fighters).

I wander through the crowds saucer-eyed and dry of mouth. I make it into the crowd just in time to hear Billie Joe Armstrong extolling the virtues of amphetamine, that most functional of street drugs whose payback is deceptively brutal. It's the summer after my first year at college and I'm in the midst of a three-day speed bender so I know what I'm talking about here. Speed is fun – for a while. A good old line of that stuff and you can clean your house, write an essay, cook a meal (but never actually eat it) and then hit the town with the confidence that everything that comes out of your mouth is of the utmost importance even if it does come cased in dry-mouthed spittle – and soon the world will know your brilliance.

And then it wears off and you're left feeling like a smoked cigarette. A smoked cigarette with no friends.

But when Billie Joe Armstrong announces to the Reading crowd that he gets his kicks from the original Seventies' punks' preferred drug of choice and that Green Day's new record *Insomniac* was partially written and recorded during these binges, the crowds roars approvingly, as do I, even though I'm out of my gourd and bending the ears of a couple of old hippies from Ashby de la Zouche. In fact, I think I've just accidentally burst one of their ear drums with my vocal enthusiasm for *everything* that has ever occurred in the universe, including this raucous trio before us.

What a prick.

Green Day are back in Britain, previewing their first new songs since *Dookie* took them global. Two months ago *39 Smoothed Out/Slappy Hours*, the combined CD re-issue of 'Slappy' and debut album *39/Smooth*, released five years earlier, and second album *Kerplunk!*, were both certified Gold. Green Day are so big that even their earliest teenage recordings bashed out in a matter of hours are currently selling thousands of copies each week.

The new record, *Insomnia*, isn't out for six weeks so while the fifty or sixty thousand people standing watching them on this warm end-of-summer night are unfamiliar with the new songs, they are receptive to them. Besides, it's August Bank Holiday weekend and in Britain that usually means one thing: a bit of sunburn and lots of drinking. When the tribes gather and no-one has work in the morning, the dormant British barbarian spirit tends to show itself and this weekend Green Day are a perfect soundtrack. Dropping in snippets of Twisted Sister and Iron Maiden songs and a now-familiar cover of Survivor's *Rocky* theme tune, 'Eye Of The Tiger', certainly helped distance the band from the many shabby grunge throwbacks or Britpop bandwagoneers on the weekend's bill.

Reviews of Reading in the rock press the following week agreed that the band had delivered a show-stealing performance, despite battling against terrible sound problems which cleared up the moment the headliners Smashing Pumpkins came onstage to deliver a set that played heavily on their recent overblown album *Mellon Collie And The Infinite Sadness* (I, like most fans, was too drunk to notice such sound problems – or care. Bad sound was punk rock.)

Insomniac then was Green Day's 'difficult' second album. Of course, it was actually their fourth, but half of the record buying public remained blissfully unaware of what went on before 'Basket Case' so such problems perceived by detractors mattered little to Green Day, though they remained quietly fearful of being remembered as nothing more than a one or two hit wonder, a flash-in-the-pan. That band that went big in 1994, then disappeared.

It was an ever-changing landscape, rock music in 1995. Spearheaded by Blur's *Modern Life Is Rubbish* and Suede's self-titled debut in 1993, roughed up by Oasis in '94 and dragged-down by all manner of Kinks/Small Faces/Beatles clones, British music once considered as plain 'indie' was now Britpop and suddenly these Isles were rocking again. Grunge, claimed may Brit bands, was dead, and American culture was irrelevant. Singing about pain and misery was not cool, whereas twatting about on scooters and being photographed in greasy spoon cafes was. But for all its parochial tendencies and vague undertones of xenophobia, Britpop was undeniably part of a wider cultural renaissance – within art, fashion, literature and to a lesser extent, film – that had risen in reaction to Nirvana and the alternative rock of 1989-1994.

Strangely, Green Day lay somewhere between the two factions that defined alternative music, at least in Britain in the Nineties. On the one hand, they were as American as a Babe Ruth chocolate bar, on the other they worshipped Britpop totems such as The Kinks, The Who and The Jam. They looked, sounded and often acted Californian, yet having spent time hanging out in Wigan or Newport or wherever, already had a better understanding of British culture than many bands whose experience is limited to a central London hotel room. They liked the beer, the curries and the people, and were well aware that the British press were notoriously snobbish, brutally honest and fond of blowing all things out of proportion. So by 1995, when Britain was dominated by local bands for local people, Green Day just had to compare their international album sales figures to those of Blur or Oasis, two bands who could make the evening news but couldn't get arrested in the US, to see there was little threat.

"In America in the whole first part of the Nineties, mainstream music was starting to get a little more interesting, you know," said Billie at the close of that year. "Nirvana breaking big, Pearl Jam – who I don't like that much, but they're still more interesting than Bon Jovi – taking off and punk rock starting to get everywhere. Then suddenly, in 1995, you get a bunch of fuckin' golf-playing fraternity boys playing music. Have you heard Hootie & The Blowfish?"

But now residing in the belly of the corporate beast where their contemporaries (and rivals) were no longer Blatz or Chrimpshrine or Jailcell Recipes, but such equally huge-selling bands as the dreaded Hootie and many other middle-of-the-road artists, there was a sense of pressure that Green Day had to deliver another album to equal its predecessor.

Their approach, perhaps wisely given the cultural climate, was to take a bunch of speed and crank out a set of songs every bit as energized and vibrant as those on *Dookie*, but skuzzier and slightly darker too. All the trademark Green Day hooks and melodies were in place in the songs they were unveiling at Reading, but they were edgier too, more sonic, more *rock*.

If the early Green Day albums were conceived while feeling stoned and goofy, then *Insomniac* was a tauter, more wired affair that seemed to reflect their sometime enjoyment of taking amphetamine and speeding their nuts off, just like the London punks of 1977 before them. A cheaply bought man-made stimulant, speed lends itself to punk rock well for a variety of reasons: its low price, its availability (particularly in certain areas of California where various towns are well-known for being home to large numbers of illegal meth labs), the way in which it suppresses appetite and, most importantly, its sense of urgency. Being worldly gentlemen with something of an appetite for life, Green Day naturally used speed on occasion.

"I liked speed because I wanted some rocket fuel," said Billie Joe. "I wanted to think. That's the difference between us and the grunge scene: we wanted to go faster."

You can tell. Lyrically as well as musically, *Insomniac* was a record buzzing with cheap energy but also trailed by the mild psychosis and paranoia that comes with the inevitable comedown – and there is always a comedown. If *Dookie* was the heart-palpitating high, then *Insomniac* was the sleepless night and hypertension that comes after such an unnaturally speedy rise to the top. For years Green Day had been whizzing their tits off on their raw energy and an ever-expanding fan base. But with success comes anxiety, and *Insomniac* was an anxious record with the fraught undertones of doses of nasty street speed.

"The main thing of choice for us – well, Tre really likes pot – but the main choice was speed," said Billie. "People think that we're this big pot-smoking band even though we sound like an amphetamine band, but I dabbled in speed for a long time."

It was there in lyrics that pulled no punches and cut straight to the chase. Billie even directly referenced meth amphetamine on 'Geek Stink Breath', while songs such as 'Armatage Shanks' sounded like the pre-dawn sleepless scribblings of a comedown.

"It's an ugly song for an ugly drug," explained Billie of the former. "We have a lot of friends hooked on speed. They're so tweaked out, man, it's ridiculous. It's not really for it, and it's not really against it. It just describes a state of mind and the effect it had on me personally."

Nevertheless, Green Day's upbeat nature was hard to suppress – they couldn't write a tuneless song if they tried and the new compositions still swung with the almost folk-ish lilt of Billie Joe's melodies and rhythm section that locked into a pounding synchronicity so simplistic sounding as to make it look like this band could do no wrong.

Insomniac had been written over the past twelve months in snatched moments between the on-going madness of *Dookie* – on tour buses, in dressing rooms and at home catching his breath and changing nappies in Berkeley – and was recorded in October and November of 1994, just as Green Day's huge summer had turned to winter and the public frenzy surrounding them showed no sign of letting up.

"I was under a lot of stress," Billie Joe told journalist Ian Winwood in 2001, of the inception of *Insomnia*. "I'd just had a new baby and I was only twenty-three years old – so I had a lot on my plate. I didn't think things would be that huge. I went from one year not even being in a tax bracket to the next year being in the highest one. All the time we had our credibility questioned – we were fighting to prove that we weren't this Disney punk band, that we were coming from some place real."

The album was again produced by Rob Cavallo, engineered by Kevin Army and mixed by Jerry Finn, who that year also worked on Rancid's excellent breakthrough album *...And Out Come The Wolves* and would soon be working with huge post-Green Day pop-punk bands such as Sum 41 and Blink-182, not to mention collaborating with Green Day on many more projects.

"*Insomniac* was a hard record and that was a reaction to *Dookie*. When *Dookie* came out we had no control over who liked it," said Tre Cool. "We had a bunch of super-fivin' marines going 'Yeah, cool, you're my favourite fucking band, bro!' You have no control so you just go, 'Oh, great, whatever.' We were playing too many Coliseum-style big shows. All these ice-rinks around Europe, the United States and Canada … it gets really impersonal after a while. It became like, 'Okay, let's play 'Basket Case' *again*'. Now it's like 'Whoo! Let's play 'Basket Case'!'"

While the songs on the album were certainly a darker shade than those of *Dookie* and the production leaning towards a slightly harder rock sound, the content was much the same as before. The usual tangle of adolescent confusion, now further complicated by the onset of adulthood and mass popularity. On songs such as 'No Pride', 'Brain Stew' (whose juddering guitar chords had drawn comparisons to both Led Zeppelin and Chicago's '25 Or 6 To 4') and opener 'Armatage Shanks', *Insomniac* practically jangled with controlled anxiety, fizzy melodies and a grinding of the teeth.

The subject of the band's fame is subtly touched upon on songs such as '86', which considered the difference between the halcyon nights and camaraderie found at Gilman Street during the early years – hence the song title, which also refers to the term for ejecting someone from a bar or venue – and the reaction to the band post-*Dookie*. There's plenty of Berkeley in the album – the song 'Stuart And The Ave' is taken from the corner of Stuart Street and Telegraph Avenue, or there's high school hang-out Tight Wad Hill in the song of the same name. Songs such as the whiplash punk thrash 'Jaded' meanwhile served to remind exactly where Green Day had come from, spiritually if not geographically.

The artwork for *Insomnia,* a square fold-out collage, was done by Winston Smith, who thanks to his work with the Dead Kennedys was already known for having produced some of the most iconic images in punk. He later revealed he knew very little about Green Day when Billie Joe first phoned him up.

The centre piece for the work was an image of a pair of figures appropriated from Flemish artist and alchemist Jan van Eyck's work from way back in 1434, entitled 'Til Death Do Us Part'. As with the artwork for *Dookie,* the band had deliberately chosen to utilise the skills of someone already established within the punk scene – another small detail overlooked by those who said that Green Day turned their backs on their peers.

"I knew Tre when he lived up in Northern California," Smith told the comprehensive website www.greenday.net. "My title for the piece, 'God Told Me to Skin You Alive' was a reference to a comic book-style religious tract that [Jello] Biafra and I used for the fold-out poster included with the first Dead Kennedys' album, *Fresh Fruit for Rotting Vegetables.* This phrase was also Biafra's first line on side one of that album. Bill instantly got the reference the moment I showed it to him. He asked how long it took me to create and I said that ... I'd spent the last 38 hours working on [just] the assembly of the composition. He asked me how it was possible for me to stay awake that long and I said, 'It's easy for me. I'm an insomniac ...'" (Smith also reveals some hidden symbolism in the artwork: as well as the two skulls visible in the collage, fans can also spot a third one by holding the artwork at an oblique angle. What Smith described as "a blurry piece of driftwood protruding from the fire" actually comes into focus as a third skull – one for each member.)

Opinions on the content of *Insomniac* vary to this day. Some see it as nothing less than an under-appreciated Green Day classic, while others found Billie Joe's lyrical tone of disillusionment, confusion and panic attacks a little hard to swallow given he'd just sold ten million albums and was now an extremely wealthy man, regardless of what happened in the future. Green Day had 'made it' – what's to complain about? Such a criticism missed the point that being wealthy or commercially successful was in no way a guarantee of happiness or a sense of ease with the world. In fact, sometimes it was the opposite. With widespread fame came bigger worries and greater pressures; a life lived under a microscope. When the album was released in October 1995, a number of reviews noted that *Insomniac* was to *Dookie* what Nirvana's *In Utero* had been to *Nevermind* – a mental (but not musical) identity crisis and an amplified embodiment of the 'be careful what you wish for...' dictum. The comparison was not unwarranted but for Green Day to have sung about anything else other than their own changing lives would have been to fake it.

Many of the same reviews also at least noted that, aside from the darker subject matter, Green Day had changed little since the previous year's release, and that this was generally a good thing. If anything, they had become more nihilistic trading in early songs about girls for wider issues of self-hate, fear and loathing. But the music stayed much the same and the usual Seventies punk reference points were noted.

It would have taken a stinker of an album to have slipped away from public consciousness so soon, and *Insomniac* was a strong work, half an hour of punk power that you could sing in the shower. "It's certainly reassuring to know that the deathless ideals of the Blank Generation have passed into such safe hands," noted *The Times*.

Insomniac sold two million copies within its first six months, a huge amount though, inevitably, not quite as stratospheric as *Dookie*.

No album could be.

Next up, the Mike Dirnt-penned 'J.A.R.' was released as a radio track and was totally unaffected by a controversial leak prior to release. It topped the Modern Rock Tracks chart soon afterwards. The song was a touching addition to the Green Day canon, particularly given its subject matter. 'J.A.R.' was an acronym for Jason Andrew Relva, a friend of the band who had died, and the song considers the effect it had upon them, such as questioning their own mortality for the first time.

The song subsequently appeared on the soundtrack to the movie *Angus*, a high school coming-of-age film far subtler and understanding than similar genre films such as *American Pie.*

But Green Day's next proper single was aforementioned 'ugly song' 'Geek Stink Breath', released in late September. As mentioned, the song was an ode to the downside of speed with references to rotten teeth, scabby faces, erratic heartbeats and all the other lovely side effects of excessive misuse, tightly-wound round an instant melody. It was all you could want from a three minute rock record, really.

'Geek Stink Breath' reached No. 27 in the US chart and 16 in the UK, a relatively low placing given the band's level of exposure, but then again, not bad all things considered.

In punk terms, Green Day remained massive. Yet they were no longer of the punk world and as such were being judged on the same level as all the biggest rock and pop bands of their time – in America 1995's biggest-selling albums included Sheryl Crow, Bonnie Raitt, Toni Braxton, Boyz II Men, Alanis Morissette and Elton John, all musically and aesthetically a million miles away from Green Day, yet all fighting it out in the same market place. In the UK, bands such as Oasis, Radiohead, Pulp and Massive Attack were the biggest sellers in the rock/alternative worlds, but were barely competing on the world's stage.

So Green Day found themselves in a strange position.

They were the reigning kings of the new punk explosion, yet were no longer considered a punk band. They were enjoying another hugely successful album, yet certain critics had deemed it a failure. And the groundswell of the punk bands of 1994 had streamlined into a select few forging forwards, almost in isolation from one another. The Offspring were still riding high on the success of *Smash*, yet teetered precariously between forging a lasting career with one of the many major labels chasing them or disappearing altogether, though the sheer magnitude of that album's success virtually guaranteed them a career for years to follow. Rancid had fought off offers from Madonna to sign to her Maverick label and recently released the critically acclaimed *...And Out Come Their Wolves*, a gritty, gutsy collection more traditionally punk-inspired in sound than Green Day's pop-orientated slant. NOFX and Bad Religion had had big underground successes the previous year (with *Punk In Drublic* and *Stranger Than Fiction* respectively), with the former increasingly finding themselves having to assert their punk rock position with self-imposed rules and regulations to ensure they stayed true to their roots. NOFX refused to allow MTV to show their videos, they only did interviews with worthwhile fanzines and just generally conducted a career that showed you didn't need to go down the Green Day route to keep your shit together.

It was NOFX's politics and general sense of irreverence, coupled with the pop sensibility of Green Day, that would be hugely influential on a new breed of bands. These new bands recognised the importance of staying independent, yet unlike NOFX, were prepared to sacrifice that credibility to achiever quicker, more lucrative success playing much the same fast, stop-start punk rock music served with a side helping of toilet humour and a loose affinity to skateboarding culture and other extreme sports lifestyles. But in 1995, many of these bands were just forming or releasing their first records – bands such as Blink-182 whose career path aped Green Day's a half decade later, yet somehow with the all-important magic missing. Perhaps its because seeing a trick done for the second time is never quite as exciting as the first …

Green Day kept their momentum rolling with another single from *Insomnia*, 'Stuck With Me'. The song was originally written and recorded with The Police-esque title of 'Do Da Da' but due to a mistake on the master copies of the recordings was given the incorrect name of 'Stuck With Me', a different song entirely. But it, um, stuck. It kind of had to. The song was a perfectly-formed new-wave punk number with a trademark sing-song element to it. It reached No. 34 in the US.

The choice of B-sides for the single over the various formats – live recordings of 'When I Come Around', 'Jaded', 'Dominated Love Slave' and 'Chump' – suggested that perhaps Green Day's collective well was maybe running dry. Or at least, the demands from a label founded on productivity *can* affect creativity.

But Green Day were still winning fans and rattling cages wherever they went. As leaders of the new pop-punk movement they remained the most credible and popular band of their ilk, helped by the fact that their live show, while often astounding, never took itself too seriously. And the one thing that many bands in the mid-Nineties were doing was taking themselves too seriously. Green Day were proving that rock culture didn't have to be about death, addiction or self-obsession, despite what the recent deaths of Kurt Cobain, River Phoenix, Hole's Kristen Pffaf, or the disappearance of the Manic Street Preachers' Richey Edwards earlier in the year had variously suggested.

Maybe if the Green Day live show wasn't so dazzling they might have had more time off to catch their breath, but the rest of the year was blocked out with dates, including a memorable show at Brixton Academy where Billie Joe berated "the shirtless macho motherfucker" elements of the crowd. The performance was also much discussed, though for much more prosaic reasons: that night Green Day elected to hit the stage for their headlining slot at the princely hour of 8.15pm when most paying customers were just arriving or getting lubricated in one of the many local pubs, or still travelling into the city from the suburbs. The reasons they gave for such an earlier appearance were that their families were with them and they wanted to read their kids bed-time stories. Another sign perhaps, that after another hard year on the road, Green Day's attention was, perhaps understandably, elsewhere.

Despite their growing family commitments – or maybe even because of them – Green Day showed little sign of slowing down. Rare was it for them to be idle. The live show had now expanded into a performance full of quirks, wanton tomfoolery, audience participation, nudity, pastiche cover versions, idiocy (Billie Joe's trick of spitting in the air and catching it in his mouth springs to mind) all wrapped around a refined set of songs that allowed no room for filler. From 'At The Library' through to '86' they had songs spanning six or seven years – and every fan already had their favourites (crucially, no two fans seems to share the same Green Day highlight).

With a growing live reputation that had first transcended punk, then 'alternative' music, the band were in the enviable position of being written about in everything from the hardest of metal magazines to the pop press to the higher-browed broadsheet papers. That they were unwittingly marked-out as leaders of a new, post-grunge sound for the Nineties could only have helped their profile.

The double-whammy of *Insomniac* tracks 'Brain Stew' and 'Jaded' was Green Day's next single, their first double A-side, released worldwide over various formats in March. At a time when people were wondering whether the album had gone off the boil, 'Brain Stew'/'Jaded' rose to the top of playlists in the US and No. 28 on the UK singles chart, an urgent-sounding reminder that Green Day should never be written off. ('Brain Stew' incidentally was the name of a friend of the band who gets a credit on *Kerplunk!*)

But live bands need to keep playing, and that's what Green Day did as the schedule ran on into 1996. But it wasn't just about increasingly longer shows each night either. Spare time was filled with interviews with journalists still asking them about Gilman, 'selling-out' and what hair dye they used. The same went for endless radio and TV interviews.

There were also soundchecks to consider, signing sessions to conduct and daily meet-and-greets with local competition winners, each day a different city and all the while living a dual existence as husbands and fathers. As such, the shows became all the more over-the-top, as they became the sole outlet for working off any worries. For ninety minutes each night convention went out the window as the band brought a bit of anarchy to the latest middle American nowhere-hole.

At a show in Milwaukee, Wisconsin, Billie Joe joined the ranks of top willy-wavers that included the likes of The Doors' Jim Morrison, when he was arrested for alleged indecent exposure after a show at the city's Mecca Auditorium. It was a stunt he had pulled many times before and it was usually his way of letting the crowd know that he thought the show was mediocre. Gratuitous nudity and rock 'n' roll go hand in hand and whenever Billie Joe takes his clothes off and moons the crowd a mediocre show usually steps up a gear – it's a great tension diffuser and, in middle America, seemingly still a sure-fire way of getting into trouble. What is dumb and comical to some (a point illustrated by Billie's hilarious excuse: "I dropped my pick!") is outright offensive to those less open-minded concert goers – the police, basically. After an hour-long set officers took the singer to a police station where he was cited for indecent exposure and bailed for $141.85.

"Mr. Armstrong dropped his pants to his knees and exposed his buttocks to the crowd," said a Lt. Thomas Christopher of the Milwaukee police department, in the subsequent Warners press release. "After the concert, Mr. Armstrong was taken into custody, given a city citation for indecent exposure. The problem was he exposed himself to a crowd of about six thousand people, including people as young as ten. That was our main reason for taking the action."

Another good insight into Billie Joe around this period can be seen in an exchange of letters dated late 1996 with an irate mother who had heard her eight-year-old son playing a copy of *Insomniac* bought for him by his grandmother and which she deemed was "trash", commenting that "it is horrifying and one of the worst interpretations of an 'art form' I have ever had the misfortune to hear." She ended by asking – or telling – "why don't you do something positive and clean up your act? All the thought you are putting into the minds of our youth is scary."

Billie's response, in his handwriting recognizable from earlier Green Day's missives was articulate and succinct: "I don't make music for parents, grandparents or eight-year-olds and I'll say what I damn well please. That's the difference between you and me – I do what I want … you do what you're told. Obviously we're not on the same planet …"

Maybe Billie Joe getting naked was a cry for help.

Or maybe not. Let's not get hysterical.

But life on the road *was* getting to them. How could it not? They'd clocked up thousands and thousands of miles since *Dookie* came out two years earlier and they'd tapped into a whole new fanbase. From the outside things were going great. Heaving arenas, another successful record, the general sense that this band could shape up to be long-term earners – all the usual boxes record industry paymasters like to see ticked.

But what the accountants and agents and publicists and managers had forgotten was just how much touring Green Day had done in the five years prior to the release of that album. It had been a lot of late-night drives and shitty motels. A lot of draughty dressing rooms. Of course, it had paid off and touring for the band now involved either far more luxurious hotel rooms, tour buses or limousines, on-the-road caterers, and a crew to keep the machine well-oiled and fully-functioning. Yet still it was hard work. Time spent away from families, endless publicity obligations to fulfill, business decisions to make and the familiarity of bashing through 'Basket Case' in another anonymous sports hall night after night began to take it toll on all three members. There was a general sense of being adrift without an anchor, a vague lack of purpose to the never-ending mission. Suddenly the themes of *Insomniac* seemed all too real.

The crowds were loving the shows – but were the players?

Halfway through their US arena tour in early 1996, affirmative action was finally taken as the band made the decision to cancel dates and head home, for their own health if nothing else. They'd already been to Europe and the Far East and were only a few months into a year that was already planned out for them. The question was asked – is a tour still a tour if it never ends?

"It was necessary for us just to go away at that point," said Tre. "It was a question of mental health on all three of our parts. We were in a bad state – not just with each other, but with the whole thing. So we just went away snowboarding for a while and forgot about the responsibility of being in a band, selling records and stuff."

"Playing for an hour a day was fun, but the rest of the day was just a blank," reflected Billie Joe. "We were beginning to not have any fun, so we decided to stop before it was six months too late and things started getting unpleasant."

The decision to cancel the tour was triggered by something that the normally adaptable band would have worked around, just as they did all those years ago when they hooked up a generator and performed for Larry Livermore.

"When we saw the hall where we were supposed to play, we knew that we wouldn't play," said Billie. "It was criminal, no electricity, no security, the floor was littered with broken glass. We'd rather have a disappointed audience than an audience that got seriously hurt or even killed. Moshing and broken glass just don't go together and a punk concert isn't fun without a pit. We were exhausted, wrecked, absolutely wrecked. At that point in time, we had been on tour for over two years and slowly our fuses blew. One after another, [we] just went bang! We were finished, fucked up. We didn't know any more who we were, where we were. We just wanted to go home."

It might have been a decision that saved the band in some small way. Recent musical history is littered with casualties who have burned out while trying to ride that first wave of success all the way to the shore. The major label music business is all about striking while the iron is hot. When an album breaks, as *Dookie* did, a follow-up is required a soon as physically possible to prevent the more fickle new-found fans getting bored or wandering off to the next big thing. Green Day achieved that with *Insomniac*. With each new album comes touring for months at a stretch and before they know it, the band are back home expected to deliver more of the same even quicker – and best hurry up because the label has just signed a younger, hungrier version of your band …

It's at this stage when tempers get frayed, bad decisions get made and bands often plunge into freefall. It already happened with so many of the grunge and early Nineties alt-rock bands who, by 1996 had either carved out their own niche (Soundgarden, Pearl Jam and Alice In Chains being obvious examples) or more likely, were already long-gone.

Green Day avoided such a dilemma by calling their own time-out. It was proof for the first time that they weren't infallible – that, whether acknowledged or not, the work-load and type of pressures they had never needed to face back in the early days, were taking their toll.

"I dived right back into being at home," says Billie. "Initially it feels like a culture shock to sit around doing nothing. But at the same time I was writing songs – we weren't just sitting around counting cheques. It can be really difficult holding a family together and doing this, but luckily my wife understands. It makes for good songwriting: you walk a thin line between everything being completely great and being completely insane."

The singer once told me an anecdote during an interview, speculating as to how he was viewed by his young son: "One time the Rolling Stones were on TV and I said 'Who's that Joe?' and he said 'It's daddy!'"

So 1996 saw Green Day keeping their lowest profile since their formation. The difference now was they had made enough videos and had enough hits for them still to be highly visible, even when they're weren't active. So even when they were resting, they were selling.

Later in the year Mike joined the ranks of fatherhood when he and his wife Anastasia had a daughter, Estelle Desiree. By the relatively young age of twenty-four, all three members were married with children, though in the case of two of them they were unions which sadly wouldn't last. The time off allowed a break from each other and a chance to enjoy the wealth that had come after a decade's hard slog.

And so it went for the rest of 1996, where Green Day enjoyed their first summer *not* touring the US or playing European festivals, not starting riots, not getting arrested and not undertaking any publicity whatsoever. It was time out of the limelight they could afford – and with little worry of their future. Despite the inevitable criticisms *Insomniac* had been a huge success.

Punk – or pop-punk, or skate-punk, or its many other variations – had fragmented in many different directions and cliques. Some of the more popular punk albums that year were releases by the reformed Descendents, Sublime, Bouncing Souls, Avail, who all offered slightly d i ffering takes on the punk sound with little threat of usurping them. Save for Refused's hardcore-leaning *The Shape Of Punk To Come*, it was not a year for punk classics. Not that it was a competition, but all bands are secretly competitive. In the UK, indie bands such as Supergrass and Ash both benefited from the interest in all things fast, frantic and youthful. Neither were punk bands *per se*, but then neither were Green Day either ...

It was a strange time for the genre – key bands such as Green Day and The Offspring were as omnipresent (and affluent) as the biggest pop stars of their time, yet those directly inspired by them enough to form bands and follow the same corporate route to stardom (The Living End, Blink-182, Good Charlotte) had not quite arrived. The punk heartland was now in the bigger clubs and theatres which the mid-ranged bands could fill with ease.

The difference now was that punk was fashion – it always had been – but the uniform was more rigidly defined by labels of the many skate and clothing companies keen to get in on the action. Long-established skate brands such as Vans and Thrasher – labels almost solely associated with skateboarders or Eighties punks – saw an increase in turnover as the new punk's ascension continued into the mainstream culture and the psyche of the world's youth. The kind of punk that was selling records was no longer about homemade clothes, DIY haircuts and charity shop budgets, but rather an amalgamation of styles – long shorts or baggy pants, golf T-shirts and sweaters, baseball caps, brand name trainers, the obligatory bog-brush haircut now carefully *coiffured* at the hands of a hairdresser, plus key chains, backpacks and all sorts of other accessories.

Just as modern day punk music increasingly began to co-opt other styles of music – reggae, ska, metal, hip-hop, dance music – to form new sub-genres, so too punk styles had become less discerning. The problem wasn't that punk had become fashion-orientated (after all, the Sex Pistols were formed in a clothes shop and The Clash's image was a major point of discussion from day one) but it had become an open market where bigger brands could gain a stronghold by smartly aligning themselves with the latest youth cultures. A more extreme comparison can be found in the way in which Nike have successfully turned their brand into an essential, must-have item within the hip-hop world and, by extension, black communities. Nike used the idea of peer pressure, desirability and clothing as a status symbol to great – if ruthless – effect. It wasn't quite the same with punk, but the mid-Nineties did see an influx of money from outside organizations keen to cash-in on the disposable income of kids happy to buy into the notion of pre-packaged rebellion – all an extension of this new-found awareness of all things 'alternative' that corporate America tapped into.

For punk, by now, was becoming increasingly middle-class. Where only ten years ago it provided a life-saving refuge for people like Tim Armstrong, and was based on a look born out of poverty, thrift stores and the squatting scene, now it was a cool look to adopt, available off-the-peg in the local mall. Punk was white and suburban. It's hard to imagine Sid Vicious or Joey Ramone turning up for a show wearing knee-high sports socks, three-quarter length shorts and *a fucking rucksack*.

So, thanks to the success of Green Day, The Offspring et al and the wiliness of a few hip young marketing men and brand managers, punk was becoming a lifestyle that could be sold to the same demographical bracket as snowboarding, which is slightly absurd as snowboarding is a pursuit that requires money to partake in. It is not for the poor kid in the street.

Nevertheless, labels such as Epitaph recognized the anti-authoritarian/anti-social connection between punk music, skateboarding and snowboarding and were open to licence their bands out to soundtracks – a major factor in the success of The Offspring, for example. Similarly, scene figureheads such as Lookout! or Fat Mike's label Fat Wreck Chords and their bands certainly benefited from the numerous compilations and soundtracks he cleverly squeezed his artists onto.

This 'corporate alignment' with punk, which would reach a zenith in 2001 when Blink-182 allowed Honda to brand their US tour 'The Civic Tour', is perhaps best epitomized by the Vans Warped Tour, a travelling punk festival with a number of stages and side show attractions, all centred around a musical policy that decreed that all bands were equal and therefore the line-up changed from show to show. One day Rancid would be headlining, the next Screw 32 (or whoever).

Started by Kevin Lyman – whose background lay in *Transworld* magazine's Board Aid charity organization – the Warped tour was quickly seized upon by Vans shoes, the company who had inadvertently entered recent rock iconoclasm through the patronage of such people as Minor Threat, Henry Rollins and the Dogtown skate team. It also didn't take long for record labels to realize that the Warped tour was also a great way to break in bands with a wider appeal in rock music – whether the Deftones or Jurassic 5, Black-Eyes Peas or Alien Ant Farm.

By 2004, among the Warped Tour 'services' taking place in the Pavillion tent were Warped Mobile and Warped Music Services (where you can listen to Warped Radio), Warped streamed music subscription services, Warped Music Store where you can spend your Prepaid Download Card. Warped – there's that word again – also recently joined forces with Apple so that festival-goers can use iMacs, PowerMac G5's and guitars (provided) to create their own music.

There are also Warped spin-offs such as tour videos, a book about its history, Warped merchandise – the whole kit and caboodle. While it's easy to be cynical, the Warped tour took an array of the best punk bands around to places they'd normally never reach and provided a sense of homogeny to a scene. For one day each year, kids could catch up on the music, get their hair dyed … buy into the lifestyle, basically. And some of that is undoubtedly down to the cash injection provided by sponsors, all of which is great for those who use the Warped tour as a sub-cultural safe-haven or an entry point into a whole new world of music. What John Lydon might think about instructions on how to dye your hair in the name of punk or the widespread corporate branding and mass-market advertising would remain to be seen, but from the mid-Nineties onwards *this* was the shape of punk to come.

So strong was Vans' association with this ever-swelling punk community that in 2002 it launched its own record label, headed up by Pennywise singer Jim Lingberg: "Vans Records is a perfect complement to the Vans Warped Tour and is a natural move for us considering Vans' long-time position at the heart of Core Sports, music and youth," said Gary H. Schoenfeld, president and chief executive officer of Vans. "Vans Records is the latest element in our efforts to forge an emotional connection and build loyalty with our core customer through sports and music."

Emotional connection? To shoes?

Things had definitely moved on since the epitome of youth cool was three hundred kids crammed into Gilman.

Regardless of what was on their feet.

When Green Day weren't touring or recording, they adopted a cheap and cheerful approach, rehearsing in the garage of a friend on a suburban street that marked the border between Berkeley and Oakland. It was here, amongst Tre's many drum kits (he's never sold a single one and has stashed them in numerous friends' homes over the years), piles of magazines, guitars and other Green Day ephemera, that any new songs would be introduced to the band, and where they felt most at home. Back in the garage, smoking weed and messing about.

Having written and rehearsed an impressive amount of new material, they gradually made moves to return to public life, starting with a secret show they played for 150 friends in a warehouse back in Oakland on Valentine's Day 1997. It was a fine reminder of the same community-minded spirit that Billie Joe sang of on '86'.

"We wanted to get them all hooked up!" explained Tre. "Boy met girl, girl met boy, boy met boy and girl met girl. We like it when people fall in love at our shows. Also, when they get knocked up in the parking lot. As long as they bring the baby to the next tour and call it Nimrod, it's fine."

Nimrod was to be the name of Green Day's new album. The traditional meaning of the word as outlined in The Bible is "the mighty hunter" but over time it came to mean idiot, geek, nerd, dork or various other Americanisms – "as good a title as any," the band would tell me later in the year. It is first known to have entered the modern lexicon when Bugs Bunny referred to his hapless hunter nemesis Elmer Phudd as a "poor little Nimrod."

Before recording the album though the band did manage to have themselves what could be considered a textbook rock 'n' roll night while staying at a textbook rock 'n' roll hang-out, the Sunset Marquis, just off West Hollywood's Sunset Strip in March while in LA on business. The night got off to a bang – at their hotel, they generally partied hard and lived up to the reputation of a mega-selling punk rock band stopping at one of the world's most luxurious hotels. But then, how boring would it be if these bands just ... went to bed early?

Alcohol probably played a part when Tre acquired the hotel's guest register and, upon finding that the Rolling Stones were in residence, made a number of late night calls to Keith Richards. Billie Joe nearly got into a fight with an Eighties pop star. Someone wandered the corridors naked. Someone else threw their TV out of a third-storey window.

"Glass was everywhere, that's all I can tell you," said Billie, "You have to live that arrogant lifestyle now and again ..."

It's usually at this point in a band's biography that you'd get to read about the experimental album, the drug excesses and the fisticuffs. But, by virtue of their unwavering dedication to a sound they had developed over the past decade – had it been that long already? – and the notion of 'the song' above everything, Green Day were unlike other bands. Here is an act who are the living embodiment of the 'if it ain't broke, don't fix it' dictum. They'd already got their drug days out of their system and any bust-up's either took the form of fights with other people or various representatives of authority, or were just plain well-concealed. Mike and Billie had been friends for well over fifteen years – they knew too much about each other to let any disagreements sour what they had built together.

"I think people thought that after *Insomniac* we were just going to go away," said Billie Joe. "But that just wasn't going to happen."

After the best part of a year resting up and writing, Green Day got back to business. And it was very much business as usual. Combining the hi-octane reckless abandon of their songs of old with a maturing, neo-classicist approach to songwriting with a serious intent that would become truly apparent a couple of years later, the only major difference when Green Day entered the studio to record their new songs was that a lot of them hadn't been road-tested to quite the extent as those that made it onto, say, *Kerplunk!* or *Dookie*.

Sticking with what they knew, Green Day once again brought in Rob Cavallo to produce the sessions that took place throughout the summer. Despite adhering to a basic Green Day formula, the band had diversified slightly, a progression evident in the inclusion of a horn section (on the zestful 'King For A Day') and various other session musician contributors. The new tunes fleetingly delved into ska, rockabilly and surf sounds in a really natural, unassuming way and it was in these broader-sounding songs that the strength of the new album lay. There was even talk of an emotionally heightened acoustic ballad featuring Billie and his guitar making it on there. 'Why not?' seemed to be the general attitude and approach for studio album number five.

By now the band were being managed by Pat Magnarella of Atlas/Third Rail management, an eminently likeable man who already had a proven track record as manager of enduring Minneapolis band Goo Goo Dolls and melodic geek rockers Weezer. He was clued-up enough to be a major player in the LA music business yet laid-back and young enough to not impose himself on the band totally, yet could command the type of respect needed between errant artists and their slightly straighter earth-based representatives.

Nimrod miraculously shoe-horned 18 songs into a mere fifty minutes. It was the band's broadest work yet, chaotic-sounding but tightly controlled too. It sounded like a band still running on seemingly limitless energy resources, but with a relaxed attitude to its own contents, as if the three members had stopped worrying about whether they were a pop band, a rock band or a punk band and finally accepted that they were a bit of all three and somewhere in the middle lay a few million floating voters.

The album's opener, the underdog anthem 'Nice Guys Finish Last' was a song that could have featured on any Green Day album. Such was the inherent energy rush of Billie Joe's guitar parts and the super-tight rhythm section that it seemed little had changed on planet Green Day; business as usual. Well, not quite.

The trio were too smart to come out with a career-suicide record, but *Nimrod* did broaden the template – there was their previously untapped ska side (thankfully more or less dormant ever since) on the aforementioned live favourite 'King For A Day', the slinky aggro-pop of 'Hitchin' A Ride', the Seventies-rock inspired 'All The Time' or the berserk breakneck punk of 'Platypus (I Hate You)', the hardcore-inspired 'Take Back' and the Beach Boys-esque twangy surf instrumental 'Last Ride In'. Phew. All layered in harmonies and melodic hooks that explode in the ear like minor epiphanies, naturally.

It was shortly before the release of *Nimrod* – September 16, 1997 to be exact and a little over five years since I had worn out my tape-copy of an imported version of *Kerplunk!* – that I first encountered Green Day in the flesh. Somehow – I'm still not sure how or why – on the very day that I officially left the UK's lowest achieving university with a low grade degree in English Literature, I was offered a full-time job as staff writer on a weekly music paper. Somebody pinch me.

So in that glorious extended holiday between completion of college in the early summer and graduation at the turn of the autumn, I found myself not sitting around adhering to a daily marijuana work-out or doing a shitty job to pay off my debts, but jumping on and off trains and aeroplanes, on tour buses, in scummy backstage dressing rooms meeting bands, always with notepad in hand.

So when I was asked if I might be interested in interviewing a flagging Green Day at the last minute as none of the other more experienced writers were available and/or interested in these three chord punkers,

I needed little persuasion. Twenty-four hours later I was digging my fingernails into the hand rest as the plane curved downwards to the right and we enjoyed a smooth touch down in Milan, city of industry and fashion and – for one night only – punk rock.

Meeting bands is weird. Meeting bands you like or care about or dare to respect under the guise of 'journalist' (or, worse, *'critic'*) is even weirder – not because they're superstars or higher beings or, indeed, any more important than the everyman on the street, but because there is no balance to the conversation. You know the band – or at least you think you do – because they've bared their soul to you through their music. You know their mannerisms and individual personality traits from TV interviews, checked their hair and clothes in the magazines. They're like long-lost friends. But to *them*, you my friend, you are just another tool with a tape recorder and a hidden agenda. It matters shit to them if you went out and bought that first seven-inch – any fool can do a quick internet search and pay lip service to get the conversation off to a good start. It doesn't matter if you dug the same obscure punk bands as they did growing up. Because when you're as big a band as Green Day, when you've sold millions of records and meet a dozen people like me per day, your defences are up and your ears are finely tuned to filter out the inanities of endless compliments and namedrops, in order to get through the day until it's either time to hit the stage or flop down in your five-star hotel room.

Meeting Green Day for the first time in a large hotel suite whose centre-piece was a large board-room table full of snacks and drinks from which they would conduct a round of interviews, my initial impression was that here was a band of three quite different personalities, yet who clearly shared enough common ground to remain firm friends as well as successful business partners. You probably know this already – that's why you bought the record, the T-shirt and now this, a book. But seeing a band dynamic in action up close when there's no-one but you and them and a couple of hours to kill provides an added insight that a TV broadcast so often fails to capture.

"I'm kind of shaky from this stuff, so excuse me if I spill it on you ..."

This is Tre Cool squeaking and *hur-hur-ing* like Beavis as he careers across the room carrying a cup of coffee, spoon rattling against saucer and nerves jangling from jet lag, too much caffeine and, well, from having to be Tre Cool twenty-four hours a day. His own cup has just been thrown against the wall, a curtain discreetly covering the brown stain he's just made in this top floor suite.

Mike is enthusiastically showing off those trousers that he deliberated long and hard about forking $10 out for. Mike enthuses a lot, it seems part of his nature. He seems like a nice guy. And then there is Billie Joe, sometimes quiet and withdrawn, other times taking charge of the conversation and swinging it back round to the original question when things get a little inane.

Playing back the interview tape now, eight years after the event, I discover a hidden message on the tape. In a deep, whispered voice comes a message from the past: "Tre Cool is *fine*, Tre Cool is *fine* ..."

Seems I got off lightly ...

Later, accompanied by an entourage that included a man-mountain of a security guard, two publicists and a photographer, we spend an eventful afternoon driving around Milan with a running commentary provided by Tre Cool. We stop outside Milan cathedral, the oldest in Europe, to do an impromptu photo shoot and the band are mobbed by fans. A street hustler sidles up close before being spotted slipping away with one of the photographer's expensive spare cameras by Green Day's security guy, who collars the street thief and retrieves the much-needed equipment. He's gracious enough not to dish out a beating.

That night, a warm balmy late summer evening, Green Day play in a small club to a crowd of around five hundred rowdy Italians, by far the smallest show they have played in a long while. After another day tirelessly spent talking about their new album, the punk scene, 'selling-out', rumours of them splitting and the usual multitude of similar questions from the Eurohacks (myself included), the band are in their element, combining the raw up-close energy of the Gilman days with a sense of projection that only comes from playing arenas where beyond the first rows the crowd looks like a beans-on-toast blur. Playing with an almost telepathic ability and flawless sense of cohesion it's in clubs like these that it's clear why Green Day have always been a cut above their contemporaries. Tonight it's Milan but it could be anywhere. Green Day are one of the few bands who could roll up to any club in the world and have the place dancing within three minutes. Billie Joe leads the crowd through a bizarre Freddie Mercury-esque call-and-response routine. They play a bunch of new songs from *Nimrod* that go down a storm. They dash out '2000 Light Years Away' and 'Christie Road' and the club goes ballistic.

Afterwards there's an aftershow party upstairs. This is Milan and the place is stuffed with supermodels keen to be seen in the presence of one of the world's biggest bands. Walking in with Billie Joe is a strange trip as all eyes turn towards the small guy with the rounded shoulders, dyed black hair and beat-up trainers. Those people that don't ask him for autographs ask him what his band is called. "I really don't know why some of these people are here," he ponders. Seemingly the promoter is friends with some of the big American model agencies and has brought in these strange, stick insect-like creatures *en masse* to hang out looking decorative, unapproachable and coolly aloof. It's the weirdest post-punk show scene I've ever encountered. And, for the band, it's something of a step-up from playing Wigan Cricketers five years earlier.

Back in the dressing room there's a telling moment when the photographer I'm with, a forty-ish ex-London punk, asks Billie Joe why, if Green Day are a punk band, they attract such a smartly dressed, *cosmopolitan* looking audience.

"I guess there are certain factions of people who are into the punk music, attitude and ideology or whatever, then there the cling-on's," reasons the singer.

"I was a full-time punk first time around in England," continues the photographer. "Arse hanging out of my jeans, ripped T-shirt, and that was just from every day wear and tear. Those people down there are wearing beautiful clothes."

"So why aren't you punk any more?" fires back Billie Joe.

"Oh, I am still mate, don't worry about that. I'm still the worst dressed person in Britain."

"That's true ..."

Conversation soon swings back round to punk as Billie ponders – not for the first time – the ethical dilemma he's long since resolved within himself, yet three years on since *Dookie*, is still finding himself having to talk about on a daily basis on this latest promotional trip.

"I've been into this for ten years now and I can't shrug it off because my band has sold however many records," he explains, sipping a drink. "It means a lot more to me than this trendy circus that is the people here today. Like I said earlier today though, I'm a songwriter and that's what I have to come back to after all this: good tunes. I've driven myself fucking crazy talking about these things. I know who I am – for the most part, anyway. I know where I come from. We can play in front of seven hundred people tonight, or the Woodstock festival, it makes no difference to us."

"Do you tire of having to justify the band's existence to people who have no concept of where the band came from to get where they are today?," I enquire.

"It's a stupid conversation. If there's such a thing as a stupid question, then that's it: 'are you still punk?' I can't just shrug off my past, man. Why change? I'm not gonna change for anyone."

The lead track from *Nimrod* was 'Hitchin' A Ride', whose simplistic descending rockabilly-ish bass line and choppy chords created the type of immediacy that has marketing men and radio pluggers rubbing their hands in glee. The accompanying video showed the band playing in an old-time theatre set, as if transported back a hundred years to a velvet-curtained corner of Paris. It was somewhat surprising then when 'Hitchin' A Ride' was released in the UK in October 1997 that it only reached a relatively disappointing No. 25 in the charts.

Mainstream rock music was in a strange place – grunge was long gone and the initial impact of the punk explosion of 1994-1995 was all but over (by virtue of the fact that an explosion is short, sharp and seismic). Newer emerging sub-genres within the metal, rock and punk scenes of the late Nineties had not yet emerged from the underground to achieve commercial fruition, though their time was soon to come.

Alongside the usual bankable suspects (U2, REM etc) the biggest rock bands of 1997 were a mixed array of disparate artists such as Korn, The Prodigy, Foo Fighters, Radiohead and The Verve, all of whom had little in common with one another. To the critics Green Day meanwhile were perhaps heavily associated with that which had passed in 1994: Woodstock, hair dye, *"Do you have the time...?"* – all of that. Unlike with previous releases, *Nimrod* was notable by its absence from any 'albums of the year' lists in the UK press at the close of 1997.

Which isn't to say it wasn't a huge success – it was. It's just musical history is often written with a type of hindsight that is always subconsciously observing the *zeitgeist* – the general intellectual, moral, and cultural climate of an era. So, at the hands of those who help write, document or comment on rock's recent history the onus is placed on social and cultural relevance of the day as much as it is on chart positions. In which case, for all its strengths, *Nimrod* was not a success.

But this is perhaps intellectualizing all the fun out of the good times. And though the band were now – yikes! – in their mid-twenties, they showed no signs of mellowing, maturing or embracing social convention.

Before the release of the album, in the summer Green Day were booked for Japan's Fuji festival and as a warm-up played a secret show as The Nimrods at Johnny Depp's club, The Viper Room on Sunset Strip. It wasn't until the band had arrived in Japan however that a typhoon hit the region and the festival-site became a wash-out of uninhabitable proportions. With the festival cancelled, the band retired to a nearby amusement park seemingly already full of the cream of Nineties rock music – Beck, The Prodigy, Foo Fighters and Red Hot Chili Peppers – taking advantage of some time to indulge the child within.

The devil makes work for idle hands, and Tre Cool should never be idle. The promise of endless rides and flashing, bleeping entertainment was not enough and a rumour later circulated that the drummer had reportedly got into a spot of trouble over hi-jinx with Foo Fighters drummer Taylor Hawkins – Billie Joe had supposedly had to diffuse the situation with a bit of humour. The image of the two drummers potentially engaging in some sort of kiddie's duel in the middle of an amusement park is certainly one to cherish.

Even greater trouble loomed in November at an instore gig/signing at the Tower Records store on Broadway in the heart of Manhattan. Seeing rock bands performing in sweaty, strip-lit shops is about as natural as buying bootleg tapes in a butchers. In such a setting, the hard-sell commerciality of music suddenly seems all the more obvious, while the heightened emotions and surge of unrestrained energy of a rock show seems somehow all the more potentially subversive. It's corny and it's unexplainable but instore gigs have the strange effect of making audiences want to smash and steal. Why, I don't fully know but it certainly has something to do with context. Bars and clubs and theatres are built to contain bands and their wild fans – record stores are not. So all it takes is a spark or two to kick-start the mayhem which in this instance happened mid-way through the forty-five minute performance: "You can start a riot," said Billie. "It's your prerogative – you can do anything you want, 'cause you're not at Tower Records – you're at a Green Day concert!"

And what a show it was. A pumped-up Billie Joe led the way by spraying the crowd and the CD racks between which they were herded with beer and water, sprayed 'Nimrod' on the store walls before crowd-surfing his way across the store to spray 'Fuck you' on the window (fuck who? New York?). Amidst more arse-flashing from Billie, chaos broke-out as the crowd followed the frontman's lead in punkifying their sanitized surroundings and Tre began to dismantle his drum kit in customary fashion – with much vigour and haste. At one point someone from the store's management was seen wrestling a two-hundred-pound monitor out of the hands of Billie Joe as he struggled to up-end it over a staircase on top of which the band were playing.

"The store couldn't handle it," laughed Tre afterwards.

Such scenes were now common place. Ever since Woodstock, Green Day had been associated with what some would perceive as anti-social behaviour. But, of course, what the security guards, the police, the more conservative areas of the press and the occasional irate parents fail to recognise is that Green Day peddle a *tightly controlled* sense of mayhem. Some would call it anarchy, though it is anything but that. Anarchy is "political disorder and confusion" or "a state of lawlessness and disorder, usually resulting from a failure of government", but what Green Day do is entertain. Political affiliations have never featured in the music and their only message is one of freedom, empowerment and the encouragement of opposition to convention (something that seems increasingly easy to achieve in America these days). Cynics would called it packaged rebellion and that if they were true punk rebels they would be more like ill-fated punk rocker GG Allin, whose shows generally centred around defecation, violence, masturbation and, ultimately, the singer's own arrest and imprisonment.

But what's the point of that?

Rock music is full of no-hopers, death-trippers and undeniable fuckwits. In riding the line between the conventional career path and the life of outlaws, Green Day have been far smarter. Even when they're wrecking things, it's done with a smile and – maybe, sometimes – an apology afterwards. But really, which record store owner *wouldn't* want the greatest live band on the planet blowing the roof off their store? It certainly sells records.

"We don't hurt people," defended Billie Joe. "I think we're actually a very friendly band. How many other bands stop shows if they see a kid falling in the pit? A lot of bands don't care about that. I want everybody to have a good time at a concert. I don't want anybody getting hurt. That's punk, playing a show, having a party, having a good time."

The band followed the Tower show the next week with a performance as equally as chaotic when they played a free gig on a tiny stage at the end of a back alley that ran behind a Toronto record store. The show attracted somewhere between two and four thousand people – and a fair few police too. Given that the alley was sixteen feet wide, this was some feat. Pictures taken by fans on the day showed an improbably narrow and deep crowd of heads craning for a glimpse of a band in this most surreal of situations.

Maybe it was the shock of the cancelled tour of 1996, but Green Day had now learnt the art of pacing themselves – in all areas. In performance, in indulgence and in work-load. The key to any touring band's success is the balance between an unerring dedication to keeping their momentum rolling for fear of being usurped by younger pretenders, and maintaining a semblance of normality – a life away from the unreal existence of a rock star. As with the Toronto show they were also in a position to do the cool things, and could now turn down the more tedious obligations that a younger Green Day might have felt the pressure to do. They had, in some respects, taken the power back. When any band is selling millions, suddenly their opinions carry a lot more weight amongst their paymasters ... *"Of course you can blow out 'MTV Cribs' because you can't be bothered to vacuum today, that's absolutely not a problem!"*

With *Nimrod's* campaign winding down, Green Day were learning their lessons well. Two albums on from *Dookie* and they had done what many said they couldn't: build a lasting career. Their newest album was certified double-platinum to mark sales of two million copies, roughly the same amount of records sold as *Insomnia*. In business-speak, Green Day were maintaining their market share nicely. But if this was to continue they needed more time off – which isn't to say they weren't doing anything with their free time.

One new project that Billie embarked upon was the start of a record label. The idea came about one lazy day when he and a group of friends and their wives and girlfriends were sitting around in someone's back yard discussing the punk rock community. It wasn't long before someone raised the notion of starting a new label to cater for the many new great local bands who had followed in Green Day's footsteps.

Those involved included Jim Theibaud, owner of the lucrative Real Skateboards company, Doug Sanglang, the aforementioned Pinhead Gunpowder's Jason White, Billie Joe and Adrienne, and a couple of others.

Between them they were certainly qualified to embark on such a venture and not long afterwards Adeline Records – named after an

Oakland street – was born. The label's beginnings were small, primarily existing in a folder of paperwork that Theibaud carried around with him, with people working whenever they could, for no money. But things nevertheless moved relatively quickly.

"It was just kind of a quick start," White explains, "Kind of a 'Hey, why not?' We started the label as a small project at first and within two years it was taking off. We didn't ask for handouts or build it on Billie Joe's name. We built it on Adeline's name."

The first bands on Adeline included the likes of One Man Army, AFI and the Criminals. While still a relatively small operation, the Lookout!-esque Adeline Records continues to flourish where other labels have struggled to survive and by 2005 had built up a strong identity within the punk scene – and a weighty back-catalogue of releases from cool, often under-acknowledged bands. Anyone quick to accuse Billie Joe of being a sell-out would do good to look into his involvement in Adeline, and the way in which he has contributed to putting something back into the East Bay scene. Adeline continues to provide jobs for its workers and a place for bands to release their records away from the world of the major record labels – just how they used to do it back in the Eighties. Maybe Green Day didn't change the East Bay punk community quite as much as some people have said.

The band were off the road again when a new single was issued, ostensibly to help plug the album. The song was 'Good Riddance (Time Of Your Life)', their most unexpected work yet. Sparse, yet underpinned by a subtle lush orchestration, it showed to many for the very first time, that there was more to Billie Joe Armstrong than three chords and tongue-in-cheek guitar solos.

"The real irony is that for years and years, when people think of us, they think of our heavy guitars and the sounds that we've had on our records," explained Mike. "But we've written most of our songs on acoustic guitars. When we wake up in the middle of the night to write a song, Billie doesn't run to his amp and plug in his guitar, he picks up an acoustic guitar and starts jamming on it."

Here was a song with far-reaching appeal, a piece of music every bit as stirring as REM or Nick Drake's finest moments and every bit as credible as Billie Joe's songwriting heroes such as Elvis Costello and Paul Westerberg. Upon its release in January 1998, the song entered both the US and UK singles charts at a creditable No. 11. Suddenly Green

Day found their music reaching places previously unheard of – at ball-games or soundtracking scenes concerning the death of young cancer patient on hospital drama *ER* ("I heard that it was going to be on," said Billie Joe, "but I kinda purposely didn't watch it because that show is too heavy for me and I don't like having my evening filled with people dying of fucked-up diseases"). The song was also reportedly played at the funeral of a US soldier who died during the invasion of Iraq in 2003.

Most famously, when the TV show *Seinfeld* – arguably one of the most popular shows in the world – aired its final show in 1998, it was 'Good Riddance (Time Of Your Life)' that they used to soundtrack the episode that collated all the show's past highlights. The show attracted worldwide viewing figures of 100 million people and has subsequently been deemed the most talked-about show finale in US TV history.

It was that type of song.

In the same month that this new career landmark came for Green Day, some tragic news rocked the wider punk community when one of its leading figures, *Maximum Rock 'n' Roll* and Gilman Street founder Tim Yohannon passed away. He had been suffering from non-Hodgkin's lymphoma cancer for some time when he died at home amongst friends.

Often controversial, always outspoken, Yohannon had provided a voice for punk at a time when it had all but disappeared off the radar. While many disagreed with his hard-line stance of total creative and financial independence for punk bands and attendant organizations – not least Green Day who suffered much criticism at the hands of *MRR* – he was nevertheless a presence who would be deeply missed. For even in disagreement, Yohannon and his adversaries all shared the same passion for this music that had changed their lives and those around them. And without him it's possible that Green Day and hundreds of others, particularly those centred around the East Bay, might not have existed.

Green Day's live performances in 1998 were a mixture of headlining arena shows and the odd festival appearance, such as their show in June at LA radio station KROQ's Annual 'Weenie Roast' at open-air theatre Irvine Meadows, which brings together the biggest vaguely alternative bands for a promotional backslapping session and a strong musical bill for fans in attendance. If Green Day still had to fulfill certain promotional duties, then this key annual event would be one of them.

This time however it was the band themselves who had a right to complain about behaviour of which they were the victim. Details about what actually happened were vague, but it would appear that Mike Dirnt got into a fight with Aron Salazar, bassist for one of the other bands on the bill, post-grunge rockers Third Eye Blind who also came from the Bay Area.

Apparently, Salazar ran onstage and bear-hugged Dirnt during Green Day's set. Dirnt, somewhat surprised and taken back (and probably not recognizing that it was a fellow musician having a bit of fun) and already adrenalised by the performance reacted and an onstage scuffle broke out. A Green Day roadie then intervened, security stepped in and Salazar was escorted off the stage. Backstage after the show Mike confronted Salazar about what had just happened. As the pair were arguing, Dirnt was struck on the head from elsewhere by a Budweiser bottle hard enough to cause a small fracture in his skull. The blame was apportioned by eyewitnesses to a fan of Third Eye Blind.

Dirnt was taken to hospital where he received twenty stitches, forcing the cancellation of their next show in Sacramento. No charges were filed, though in the aftermath Green Day reportedly hired their own Private Investigator to look into the incident. Third Eye Blind's management were quick to issue an apologetic statement in which Salazar respectfully said, "I am sorry that my attempt at doing something I thought would be funny escalated into Mike getting hurt. That was never my intention. I simply had too much to drink and made a very bad decision. If I had been in Mike's place, I'm sure I would have acted similarly. My heart goes out to him and I hope he recovers quickly. We have many friends in common and I just hope that he can accept my sincerest apology. I am sorry, Mike."

Meanwhile, a new Green Day single came in the form of album track 'Redundant', primarily because the band were out on the road again. It reached No. 16 in the US charts, the lowest performing single from *Nimrod.* While the album had now sold in excess of two million copies, it was still nevertheless a fraction of *Dookie*, and low enough to prompt certain critics too publicly wonder whether Green Day's future was to see an ever-depleting fanbase. It was a reasonable enough question – few acts can maintain huge sales over a number of albums – but the band had one saving grace that distanced them from many other bands: they were now consistently one of the greatest live bands in the world, a fact recognized by *Kerrang!* who awarded them just that at their annual awards ceremony in August. So long as they were still a major live draw they would still have a career. Besides, any doubt that their future was nothing less than assured so long as Billie Joe Armstrong kept writing songs came from outside the band camp (though, tellingly, in an interview with *RIP* magazine in 1996 at the height of exhaustion he had admitted: "There isn't a day goes by in the past year and a half that I haven't thought about quitting").

In September, Billie Joe and Adrienne became parents for the second time with the birth of another son, who they named Jakob Danger Armstrong.

Pictures from around this time show the frontman carrying a bit of excess weight – he would later brilliantly term this as his "fat Elvis period" in tribute to the former King's gluttonous latter days. Always short of build with rounded shoulders anyway, the speed-skinny cheekbones of old were now hidden behind jowls that he attributed to his fondness for beer and his wide-eyes had recently taken on the slightly worn look that comes from endless late nights. In short, Billie Joe looked increasingly like the gas attendant or handyman whose clothes he always favoured anyway. It was no big deal, but the loosening of waistbands did seem to correspond with the winding down of the band after *Nimrod* and the start of another relatively fallow period for Green Day, a time from which they would emerge with a more refined direction befitting of their visible maturity.

"I kind of became everybody's weird uncle," said Billie in 2004. "I was just drunk all the time and wearing a fucking leopard G-string. What's not to love about that? So I cut back on drinking beer. I had no balance in my life – I had to start taking better care of myself. Just going for long walks and listening to Tony Robbins."

In their late twenties, with an entourage of wives and children and several million each in the bank, Green Day finally stopped being teenagers, a progression marked by Billie Joe's decision to give up drinking the beer that had been helping to fuel him for the past decade.

Unbeknown to them, the band were moving into the rock 'n' roll equivalent of middle age.

PART III: NOT THE END

"Adults are obsolete children."
Dr Seuss (1904 – 1991)

Five years after it had been released, *Dookie* went *ten times platinum*, a rare feat that recognized sales of ten million copies. And rising...

Commercially, it is now a greater success than Elvis Presley's *Christmas Album*, Britney Spear's *Oops! I Did It Again*, Michael Jackson's *Bad*, Fleetwood Mac's *Greatest Hits*, Eminem's *The Marshall Mathers LP* – even the *Grease* soundtrack. Green Day weren't just competing with all-American icons, they were becoming ones themselves.

The rock world – and certainly the punk scene – were very different places. *Nimrod* had seemingly eased the band into the next phase of their career, an elevated level where the only thing a band can do wrong is forget who they are and why people like them. That didn't happen.

Green Day remained strangely humble, their interviews totally devoid of any airs of pretension or the type of self-aggrandisement it must be difficult not to indulge in when you have the hearts and minds of a generation at your disposal – and are still considered a major earner by those who pay the wages. The figures are staggering: *Dookie* has grossed over a hundred million dollars on sales alone and that was just one record. Factor in merchandise, performance fees, publishing royalties and residuals accrued by three men in their twenties with little or no academic qualifications and you have an unquestionably profitable business consistently maximizing its potential.

By 1999 they had options. Options that might allow them to explore further new directions first hinted at on *Nimrod* and their recent surprise hit 'Good Riddance (Time Of Your Life)'. When rumours circulated that Green Day's new songs were taking an acoustic direction, it seemed strangely out of step with the time. In the rock world the final year of a decade that had begun with the likes of *Kerplunk!* and *Bleach* was being soundtracked by an ugly breed of bands dubbed 'nu-metal' for their fondness of updating classic Slayer-inspired thrash and metal sounds with rap, industrial and electro influences. The biggest exponents were

147

bands such as Limp Bizkit, genre-founders such as Korn and literally hundreds of lesser emerging bands who found, for a while at least, that wearing their angst on their sleeves and bashing out down-tuned riffs was enough to wangle a record deal.

Once again, a lot of fun had been pummelled out of rock music, as had the wit and intelligence hinted at by Nirvana. Nu-metal was okay, but it was boys' music and highly fashion-orientated, and therefore had an inherently limited shelf life. The most interesting bands to be associated with nu-metal were: LA quartet System Of A Down, whose wide array of influences, precision musicianship and politicised content immediately distanced them from their low-browed contemporaries; and Slipknot, whose outfits and masks used horror film imagery to absurd effect, yet were dedicated enough devotees of metal to have the songs and explosive live show to back up their 'anti-image'.

Poppy-punk blasts or introspective acoustic songs seemed highly incongruous by comparison, so it's perhaps just as well that Green Day spent a large portion of 1999 out of the spotlight. When they did do interviews they found themselves having to give opinions on bands they had little or no time for – at an instore at London's Virgin Megastore, Billie Joe had donned a Slipknot mask and sarcastically ranted at the crowd. Green Day had grown up loving punk, metal and rock equally, but found themselves with little in common with the new wave of contrived angst-peddlers. Even punk's latest scene of post-hardcore or 'emo' (emotional hardcore) bands, many of whom, though they might not admit it, had been turned onto punk via Green Day as much as they had by Fugazi, seemed a million miles away. Because at the heart of it Green Day remained a pop band – but it was a new kind of pop music that they would explore on their next record.

In the meantime throughout 1999 the trio took some much needed time off to catch up with their friends and families and do a whole load of not much. "I spend all my time at home parenting," says Billie. "I have no kind of rock star lifestyle whatsoever. Call it a curse, call it a blessing. But when I'm at home, I'm Daddy. I rarely go out. I get up at 6a.m. I do a little lawn-mowing now and again. I don't think I really do anything my broke friends can't do."

"I played a little bit of golf," said Mike. "Do you know why? Because a bunch of my friends said 'Dude, c'mon, man, we drink as much as we can!' You've gotta picture this, there's all these guys in leather jackets digging holes in the course and pissing off all the other golfers."

They weren't quite living a Stepford Wives-style suburban existence then. Billie Joe told me about hating one of his neighbours, and Mike too failed to ingratiate himself when he bought a new dog home.

"I moved into a new neighbourhood and [one] neighbour said, 'Are you going to shut your dog up or what?'" explained the bassist incredulously. "I said, 'Well, first of all you better take a step back because I'm going to knock your old ass the fuck out and, second of all, is that how you introduce yourself to a new neighbour? You should be ashamed!'"

The members all enjoyed holidays too – Billie Joe went to Minneapolis, Mike to New York and, later, Tre to Alaska on a honeymoon when he married for a second time, to new fiancée Claudia in May 2000.

Before that, the band broke their relative radio silence when they performed their first ever acoustic set – and their first public performance in months – at Neil Young's annual Bridge School Benefit concert at the Shoreline Amphitheatre, alongside such esteemed acts as Pearl Jam, The Who, Tom Waits, Brian Wilson and Neil Young himself. The show was to raise money for an educational programme for children with severe speech and physical impairments. Interestingly, given the record they were about to make, years earlier the band had joked they'd "never do a Neil Young" – meaning you'd never see them going mellow and acoustic. This one-off performance provided a glimpse into the near future for the band. But for the moment they were in no major hurry to return to the fray.

Never ones to disconnect themselves from their art completely, back home it wasn't long before they began pursuing other non-Green Day musical interests with the enthusiasm of teenagers involved in music for the first time – perhaps playing 'Welcome To Paradise' night after night for a decade does that to you. Certainly by the end of the millennium the band were in need of a break, from Green Day and from the constant whirlwind that surrounds a band doing everything they can to remain at the top of the pile. Whether unwittingly or not, the band used their down-time to reconnect with their punk roots, or at least go back to the grass roots level where music is recorded for the hell of it and record sales or tour logistics play no part in the creative process.

Throughout their prolonged hiatus, Billie Joe involved himself in the recording of albums for two bands on Adeline, producing *Burning Flesh And Broken Fingers* by The Criminals (who featured former members of key East Bay punk groups Blatz and The Gr'ups) and fellow blue collar pop-punks One Man Army's *Last Word Spoken* album.

Mike took a similar route but went one further when he formed a new band with three friends who he had met on tour and who had relocated from New England out to California. The three had previously played in the unknown bands Waterdog (who in a tenuous link to Tim Armstrong had shared a guitarist with the Dance Hall Crashers) and Violent Anal Death (nice). The Frustrators' first EP, 'Bored In The USA' came out in 2000 on Adeline. They might have temporarily gone their separate ways but Green Day were still keeping it in the family.

But by the summer of 1999 Billie Joe began piecing together ideas for a new Green Day record. The ideas he was having strayed from the usual template. Up until then diversity was not generally a word in the Green Day canon – like The Ramones before them much of the band's appeal was that they changed very little. Whatever was going on in the world or whatever stage they were playing on, the sound was always the same whiplash combination of simple chords and memorable choruses set to a pretty unvarying tempo (OK, maybe not *always* – 'Good Riddance (Time Of Your Life)' had already exposed Billie's soft, sensitive songwriter's underbelly). This is no criticism – even their staunchest critics couldn't accuse Green Day of betraying themselves musically – merely a way of recognising that after ten years of releasing records, a change was needed. If not for the fans, then for themselves.

Warning was to be that record.

"We didn't go to band practice and try and pound out songs," said Mike. "Billie really waited for inspired moments, especially lyrically inspired moments. And you know, we weren't forcing songs. When we'd have two, three songs, we'd start another one and we'd go, 'Uh, that's not working today. Let's go work on the ones that do work.' Whereas on the last record, we were just pounding songs out, as many as we could."

In June 2000, I flew to LA to interview Green Day during their final mixing days of their sixth album in Ocean Way studios. Occupying the former United Recordings Studios on Sunset Boulevard in the heart of Hollywood, Ocean Way is a place steeped in recent American musical history. The Beach Boys recorded 'Good Vibrations' there (and left behind a mixing desk that's still in use today), The Mamas & The Papas cut 'California Dreamin' and everyone from AC/DC to Eric Clapton and Bob Dylan to Red Hot Chili Peppers have recorded there in the fifty-odd years that it's been open for business. Photos of the hundreds of artists who have recorded there adorn the walls.

I joined Green Day for the mix of what would prove to be an altogether mellower and more thoughtful album than what had gone before. If 'Good Riddance (Time Of Your Life)' had taken the band to a much wider middle-of-the-road audience, it had also seen off many floating voters from the punk community – those who felt a sense of unease listening to a Top 10 band, yet couldn't fail to be seduced by the music. But in embracing that introspective, downbeat streak they'd always hinted at, on *Warning* the band felt a sense on freedom that showed. Simplicity had always been the key, but now Green Day were carried along by their own sense of ease and natural musicality.

The word was that the recording sessions hadn't got off to the best of starts. For the first time the band had decided not to work with Rob Cavallo, and instead hired producer Scott Litt. The band hadn't fallen out with their collaborator, but instead thought a swerve in musical direction might benefit from some new input. Litt had an illustrious production past, most notably having worked on REM's 1987 breakthrough album *Document* and their 1989 release *Green* and also Nirvana's *MTV Unplugged*. But it was his work on The Replacements' final album *All Shook Down* that perhaps swayed Billie Joe. Litt meanwhile had seen the band's acoustic set at the Bridge School show, and was impressed.

"He seems like the right person for the job," Billie Joe said at the time. "As long as he can put up with Tre, I think he'll be fine."

Recordings began in March, but it soon became apparent that the band weren't entirely happy with the way it was going. After some deliberation they decided to tackle production duties themselves. Aided by a number of engineers and mixers, a G3 operator, a production co-ordinator, equipment technicians and a studio consultant and a number of other behind-the-scenes people, they did just that.

"I don't want to put any unnecessary hype on ourselves because we're not politicians but we had a really great time with this record," Billie confided. "It's an album you can really get into. It doesn't have to grab you or pummel you into submission, you can just kind of fall into it."

Hearing the songs coming out of the mixing room after I'd been given a quick guided tour of the building, it was evident that this would soon be quickly dubbed Green Day's 'mature' album, Billie Joe's personal addition to a lineage of American songwriters such as Bob Dylan, Bruce

Springsteen, Husker Du, The Replacements; it had a timeless feel to it. But 'mature' was probably the wrong word for the music that was pumping out of the speakers; this was, after all, the work of three men still in their twenties and which featured a farfisa, a dominatrix, the odd unabashed musical homage to works that have gone before and a general upbeat sense of musical abandon.

"We wanted to bring in new instruments, but we didn't want to really lose the edge or the energy that me, Mike, and Tre have," said Billie. "That's definitely the one thing that we want to keep intact, is the glue that we have between the three of us. But it's fun to bring in harmonicas and mandolins and, you know, a Mariachi band, Italian funeral band, or whatever. I think in essence this is the most rock 'n' roll record that we've ever made."

Green Day were using a new environment to mix an album that was something of an understated milestone for them. Mixing it was Jack Joseph Puig, who had previously worked with No Doubt, Beck and the Black Crowes.

"Jack has done a million things we've never even heard of, huge orchestras and all sorts, but we didn't hire him for his resumé or pedigree," said Billie Joe. "We'd met him and liked his style. Jack really gets inside the songs. He would ask me about the song and talk about the meaning of it to me, which we've never really had with other people mixing our records – usually they just want to crank it up …"

Ocean Way was Puig's domain so when I arrived in the studio, despite a tight deadline on the album – it had to be finished in the next 48 hours – there was a relaxed air about proceedings. The band were milling around, Tre playing the joker, Mike talking about his latest punk rock purchases or something dumb he'd just seen on TV, Billie hunched over the mixing desk with Puig and his assistant, all three listening to the same drum loop over and over again.

Warning might have been an altogether more serious affair, but its creation wasn't without the expected japes. For the recording of 'Blood, Sex, Booze' they decided to spice the soundtrack up, if only for the hell of it. Tre got on the phone to a local Hollywood dominatrix called Mistress Simone and called upon her services to "beat the shit out of" their twenty-year old sound engineer, Tone. Listen to the song and you can hear the dominatrix humiliating the fearful young engineer at the start of the track.

"It was fucking cool," laughed Tre. "She was kicking him in the nuts, stamping on his nipples with big ol' fucking heels. He was scared but now he's into it!" he joked.

"Because we produced this album ourselves there was a real sense of independence that goes along with it," explained Billie Joe when we retired to an upstairs lounge in Oceanway. "Just the three of us getting in there and doing it together as a unit. It's a gang, it's *our* gang. This is what we do. There's a sense of hope in this record, on a personal level and for humanity in general. I don't think there is anything on here that is too self-absorbed or dwells on the negative."

Is there less angst on *Warning*?

"Angst is something that is looked at in so many different ways. There is Fugazi's angst which is looked at as something really positive, or there's the type of angst that Marilyn Manson deals in, which is sort of trivial. There are a lot of angsty metal bands around right now, but I want to know what they are angry about and what they're going to do to make it better. If it's angst that is being used for showmanship then I can't take them seriously because there's no sort of intellect being applied, it's just testosterone. I don't know, it's weird for me to talk about this because after working on the lyrics and music for two months straight I feel that I can't really do it justice in a couple of sentences, you know? I'm too close to it to tell what kind of a record it is."

"The listener can definitely expect multiple audio orgasms and to cum out of their ear-holes," enthused Tre. "You won't need Viagra when *Warning* hits the stands, man."

"What we need to do is work out what this records smells like, what its scent is," Mike helpfully suggested. "Then we can put it out in a scratch 'n' sniff sleeve. So what type of funk does this record portray?"

"OK, well it's kind of like a dog, sorta ..." offered Billie Joe.

"A wet dog?" asked Tre expectantly.

"Yeah," said Mike. "A wet dog. It's funky but it's kinda cuddly. And it's got a puppy breath thing going on."

"But not a dog that's just licked its nuts, right?" says the drummer.

"Right. That's exactly it."

It was also during this interview that Mike chatted freely about his other project The Frustrators and their music, including a new song they were about to release called 'Great Australian Midget Toss'. When I subsequently reported these details back in the UK for a brief news story for a magazine he later expressed disapproval at the irreverent tone adopted to describe a song about throwing midgets. He soon had greater concerns though – when the song was aired on TV during a basketball game an organisation called The Little People Of America complained at what they argued was a negative portrayal of, um, little people.

Though the repeated sound of a click track had been looped in the background and the same few seconds of one song played over and over in the distance for far too long, I actually first got to hear a carefully selected collection of songs from the album at the headquarters of the band's manager, the next day, for my own personal playback while sitting on a plush couch in a room with various awards, tour posters for Green Day and the Goo Goo Dolls and guitars. Cool.

The official playback is not uncommon for journalists, particularly in Hollywood where the industry tries to exercise as much control as possible. Given that most music is either listened to out at a club or a show or at home while doing something else – writing, cleaning, drugs – it's not a natural experience. And when you have close associates of the band asking what you think of a particular song having heard it once while jet-lagged, it's hard to know whether to be honest/rude or dishonest/courteous. The level of hospitality is such that you're thrown into something of moral dilemma. But this wasn't the case with *Warning*.

Five years on from the playback and I see that my notes from the time are filled with adjectives scribbled with the type of haste that suggests I had just minutes to listen to an excerpt of the album in order to write a lengthy cover feature story for a magazine. Pleasingly the first impression seems to stand-up today: *"simple, direct, immediate, sharp and crisp, anti-fashion street music, like when Bob Dylan went electric – only in reverse ..."*

Repeated listenings – and *Warning* definitely benefits from deeper investigation than some of their other works – revealed an album of rich songwriting with a pan-international flavour and lyrical subjects that differed from the straight-forward angst and paranoia of before. The opening title track was a seemingly innocuous strum-along based around a circular-sounding acoustic guitar riff, that touched upon ideas that came from viewing the world through a wider lens.

"Warning' is a song about being surrounded by outside information, about warning labels and signs that direct you where to go in life, but are really just representative of this general false sense of freedom that America seems to exploit all the time, probably now more so than ever," explained Mike. "America is built on boundaries and disclaimers. The message of the song is that rules are there to be broken and laws are meant to be disobeyed."

"A good example of what Billie is saying is that one difference between America and Europe is that in Europe you can go and squat a building if you have nowhere to live, but if you do it here the authorities will come in, beat the crap out of everyone and bomb you out – just look at what happened in Waco, Texas."

'Blood, Sex And Booze' – the dominatrix song – was about sado-masochism but explored in an upbeat, accessible manner in keeping with the approach of the album. Witness the effervescent 'Church On Sunday' that had definite hints of Elvis Costello's 'Oliver's Army' (inspired by the occupation of British troops in Belfast) or 'Waiting', which aped Petula Clark's 1964 hit 'Down Town', one of the greatest pop songs ever written (and the first by a British woman ever to reach No. 1 in the US), both effortless, understated works).

And as the band explained, 'Fashion Victim' had been indirectly inspired by the recent shooting of fashion designer Gianni Versace. "There was this T-shirt that Tre had on that had bullet holes in it and a slogan saying 'Fashion Victim #1'," Billie said. "Versace had just been shot, and I thought that was a pretty harsh statement to put on a shirt, but I like things that are extreme or bizarre. So that led to me thinking about the fashion magazines and the portrayal of celebrities on television – you know, like twenty-five-year-olds who are advertising nothing but themselves and targeting very young audiences. The funny thing is, the groove to this song is so infectious that catwalk models could probably go down the catwalk to it without ever getting the irony of it."

Elsewhere, the influence of The Beatles and Dylan loomed in the background (most noticeably on the harmonica-smattered 'Hold On'), but the album had a distinct voice of its own and a truthfulness about the band's shift in perspective – which is all a songwriter can really aim for.

The album closer 'Macy's Day Parade' was another acoustic song, a simple maudlin musing on the hollowness of commercialism – as Billie put it: "It's about the lies and deceptions that you have growing up, and [how] you have to find your own way around; it's sort of a make-or-break situation in your life."

Without any breakdowns, OD's, changes in personnel or major lifestyle overhauls, Green Day had just casually reinvented themselves. From punk kingpins to earnest commentators sitting atop stools in the spotlight. They'd distanced themselves from increasingly commercial contemporaries such as The Offspring and Blink-182 and gone back to being the underdogs, the outsiders.

To many enthusiastic, long-term Green Day fans, *Warning* is still considered one of their finest works.

There's an interesting – and appropriate – footnote to my brief time in LA with Green Day. The day before mixing on the album was finished they had been invited to film a slot for MTV where they were to perform a live session in a natural, no-frills setting for some new feature the channel was running.

The truth be told, as is almost *always* the way with any band, the interviews hadn't happened as planned. First they were delayed a few hours, then postponed until the next day. Then after another twenty-four hours of phone calls, messages, rearranged rendezvous points, and subsequent cancellations, by way of compensation I was invited along to take in the scene at the recording in Swinghouse Rehearsals, a generic-looking LA rehearsal space scummy enough to achieve the authenticity that the channel was no doubt hoping for. The band, though distracted by filming and the chaos of a set cramped with cameramen, runners, sound men and various unidentifiable MTV types, were their customary welcoming, friendly and high-spirited selves. Tre had climbed up onto the roof of the building, Billie was running through a version of Husker Du's 'Don't Want To Know If You're Lonely' and Mike, endearingly true to form, was doing little to deny that he's one of the most élitist and old-fashioned record collectors around. "I'm no purist," he tells me without a trace of irony, "but fuck twelve-inches, man!"

It doesn't matter because there's something else to preoccupy the endless dead hours on a TV set. The LA Lakers are playing their final game of the season and if they win the NBA Championship is theirs. The film crew are interested, as are the band to a lesser extent. We gather around to watch the dying moments with a passing Cool occasionally providing a running commentary.

The Lakers' star player Kobe Bryant sealed it and everyone was happy. So happy in fact that six thousand fans, many of whom had been watching on screens outside started rioting in the streets surrounding the Staples Center, a mile or two down the road from where we were. First they burned T-shirts and posters, then cars. Then the police began to pile in and things began to turn nasty. Running battles. Tear gas. Injuries. All the usual symptoms of wanton public disorder.

"Wow, is that the smell of burning pork?" chuckled Tre as a cop car went up in smoke.

It was when the riot began to escalate and edge ever-closer to where we were, still on set late into the night, that the band began to pay true attention, shifting between nervous laughter and outright bewilderment, and joking that, for once, they weren't to blame. A nice little riot seemed like a fitting end to a punk rock few days and everyone made it back to their beds that night with barely a scratched – ahem – limo in sight …

As I departed for the night, Tre patted me on the back with a suspicious degree of sincerity. It was only the next day that I discovered a big Green Day sticker stuck across the back of my jacket: *Warning*.

Brief breaks to watch rioters aside, by the time the album was finally finished and ready to be pressed, cabin fever had set in after months of working in close proximity. When they were asked to take part on that summer's Warped Tour the band gladly accepted, appreciating both a chance to play in front of audiences who had now come to understand Green Day as elder statesmen of the new wave of pop-punk bands but also, as Mike put it, get outside and "play at immense levels of volume, just cranking our amps up and going ballistic."

Green Day had been invited on the tour on numerous occasions but had always declined, some in the punk community seeing their refusal to take part as something of a rebuttal to the scene. Or perhaps they just didn't want to be associated with a mixed bill of bands that contained its fair share of cookie-cutter punk-lite clones that Green Day had inadvertently spawned. Either way, the time was now right. Maybe after *Insomniac* and *Nimrod* Green Day needed to remind themselves why they were doing this music thing in the first place. Maybe, despite all their best intentions, they had drifted away from what they once were and now simultaneously had one foot in the mainstream pop world and the other tentatively dipping a toe back into the scene from where they had come. Not that Warped, with its extreme sports association and heavy corporate branding and sponsorship, is that underground, but it was a move back in the right direction – a band used to doing things on their own now acting, albeit temporarily, as part of a wider community.

The tour started on the Friday [after the final mixes for *Warning* were completed], in Fresno, California, in scorching temperatures well over 100 degrees. Also on the bill were a mixed-bag of bands, from old favourites like NOFX and The Mighty Mighty Bosstones, hip-hop crossover bands like Jurassic 5, up-and-coming bands such as The Donnas and then-current MTV favourites like Papa Roach getting down and dirty with the punks. The band decided to go straight for the jugular – they played no new songs on the entire tour, instead relying on old favourites. Now, in front of the punk youth of America, was probably not a good time to be unveiling their more acoustic-leaning, 'mature' sound.

"It was fun," said Billie Joe, upon the tour's completion. "There's a certain sort of club-like atmosphere from playing those shows, even though they're outdoors playing to between five and ten thousand people. Playing during the daylight without lights and all that stuff made a difference too. We could see the crowd for once. And they could sort of see us through all the dust clouds …"

"There was a certain amount of solidarity there," added Mike. "On other festival bills there's sometimes a sense of 'celebrity' about it, but Warped was about a bunch of punk rock bands getting together. A bunch of drunks in baggy Dickies pants."

Some international promotional activity surrounding *Warning* was called for and by September Green Day were back in Europe again facing the endless parade of unblinking cameras and tape recorders thrust into their faces at every turn.

Our paths crossed again when I was offered the chance to spend some time with them, trailing them around London for a few hectic and increasingly absurd days. Beer would be involved, as would minor celebrities, the BBC censors, a large Samoan, a limousine, a drummer called Edwin and general scenes of everyday chaos that Green Day tend to leave in their wake.

The first stop was a hotel in Elstree just outside London where the band had day rooms in advance of a *Top Of The Pops* appearance at the BBC studios just down the road.

Green Day arrive in the hotel lobby in different stages and in various states. Tre barrels in wearing a doctor's stethoscope that he's liberated from the set of BBC hospital drama *Holby City* and tells anyone who is listening that he's giving up rock 'n' roll for a career in medicine – specifically, gynaecology and the study of 'lady parts'. The tourists checking in at reception don't appear to be particularly amused.

Trailed by his huge Samoan bodyguard – if memory serves me, the same guy who stopped our camera being stolen in Milan three years earlier and here "to protect the public from Tre" – Billie Joe sits quietly thumbing his way through a copy of *Maximum Rock 'n' Roll* and enquiring as to whether I have heard Rancid's new record, and what I thought of it. The type of conversation that fans of punk rock have when they don't really know one another. Mike arrives last, bright and breezy, refreshed and ready for action.

On our drive to the studio, a restless Tre is quizzing the driver on what music he has on his in-car stereo for our listening pleasure.

"Pink Floyd," he replies. "And Manfred Mann."

"Keep talking buddy ..."

The pre-show corridors of *Top Of The Pops* are busy with various presenters, pop stars and dancers. In their leather jackets, battered Converse and home dyed haircuts Green Day seem strangely out of place, though, bar Kylie Minogue who is on after them, have sold more copies than all the rest of the artists in attendance put together.

Upon arrival at the studio one thing becomes increasingly apparent. TV shows are boring to be a part of. Or rather, for the performance of a three-minute song, the artist must endure endless dead hours. To achieve such a veneer of youthful irreverence and spontaneity takes a lot of planning – and a hell of a lot of time to kill for those guests involved.

"They always make us get to these things really early," explained Mike. "It's the usual case of 'hurry up and wait'. They tend to start panicking: 'Quick, you're on in six hours!'"

So there was at least plenty of time to hang around, shoot the breeze and soak up the atmosphere – like another typical day in Green Day-land.

Having been pro's since their teens they had long since settled into such situations with ease, having clocked up hundreds of TV appearances, radio interviews and signing sessions. So Billie Joe spends his time evading a BBC news crew who are after him for an interview, by hiding in their dressing room. For reasons not fully explained Mike reveals that his actual name could nearly have been Mike Warman ("Which would have cool, because I could have had 'war' and 'man' in my name!") and Tre is pondering whether to ignite the fat joint that is tucked behind his ear. "If I smoke it, my drumming might speed up or slow down," he ponders. "Then again, I do play pretty good when I'm high. Although maybe I could disappear off to the bathroom and twist one off? Damn it, I could do both!"

The band are soon called on set and I find a spot near the back, having a sudden mini-dilemma as to whether being spotted on *Top Of The Pops* (whilst, admittedly, a little bit stoned) by friends would be either highly subversive or just plain embarrassing. The crowd is predominantly girls in their early-teens dressed in their best school disco outfits and the odd curious star of soap opera *Eastenders,* who have wandered over from that show's nearby set. A few recent late nights and with few opportunities to bath or shave this week have left me feeling somewhat incongruous and under-dressed so I slip off to the side to watch the show and avoid the clutches of the floor manager who is shepherding the crowd like they're cattle and giving them the nod to 'clap and go crazy!' on cue – which is exactly what they do as Green Day bounce onto the stage and rip through new single 'Minority'. Live, it sounds satisfyingly raw given the sterile surroundings and as quickly as they started they're done. One take, and out of there in three minutes. Excellent.

"I'm a collector of videos and have a whole bunch of video tape stuff like Generation X on *Top Of The Pops*, so in that respect it's kind of a cool thing to do," Billie Joe says afterwards as we depart from Elstree. "And here we are now on it ourselves, so maybe fifteen years from now some kid will be collecting videos of us on TV. I don't mind doing those types of things so long as we can play live. We've seen old *Top Of The Pops* shows where people were failing to lip-sync pretty badly and it just looks stupid. After we were done playing and actually had a chance to see the scene that was developing I said, 'You know what? The sooner we get out of here the better …'"

"Besides, it's too hard to mime and do the dance moves at the same time," deadpans Mike from the back seat.

The following night – Friday, September 15 – I went to see Green Day play a secret show at King's College in London, in an intimate student union that has been host to many an American rock band looking for a low-key venue to connect with the London crowd (Foo Fighters famously played their first UK show there). The gig was sponsored by Radio 1 and was being broadcast on Steve Lamacq's *Evening Session* show and was ostensibly a chance to showcase the new material for record label, music industry types and those select fans who have got in by winning competitions or through more imaginative means. Expectations weren't particularly high, perhaps Green Day had been away for a while and the new-found temperate nature of *Warning* suggested to many that Green Day Mk1 was over and it was to be only nice, thoughtful, radio-friendly songs from hereon in.

It also happened to be the first occasion that they publicly played new tracks from *Warning* and for the occasion the band had recently decided to beef out their live sound and do the new material justice with the addition of a second guitarist, Jason White, who would remain with the band on and off to this day.

Originally from Little Rock, Arkansas, Jason had been a friend of the band for years and had played in both Pinhead Gunpowder with Billie and in The Influents, who he formed the previous year and who were now signed to Adeline Records, the label he helped launch with Billie Joe and their circle of friends. White had moved out West to the East Bay in 1992, attracted by the number of good punk rock bands out there, and soon made a lot of friends in the scene. After briefly moving back to Arkansas in 1996, he was soon back in the East Bay again to join Pinhead Gunpowder, before getting the call to join Green Day. Like the band members, he was a major fan of The Replacements and their chief songwriter Paul Westerberg and shared many other such similar musical reference points. Jason also added a new element to the band's sound without changing it or imposing his personality upon the band's long-established dynamic. He was easy-going, fun to be around and a great guitar player. He fitted right in.

After an impassioned introduction from Steve Lamacq, Green Day played a fantastic show. It was a necessary reminder of the band's raw appeal and total command over their performance. The set comprised of requests from the crowd and included a cover of Generation X's 'Dancing With Myself', in recognition of London's musical influence on the band. *Ah yes*, nodded five hundred fans. *This is why we like them.* The critics seemed to feel the same as the reviews that followed in the press over the next few weeks almost unanimously declared that the show was a near-legendary performance in the band's rich live history.

"It was the best show we've ever played in the UK," Billie Joe told me a couple of days later. "Doing interviews gets really monotonous – I think people can find out more about us and our individual characters by coming to see us live than sitting talking to us. Our music really needs to be seen live to understand."

Midday, Saturday, and I'm in another hotel lobby, this time the Royal Garden in Kensington, a popular place for passing American bands to hole up in. Green Day have another TV show to record.

Billie Joe has already disappeared off down the road to find some decent coffee so it's up to a bleary-eyed, but nevertheless ebullient Tre Cool to fill in the gaps on what the band got up to last night after the show when he'd headed to intimate central London venue The Borderline.

"Some girl invited me to a sex and drugs party at her flat," he says. "She said she figured I was someone important because I was the only person in the club wearing shorts. And because I was American." [He didn't go, obviously] Mike meanwhile had avoided a night of drinking in order to rise early this morning so he could do some whistle-stop visits to the capital's finest second-hand record stores.

He waltzes into the lobby, looking pleased with himself. He has, he enthuses, just purchased fifty-five rare seven-inch UK singles for £90 – Lou Reed, the Rolling Stones, the Rezillos … all sorts. As previously demonstrated, it's safe to say Mike is something of a purist – he prefers to listen to his music on a jukebox at home and will only DJ at parties with his trusty seven-inches. We spend a good twenty minutes outside the hotel, discussing obscure Seventies UK punk rock bands, waiting for the Green Day troops to assemble.

On the drive to the studio while conducting an interview in their people-carrier we witness the aftermath of a nasty motorbike accident in central London – the second the band have witnessed this week – and everyone is temporarily silenced. It's hard to ask another dumb question about rock 'n' roll when someone is lying splayed in the middle of the road only yards away. "Let's try and not think about what we've just seen," says Billie, stoically trying to get the conversation back on track.

We take a detour to a scrap of wasteland beneath the iconic Westway flyover of west London for some impromptu magazine photos. Mick Jones of The Clash was raised in a tower block overlooking this twisting strip of concrete, once a futuristic vision of the city and now a functional and strangely retrogressive-looking part of the cityscape. Naturally, the conversation turns to The Clash and the direct effect this area had on their music. Billie and a Guinness-drinking Mike in turn discuss the impact Strummer and Co had on them as youngsters. Desperate to use the toilet but with none in reach, Tre is considering standing on his head "to make the shit go back up again …"

And onto the next studio, this time Channel 4's youth/entertainment show *T4 On Sunday*, for more hanging around, talking shit and awaiting further instructions. There was a barbeque set up on a terrace outside the back of the studios. Tre was inexplicably tucking into a plate of boiled potatoes while waving at a small row of heads that kept popping up from behind a perimeter hedge. Pretty much everywhere the band went there seemed to be some small following of fans, autograph-hunters or curious non-fans drawn in by the brightly dyed hair and inevitable japes on display.

The show's producer, Andi Peters, came over to introduce himself to the band. "Hi guys, it's so great to have you on the show!" he said. "I'm Andi, the producer!"

"I know who you are," fired back Tre. "I saw you on TV this morning. You were painting a duck or something."

Meanwhile between note-perfect rehearsal takes of new single 'Minority', Billie was telling me about one of the scarier aspects of his fame. His notoriety. "I had some girl threatening to assassinate my wife this year," he confided. "She said she wanted to assassinate her so that she could become my new wife and raise my children instead. Did I take her up on the offer? No, I actually called a Private Detective to find out who this person was. It turned out to be an artist who wanted us to use her artwork and that was their way of trying to get me to take notice. Scary. What else can you say to that but 'fuck off'?"

The band run through the song again to an audience of various contestants from the first series of reality TV show, *Big Brother,* before word reaches them that the people in the control room are concerned about the use of the 'f' word in the lyrics and would they perhaps consider changing it? "Forget", perhaps?

A quick decision is made: absolutely not. And that's that.

So the band record the song as it was meant to be and it's up to the producers to come up to with something broadcastable.

Back in the band's dressing room they gather around to watch the show, recorded with a one-hour delay before it aired. But they're only mildly interested – they've seen and done it all before. One youth TV programme is like another. The show cuts to the band performing and when the offending word comes up it is beeped, although obviously by someone with a bad sense of timing as it misses the word by a fraction of a second and makes the expletive all the more obvious.

"Cool," grins Billie Joe. "I've just sworn on national TV anyway."

"Always a good thing," says Tre, wandering off, ready to move on to the next thing.

That night, Green Day's hectic time in the UK's capital came to an end with a late-night instore appearance at the Virgin Megastore on Oxford Street. It was run with military precision as detailed in my notebook at the time: *"10.30pm – doors open, 11.20pm – MC5's 'Kick Out The*

Jams' over the PA, 11.25pm – Green Day open with 'Minority', 12.40pm – smash everything and leave, victorious."

The jaunty, anti-authoritarian song (which some of the less enthusiastic critics had already compared to The Levellers) that I'd heard played about fifty times in a couple of days, and which the band had tirelessly run through seemingly almost as many times for TV cameras, entered the UK charts at 18 two weeks later. More significantly, back in the US, where Green Day relied less on positive press and more on radio play in America's vast impartial heartland, it topped the Modern Billboard Rock charts in the US for weeks.

"George Bush was not elected by a majority of the voters in the United States. He was appointed by God."
James Watt, Republican Secretary of the Interior.

Back in America other great changes were afoot. While Green Day were out doing their bit for international punk-pop diplomacy, changes that would resonate across the globe for years to come were being implemented. In the same week that Green Day enjoyed a hit with 'Minority', Bill Clinton stepped down as US president to make way for a wide-eyed cowboy from Texas called George William Bush.

Bush was an all-too familiar face, the son of pre-Clinton president George Bush Senior and the latest rising public face of an oil-based dynasty that stretched back for generations. The Bush family were hard-line Republicans, their philosophy entrenched in Christianity, separatism, a dangerous level of patriotism and who had much support from the leading figures of corporate America. Next to the Bush's, the sax-playing, dope-smoking Democrat Clinton had seemed like a bare-footed commie pinko. But he had blown it by lying to the American public over his sexual encounter with White House intern Monica Lewinsky. The blow-jobs they could just about take, the bullshit they couldn't.

Discounting the fact that, in the words of esteemed Nineties comedian Bill Hicks "all leaders are liars and cocksuckers", Clinton's subsequent political downfall was the end point to a craftily-manipulated campaign by the Republicans to discredit the president. At that point a straight-forward election would not have swung it for their party. Clinton served his two terms (the maximum the Commander-In-Chief is allowed to serve) but, to many voters, by 2000 had besmirched the name of his party. As president, Clinton had done some good and plenty bad. He was reasonably liked by liberals and hated by the neo-Conservatives. While his foreign policy was highly questionable, he at least possessed the intelligence and charisma to enter into much-needed dialogues with world leaders on such all-important issues as oppressive regimes, climate change, world debt and weapons control.

And now he was out.

Enter the Idiot.

The US election of 2000 will go down in history as one of the most divisive, dirtiest and most controversially contested election campaigns, *ever*.

Chosen as the man most likely to keep the Democrats in the White House, Clinton's deputy Al Gore stepped up to do battle, with the wily contender George Bush, reformed alcoholic and born-again Christian. Gore was no hero in white – his wife Tipper Gore's associations with the anti-rock 'n' roll, pro-censorship Parents Music Resource Center (PMRC) lobby group alone was enough to tell many young voters the standpoint he was coming from – but he did seem a smarter, more trustworthy guy than his opponent. Unfortunately trust and intelligence are not the key factors when American voters enter the booth.

What followed next is well-documented and still open to discussion. The election was so hard fought that it came down to a matter of hundreds of votes. In a country whose population numbered 295,000,000 people, this seemed incredible and quite unbelievable although opinion certainly suggested there *was* a fairly even split. Amid controversy that many of the new automated vote-registering machines weren't functioning correctly and that re-counts were required, the election descended into a legal battleground fought by a front-line of lawyers on both sides. After weeks of delays, re-counts and calls of foul play from both sides, the outcome came down to the key state of Florida, whose Governor was Jebediah Bush, son of George Sr and brother of George Jr.

And the rest is dirty history.

Two months later in January 2001, George W. Bush was sworn in as the 43rd president of the United States of America.

So what does this have to do with a seemingly apolitical band such as Green Day?

Only everything.

With the Republicans back in the White House again, the climate suggested that the Nineties had barely happened and Bush was back to clear up a lot of unfinished business, not least in the Middle East where natural resources that were much-needed to support the American economy were available in abundance to those who wanted it badly enough. In fact, the general tone of heightened conservatism and the most basic sense of patriotism similarly recalled Reagan's rise in the early Eighties (one only has to listen to the work of the Dead Kennedys to see the counter-cultural reaction to 'Bonzo's' term in office).

To say that Bush was hated outright by musicians, actors, writers etc though would be untrue. Interviewing Marilyn Manson on the eve of the election, I was surprised to hear The God Of Fuck say that, of the two candidates, he was rooting for Bush because of Gore's links to the PMRC and because his running partner Joseph Lieberman had branded his work "the sickest music he had ever heard". A year later he told me he had been joking.

Nevertheless to anyone who didn't necessarily agree that America was the land of the free (so long as you can get credit) and that all foreigners were plotting the downfall of the empire, to anyone who agreed in freedom of speech and the basic principals of peace and harmony on a world-wide level, things were … well, they were fucked.

In a little over a year's time, such feelings would be further amplified to symphonic levels, and rock stars would find themselves in the most difficult position since the McCarty-led 'witch trials' against any citizens perceived to be 'anti-American'.

But for now, America was entering a new age under a new regime.

The question was, from their elevated platforms would the artists dare to comment?

"You know, I knew the day that George Bush was elected president that we were in deep, deep shit," said Tre Cool. It was a worthwhile philosophy – an expected one from a punk band – and one that extended to America's many disparate disenfranchised. It was also at this point, in late 2000, that we can pinpoint the first stirrings of a new disenchanted, previously apolitical youth voice making itself heard amongst liberal-leaning actors, artists and musicians. For if the rise of George W. Bush was good for something, it was the awakening of a once abstract sense of protest that now had very real complaints to air – namely, the new President and corporate America that backed him. Out of this would rise a grass-roots movement to mobilize the youth of America making sure this didn't happen again.

"There's a lot of people that [didn't] vote this year just because of a lack of a better selection," reasoned Billie Joe shortly afterwards. "The way I look at it, every dollar that I spend is a vote. Where are you going to put your dollar into? What is worth investing into? Is it gonna be the Starbucks in town, or is it gonna be your local coffee place, or small business people that are trying to just put food on the table?"

Soon though, Green Day would do more than offer the odd vaguely-controversial soundbite on the subject of their leader or the state of the nation. But no-one could anticipate quite how just much America and its relations with the rest of the world were going to change over the coming couple of years.

But in the meantime, Green Day busied themselves on a practical level – the very best type of political contribution   when they headlined a free Sunday afternoon event in the Bay Area entitled 'Take Back San Francisco', organized to raise awareness for the plight of renters, particularly struggling musicians. Like cities such as London and New York before it, San Francisco had been hit by a real estate upswing that was sending property prices and rent in the city through the roof, with little in the way of affordable housing to compensate. The knock-on effect was that many of those involved in San Francisco's fertile music scene were forced to move out of their premises or out of the city. Similarly, rehearsal space was increasingly hard to come by or just plain overpriced. Business was triumphing over the support of the city's indigenous arts, and Green Day lending support was their way of letting people know that if the property situation carried on the city could never produce a band as successful as theirs, and that if they had formed today they would be struggling to survive. Afterwards, local musicians marched in protest on San Francisco's town hall.

Warning was released in October 2000, the month before Bush won the election, to a curious reception. Apart from the endless tired questioning as to what constituted punk and whether Green Day had peaked, the general critical reception was warm enough to acknowledge the strength of the songs on display. Many picked up on the obvious historical presence of undeniable accomplished musical craftsmen such as Bob Dylan, The Beatles, The Kinks, Tom Waits (whose *Rain Dogs* album had recently had a profound effect on Armstrong) and even the everyman, humanist lyrical approach of Bruce Springsteen. Suddenly perhaps for the first time, by association, it was not completely absurd to now place Billie Joe in the same category.

The album reached No. 4 in the UK (Radiohead's *Kid A* held the top spot) and No. 4 in the US. After the success of that summer's Warped tour shows, Green Day hit the road again. The latest leg took in eleven dates across Europe – including a show at London's twelve thousand-capacity Wembley Arena – and a clutch of US radio festival slots, then, after two weeks break for Christmas, straight into a month-long tour throughout January 2001 that traversed fifteen American states in twenty shows.

Around about this time papers reported that an unknown English band called The Other Garden were suing the band because of alleged striking similarities between 'Warning' and the band's own composition 'Never Got The Chance', particularly the bass part and the overall melody, the former claiming they were due $100,000 in royalties (accordingly the approximate figure any artist should hope to receive through publishing from one track on a gold-selling album).

"People might rightly ask how Green Day would have heard a small Cambridge band," said the band's lawyer Alastair Nicolas in a statement for the press. "But the track was from a 1997 promo sent out to labels and radio stations throughout the country. It had airplay on at least 40 stations, including Radio 1, and was also played frequently on Avalon FM, the official station of the Glastonbury Festival, during 1998, 1999 and 2000. Green Day were in the UK in 1998, we just have to establish exactly where and when." The issue didn't get very far – nor was it ever revealed whether Green Day had ever heard the band, though it's highly unlikely.

The singer also discovered that just because he's loved by millions, the life of a rock star doesn't guarantee immunity from the tougher aspects of everyday civilian life. Early in the year he was mugged in the street at gun point – the incident has understandably instilled in him a fear of firearms ever since.

It was the first in a number of sad events that would mark 2001, continuing in April with the death of Joey Ramone, frontman for the iconic and influential granddaddies of punk rock. Born Jeffrey Hyman, Ramone's death resonated throughout music as everyone was reminded that even the largest of life figures aren't immortal.

"I can firmly say that rock 'n' roll will not be the same without Joey Ramone alive," Billie Joe Armstrong told MTV. "The one thing no one will ever be able to [capture] was how cool he was. He was rock 'n' roll coolness. The glasses. The leather jacket. And he barely moved a finger.

He just stood there."

Most notably for Mike the year was marred by the tragic death of his mother in June from an alcohol-related illness – something he pointed out when the band were approached about advertising beer shortly afterwards.

The worldwide biggest event of 2001 was, of course, the terrorist attack on the World Trade Center in New York on September 11, part of a series of actions that have single-handedly changed the way the people of US – and beyond – look at security, government, immigration laws, weapons budgets, patriotism, censorship and foreign policy. Thousands of tragic deaths were consequently used as justifiable reason for the US government to push through a number of economic and legal policies through the senate that they otherwise wouldn't have attempted, sometimes contravening United Nations and Geneva Convention laws along the way. A climate of fear permeated the Western World – and continues to this day.

The knock-on effect was that everyone in the public eye was asked their opinion of developments. While everyone from Bruce Willis to Britney Spears adopted the standard patriotic, party line, the sense of unrest that had been bubbling under with the more liberal-minded actors, musicians, writers, journalists and film-makers rose to the surface and the idea of what constituted being 'American' was placed under greater scrutiny than ever before.

"I was on West Coast time, so it was really early in the morning for me," Billie told *Kerrang*! at the close of 2001 of the fateful day. "I saw the towers fall, and it felt like the world was gonna end ... I can't really see myself as a patriot. I don't see what happened in New York as an act of war, it's an act of terrorism. Every country has to deal with terrorism in some form, and this is the first time America has ever seen it and they don't know what to do, so everyone is clinging to these war slogans. All the flags in people's cars and homes – it just seems kind of gross to me. America has these feelings of its days being numbered. It's like a country that just got cancer, the cancer's in remission. A lot of people are doing the thing they always talked about doing."

"I object," said Tre Cool. "I object to any killing at all. You know, it's terrible what happened and I think retaliation definitely makes sense and it's definitely one option. But, personally, I prefer peace. You know, maybe I'm just being ignorant and short-sighted, but I just don't think that killing people is a good way to remedy people dying. Martin Luther

King Jr. said that you can murder a murderer but you can never murder murder itself."

"I hope some good stuff comes out of this," added Billie Joe. "People have become so self-absorbed and dedicated to their careers. I'm not a person to wave a flag for family values or anything like that, but there comes a time when your relationships and your family is your most important thing, not whether you're making $100,000 every year. That's what I hope comes out of it – that people realize the important things in life."

Unbeknown to the band at the time, this seismic change in the psyche and outlook of a nation – the general shift back towards an overt, amplified sense of patriotism and a need to reinforce the idea of America as the world's sole imperialist superpower – was to be a massive influence on the band's next work.

Things changed forever after September 11.

Not least, to many, the perception of their president. Suddenly their simple-minded cowboy leader was waging a war on unseen, unidentifiable 'enemies of America' – suddenly there was a point to prove and 9-11 provided the perfect get-out clause for some despicable anti-diplomatic behaviour on the world's stage. A culture of fear prevailed into which the White House was able to plunge into unfinished business and settle old scores.

Despite outward appearances, America was more divided than ever before and things were going to get much worse before they ever had any hope of getting better. Seven words was all it took for George W. Bush's speech-writers to reduce all manner of complicated national and international diplomatic – not to mention religious, racial and socio-economic – issues down to a black and white argument that precluded the opinion of that vast middle ground who were neither for or against America. *"You're either with us or against us."*

Such a cleverly constructed confrontational stance was enough to want to make intelligent people take moral sides, whether they wanted to or not. What about the millions of people who were simultaneously against terrorism, unnecessary death, religious fundamentalism *and* those extremists who perpetrated the attacks.

What Bush neglected to account for was this frustrated majority who opposed the twin totems of American Imperialism and religious extremism, George W. Bush and Osama bin Laden.

It was to these people who Green Day would be speaking to on their new album, the band themselves a perfect example of a group of young adults forcefully politicized by world events in an attempt to do something – anything – about what was going on. The first seed of their forthcoming career-pinnacle album, *American Idiot*, had been sown.

Maybe it was the damaged national psyche and vague sense of unity against their adversaries in the days that followed the attack on the World Trade Centre, but five days later Green Day played an impromptu show at 924 Gilman Street, their first in eight years. The occasion was an Adeline Records showcase and the band used instruments borrowed from the other bands, even taking requests from the crowd. For once there was little animosity, all "Billie Joe must die" scribbles temporarily forgotten as band and crowd enjoyed the evening for what it was – a punk rock show.

Perhaps somewhat appropriately it was their final performance of the year. By the close of a chaotic, tumultuous year, twelve months in which rock music suddenly seemed as if it was the most frivolous, decadent pursuit imaginable, yet conversely at the same time was a more necessary conduit for information than ever, particularly for the young and the cynical, Green Day had laid their latest album to rest. *Warning* had been their lowest-selling album for Reprise to date, its more straight-forward downbeat approach finding mixed favour but not massive sales by their usual staggering standards. But it still sold a small shit-load – and continues to today.

When the band then announced details for their forthcoming compilation album *International Superhits!* in November the inevitable rumours of a forthcoming split began to circulate. Though the title was partly tongue-in-cheek, it was nevertheless a straight forward collection of their biggest songs, with two new tracks – 'Maria' and 'Poprocks And Coke' included to entice those who already owned the back catalogue. The 'Greatest Hits' has long since often marked the passing of bands, a final record company cash-in before a band is sent off to the knackers yard, and though some were wondering whether Green Day might slowly be winding down, the band were too young and vital to give up. Their career to date had been played out at fast-forward speed; many had simply forgotten that this was a band whose members were all still in their twenties. They were hardly the Rolling Stones.

International Superhits! brought many of the band's finest moments together in one place, but tellingly only featured those songs recorded for Warners therefore – bar 'Welcome To Paradise' – the album entirely overlooked the band's equally worthy songs recorded for Lookout!, and even then it was the re-recorded major label version. So, though it read like a radio programmer's wet dream ('Longview', Welcome To Paradise', 'Basket Case' in rapid succession) it only told half the story – and that half which many were already familiar with. An accompanying *International Supervideos!* collection was also released on VHS/DVD. Again, though essential viewing for any fan, it still nevertheless only covered the band's visual history from 1994 to 2001.

The collection certainly had a perfunctory feel about it, either released to signal the band's steady downturn in sales, or more likely, with no new recordings on the horizon, plug a gap and keep the momentum going. Given that it reached No. 15 in the UK charts and 40 in the US (where it soon went gold) ... why not?

"Yes that's right, punk is dead, It's just another cheap product for the consumers head."
'Punk Is Dead' by Crass, 1978.

If the cultural commentators were to be believed, punk had died every year since it first went overground in 1977. And the new punk explosion which had begun in 1994 was no exception. It took less than ten years, a whole bunch of bands and a handful of record labels to bastardize another movement so spectacularly. Less than a decade on from the release of *Dookie,* through a slew of polished pretty boys from Blink-182 downwards in the late Nineties, to a generation of manufactured twenty-first century pop bands co-opting a look for their own evil purposes, even the new punk was further diluted until it morphed into something else entirely.

Yesterday it was Busted, three self-confessed Tory-loving poshos doing star jumps, today it's the pubescent pop and spiked hair of McFly. Tomorrow's tide will bring more detritus, no doubt.

But should we – those who might consider ourselves punks in some loose way, or maybe 'old school' (yuk) fans of Green Day – be losing our lunch over such matters? Should we still be screaming at the TV screen when they parade out the latest gimps in Ramones T's (cheese-gratered for that authentic look) to twist and gurn like they've just caught one of Billie Joe's loogers? Does this shit matter? Well, to many, yes. Because there's no going back. Punk as we know it is dead and gone. It is in the hands of the pop world now, financed by Sony or Warners (or whoever), or clinging to credibility through independence in the rosters of Epitaph Records (itself now part-owned by a major), forever selling itself on extreme sport soundtracks or selling sneakers. To many, punk today is New Found Glory whining about some girl or forgetting to take that *Back To The Future* DVD back to Blockbuster. It is The Offspring creaking their way through their latest seemingly calculated pop hit to crowds of rambunctious eight-year-olds. It is the Warped tour, a fine concept gone predictable. It is Good Charlotte, a band whose career follows the exact same hard-sell marketing campaigns of their pop contemporaries. It is Avril Lavigne, stifling a smile just to look that extra bit 'street', then switching to the ballads for album number two. Indeed, it's the surly Canadian songstress who perhaps best illustrates this convoluted argument calling for more élitism in music, a return to the short-lived groundswell of colour and noise of CBGB's or the 100 Club or Gilman Street, a genuine need for a bunch of bands to burn brightly and get the fuck out of Dodge to let the new breed in.

When launched in 2002, Avril Lavigne was touted as a post-Green Day teen punk pin-up, a voice of a generation in a skinny tie and battered vans. Her big hit, 'Sk8er Boi', was a sugary, star-crossed Romeo & Juliet on skateboards, and the world's mainstream media lapped it up (though Tre Cool once quipped "I'll choke her with her fucking tie if I meet her"). By the time her debut had topped ten million, the music was slowing down and the videos becoming increasingly windswept, stylised and 'mature', all lingering shots and mid-tempo choruses ... and suddenly a young Alanis Morissette was in our midst. Urgh – how vile. The punk angle was dropped, discarded, spent. Bland-rock for the masses was in.

Once again punk had been flirted with for more cynical reasons. It had been softened and made pliable in grubby hands, its energy and ideologies rendered lifeless, simultaneously killing all sense of community and solace for that next confused street kid with nowhere to go – that next Sid Vicious, that next Billie Joe Armstrong – while drawing in money from the suburbs, from the MTV babies.

But who wants a musical scene to remain stagnant anyway? Punk works best as a flash-in-the-pan movement, a sudden surge of activity that by its explosive nature can only be sustained for a certain short period. It was there in London in 1977, in Washington DC with the birth of hardcore in 1981 and in 1994 with Green Day and the new punk rock explosion. And shortly after each re-birth came the inevitable death.

It is the chapter entitled '1994 and all that' in the imaginary musical history books from which many of today's bands take inspiration. Bands such as Good Charlotte and Sum-41 have openly admitted that it was Green Day, NOFX and Rancid who inspired them to form bands in the mid-or-late Nineties, and it was they who then lead them to investigate the Sex Pistols, The Clash and The Ramones. Which is fine. What's missing from the most successful bands though is a desire to take the slow independent route rather than the quick corporate one. Recent artists as diverse as At The Drive-In, The Strokes, Franz Ferdinand, The Hives, Bright Eyes, The White Stripes and Dizzee Rascal have enjoyed huge success on independent labels, so it can still be done. But, the new punk bands might reason, if such a great band as Green Day can conduct a successful career on a major label with a degree of credibility and respect, then why not us? Why not indeed. After all, it's a buyer market. I know that Rancid and Green Day's apprenticeships in Gilman have informed their music in ways Good Charlotte will never know. Which is why, though they have worked together and are friends, Rancid make regular appearances on my stereo and the music of the Madden brothers does not.

So punk is a mixture of contradictions and arguments and hypocrisy and some of it stinks of dirty money and salty pretzels, and Green Day have undoubtedly played a major part in punk's slow dilution into what it is today, but that's okay too. Because what began with the Pistols has gone through endless changes, scenes, cliques, sounds and styles so much that today's visible punks are the mall rats in their uniform; not challenging but conforming without even realizing it. It needs to be anti-fashion again if it hopes to stir things up as it once did. 'Punk' has been homogenized – it's Gap, it's Starbucks, it's a dead corpse.

But again, who cares. That's just the tip of the iceberg. A whole generation of cool bands also followed in Green Day's wake and the punk spirit lives on in other forms. People who would otherwise be flipping burgers or shooting smack or working in advertising have formed bands and seen the world. They've formed labels and fanzines and websites. They've avoided the drudgery and the slow suicide of the nine-to-five that people like Mssrs Armstrong, Dirnt and Cool – and millions of others – were just not made out for. Through association, Green Day have brought wider attention to deserving bands like The Living End and The Donnas and given people access to bands like Pansy Division or Operation Ivy's back-catalogue – maybe even Watt Tyler. They've brought money into local venues and labels and donated to charities. They raised political awareness without ever being dogmatic. And night after night on tour they have given away hundreds of guitars to teenagers to go and do their own thing with.

Most importantly, Green Day have dyed the world day-glo in some of the most drabbest of times. And for that alone they should be saluted.

Artistically Green Day had entered their quietest period yet. Live, they were still a huge draw, yet no band can tour 365 days-a-year, especially when raising young families and getting married and divorced. They could also still sell a million albums. But, wondered a speculative press, did they still want to?

Billie spent some time collaborating with a reformed Go-Go's, the excellent all-girl LA punk/new wave band, who had gone from Sunset Strip in the Seventies to spawning Belinda Carlisle and Jane Wiedlin in the Eighties. The frontman co-wrote the band's come-back single 'Unforgiven', from their *God Bless The Go-Go's* album, their first since 1984 after going to see them play a couple of shows in the Bay Area in 2001. "They were influenced by us, and we ended up getting re-influenced by them," commented Wiedlin reasonably enough.

Seasoned road dogs that they were, in the absence of a new record Green Day headed out on the road where they could by now command huge fees from promoters. Interestingly, their next tour was a joint headline jaunt with men-of-the-moment Blink-182, the San Diego trio who had polished Green Day's sound to even greater pop appeal and perhaps more than any other had found themselves to be marketed in much the same way that a boy band would be.

Named the 'Pop Disaster' tour, the forty-show double-billing of April 2002 was a wet dream for many young punk-pop fans, while for others it was total confirmation that Green Day had lost it and were resorting to touring with their own lightweight doppelgangers.

The irony of two punk bands filling arenas with over-the-top, pyro-packed performances was not lost on reviewers, many of whom made comparisons with the glam rock bands of the Eighties who favoured flash, swagger and cheap thrills over content. It was a fair point. The audiences was heavily comprised of teenagers and pre-teens – punk boys in their shorts and baseball caps cocked at jaunty angles or girls drawn to

Blink-182's nice boy sex appeal and basic blue humour. Many hadn't been born when Green Day had released their first single. Nothing wrong with that of course – pop is the preserve of the young. But the Blink-182/Green Day billing (supported on some dates by rising melodic emo-ish band Jimmy Eat World) was as far removed from punk as they could get without breaking into dance routines and featuring a guest vocal from Usher. So while the tour served the fans well, it did little to enhance Green Day's slightly flagging reputation as stand-alone leaders of the new punk.

Such thoughts hardly subsidised with the release of the second Green Day compilation in twelve months, the B-sides, cover and rarities album *Shenanigans* in July 2002. Though clearly not their greatest work (for obvious reasons) *Shenanigans* did remind that Green Day were in possession of one of the greatest songwriters in rock music – and Mike Dirnt's lyrical contributions on 'Scumbag' and the previously unreleased 'Ha Ha You're Dead' weren't bad either, even if they seemed more or less written to order. As website www.allmusic.com put its: "Green Day knew what their best songs were, and apart from 'J.A.R.,' which they threw out to the *Angus* soundtrack, they kept 'em on the albums … they turned out material for B-sides largely because they *had* to; that was the game in the '90s – you had to make sure the multi-part singles in the UK had unique material, and if a soundtrack came calling, you had to ante up."

Nevertheless for a bunch of songs not deemed strong enough to be released in their own right and recorded in various studios at many different points, it was a welcome enough addition to Green Day's body of work. And just to point new initiates back in the direction from which the band had come, they also included versions of 'I Want To Be On TV' by Eighties hardcore band Fang, The Ramones' 'Outsider' and an alarmingly accurate rendering of The Kinks' 'Tired Of Waiting For You'.

The cover was cool too – a spray-can and stencil graffiti image of the trio sporting matching peroxide hair, recalling images of the similarly-styled The Police and the style of enigmatic UK graffiti whiz Banksy.

Given that the album was more likely to appeal to core Green Day fans or recent converts, surprisingly the record charted higher than the *International Superhits!* collection.

Inevitably the album required promotion from the band and yes – you've guessed it – they went on tour again, including eight dates in the

UK at a variety of large outdoor venues. Though Green Day tended to avoid major criticism and never experienced a dramatic fall from grace that many million sellers suffer, they did find themselves in a strange position, comparable to their *Nimrod*-era four years earlier. So they could play two nights at Wembley Arena or headline Scotland's T In The Park festival as they did in July, yet the press were less interested in what the band had to say when there were new bands emerging every day. Green Day were on auto-pilot. They were playing great shows to big crowds, but they were also, to a degree, going through the motions. Night after night they delivered the expected, when rock 'n' roll should be anything but that. "Breaking up was an option," Dirnt told *Rolling Stone* in 2005. "We were arguing a lot and we were miserable. We needed to shift directions."

Also, punk as a genre – the type of punk Green Day played anyway – was now associated with the fart jokes of Blink-182, the punk-rap-cock-rock hybrid of Sum 41 and the generic, sleek sounds of Epitaph and Fat Wreck bands, as well as newer labels like Drive Thru, whose entire roster seemed, in my opinion, comprised of lightweight punk bands ever-happy to emote on cue.

It was safe.

It was boring.

It needed to get angry again.

The band were stuck in a creative rut, not helped by Billie Joe's approach to music. As frontman and songwriter Billie was the band's natural leader, quietly casting his eye over all areas of their business but especially guiding the band's musical direction. Mike and Tre consequently felt marginalised on occasions – the source of a number of disagreements. As these divisions became more frequent, their singer found his confidence in his own new music in question for the first time. In light of the relatively muted response to *Warning*, could he keep up to the multi-million selling standards he'd inadvertently set for himself?

By 2003 something had to change – maybe their individual attitudes?

Finding that writing and rehearsing songs just wasn't happening, Billie suggested that they allocated a certain amount of time each week to conversation, in order to address any grievances, insecurities or issues that they might have each been harbouring. While it might seem odd that the three childhood friends would resort to such a *Californian* approach of self-help and 'sharing', it's maybe also surprising they didn't attempt it earlier. It certainly seemed to work as the band got back in touch with themselves – and each other.

"Before we started [the new album], we had to sit down and really talk about why we should be doing this," explained Billie Joe. "I love those guys, but it was like, 'How come everybody treats me like a decent human being except these two guys, who treat me like I'm 17?' We had to say, 'Hey, we're grown-ups now, it'd be nice if we treated each other with a bit more respect.' Then we made love."

"Before, Billie would write a song, get stuck and then say, 'Fuck it,'" says Cool. "The imaginary Mike and Tre in his head would say, 'That song sucks. Don't waste your time on it.' He stopped doing that and became totally fearless around me and Mike. Admitting that we cared for each other was a big thing. We didn't hold anything back."

As a result of this self-induced self-group analysis, Green Day actually *lightened up*. For the next four-and-a-half months they regularly jammed in their Oakland studio, writing a new set of songs that experimented with polka rhythms, salsa tunes, even ridiculous versions of Christmas songs for the hell of it, recording it all along the way.

The new songs were at the mixing stage when they arrived at the studio one day to find that the master recordings were gone. Someone had broken in and taken the lot – at least twenty new compositions in total. "We were really pissed," says Billie Joe. "But it ended up being good because we were readying ourselves to go where we hadn't gone before."

As it happened, extra CD copies of some of the tracks had been made but the set-back prompted a change in direction when they had least expected it. They decided to start the album again. Only not just yet.

Billie reacted by going on a trip to New York that turned into a month-long, boozy stay; a prolonged missing weekend where he "drank a lot of red wine, and vodka tonics – I was searching for something. I'm not sure it was the most successful trip." "He was really questioning what he was doing," says his wife Adrienne Armstrong. "It was scary, because where he had to go to get this record wasn't a place I'm sure I wanted him to be."

By the time Billie returned to Oakland the country was at war. Or rather, it had started a war when George W. Bush decided to refute international diplomacy and invade Iraq.

One good thing did come out of their tumultuous time in the studio in 2003. In September an album emerged on Billie Joe's Adeline imprint by a curious-looking new five-piece going by the name of The Network who were shrouded in mystery and disinformation and came with an elaborate story of various members' crimes and misdemeanours, origins and their supposed involvement in the mythical 'Church of Lushotology'.

Entitled *Money Money 2020*, the album was a new wave/synth punk collection of songs clearly heavily influenced by bands such as Devo, Gary Numan's Tubeway Army, and Kraftwerk. Packed full of jerky, rhythmic pop songs with titles such as 'Supermodel Robots', 'Spastic Society' and 'X Ray Hamburger' delivered in a suitably monotone voice, though something of a pastiche *Money Money 2020* didn't seem that out of place in a time when bands such as Yeah Yeah Yeahs, The Faint and Hot Hot Heat were all releasing records that drew heavily on the music of the early Eighties.

It was only that the band were clad in PVC day-glo, all wearing old-school wrestling masks and using the names Fink, Van Gogh, Captain Underpants, the Snoo, and Z that it became clear that The Network weren't entirely serious. And that *Money Money 2020,* licensed through Warners/Reprise, might be the work of imposters, albeit ones seemingly incapable of writing bad songs.

The band's musical ethos was summed up in their own, occasionally hilarious biography which they issued with the album. *"The Network is the future and if it so happens that the future is the 1980s, so be it,"* it read. *"The Network asks you, have we really progressed since then? And the answer is NO! Get out of the 90s people! Put away the flannel and the grunge and join us in the future! The 1980s! The Me Generation."*

Green Day fans who came across the album picked up on certain hints that The Network was in fact the work of their favourite band, recorded and released for the sheer hell of it. One of the album's highlights was 'Spike', a monologue delivered by way of a phonecall from a hapless punk kid in search of a fix, set to a Hives-style garage punk backbeat. One listen and you can tell it's Billie Joe. But the other signs were there – the inclusion of a version of The Misfits' 'Teenagers From Mars', the lyrical intonation, the fact that is was recorded in Oakland and released on Adeline, and that the many bands so lovingly referenced had always been particular favourites of Billie Joe and Co. Even then though, many were not convinced and Green Day message boards were awash with discussion, some fans saying it could never be Billie Joe and friends, for all sorts of contrary reasons – the songs were shit, they were wearing masks (despite publicly hating Slipknot for doing so) and so forth. Many others claimed it was actually a collaboration between Green Day and Devo.

Whatever. They did an excellent job of perpetrating the secrecy of The Network, to such an extent that they posted 'Fuck The Network!' messages on their website and even manufactured a feud between the two bands, complete with footage of The Network causing mayhem at the mere mention of Green Day during a press conference.

How and why The Network actually came about – and who the extra two members might be – remains open to speculation, though it's likely that Jason White is also involved. Further 'details' can be seen on The Network's accompanying *Money Money 2020* DVD. Perhaps the sweetest irony though is that, as I write in 2005, certain bands are finding favour in the charts with a sound even more akin to The Network, only today's synth-widdling, pouting boys' homage to the early Eighties is done without an ounce of humour.

Besides, what probably started out as a joke during studio down-time had excited its players enough to make them plunder headlong into a new album proper.

"We're fighting against humanism, we're fighting against liberalism, we are fighting against all the systems of Satan that are destroying our nation today. Our battle is with Satan himself."
Reverend Jerry Falwell, Christian TV evangelist and founder of the Moral Majority.

The controversial presidential election of late 2000 and the reaction to the attack on New York of 2001 had confirmed to many what they had always believed: that something was rotten with Uncle Sam. That perhaps the American Dream didn't exist, or had long since turned into a nightmare. Similarly, millions more felt that they were living in the best country in the world and that whatever their government did overseas was fine because it was in the name of our Lord Jesus. The President said so and everyone knows he doesn't lie. And you'd be a terrorist to suggest otherwise.

So, despite America's constant assertions that they were "spreading democracy" as if it was as handily attainable as margarine, the world seemed more divided and unstable than ever. Out of a general sense of dismay and disgust (or to paraphrase the crass words of the president, "shock and awe"), rose a protest movement that brought together many diverse socially-aware groups and even more individuals, from every background and social status possible, united in defiance. The common bond was that they were against America's aggressive foreign policy and a president on a mission.

This anti-war/anti-Bush movement produced its own unlikely heroes and figureheads, most notably in the shape of documentary-maker and agent provocateur Michael Moore, a whining, meddlesome, bleeding heart liberal to half of America, a bold and intelligent satirist to the other half (and large portions of the rest of the world). Moore had incurred the wrath of the right-wing National Rifle Association when he tackled gun control with his 2003 film *Bowling For Columbine* and long-since made enemies in high places – right-wing corporate America and its many shady enclaves, mainly – with his earlier documentaries and TV series *The Awful Truth*. Regardless of his overly humble, everyman presentation, Moore presented chilling facts about America that could not be ignored by anyone with a conscience.

"I've learned more through Michael Moore than I have through a textbook," Tre said. *Fahrenheit 9/11* had an impact on me before it even came out. I knew that movie was going to have a lot of information behind it."

And if Moore was too schlocky, there were writers such as professor of linguistics and political dissident Noam Chomsky and investigative journalist John Pilger to present the case against America in reasoned, informed terms for mainstream accessibility.

Inspired by the events of the day and the works of people such as Moore, Chomsky and politically-engaged bands such as Dead Kennedys and Crass, NOFX frontman Fat Mike Burkett brought politics to the punk community again when he established Punkvoter, a mass drive to get young people – specifically punk fans – into the voting booths for the election of 2004 (centred around their website of the same name). NOFX might have long been established as some of the finest entertainers around, but college graduate Fat Mike had always held strong political beliefs that crossed over into the songs he wrote. But by 2002, like so many others around, he began to put his philosophies into practice with Punkvoter, and a couple of compilations entitled *Rock Against Bush*, that included bands such as Bad Religion, Blink-182, Circle Jerks, Foo Fighters, Mudhoney and Green Day, whose unreleased track 'Favourite Son' appeared on *Rock Against Bush Volume II.*

"Bush, Cheney, Rumsfeld, Ashcroft and Co. are intent on fucking us," Fat Mike wrote in the sleevenotes. "The least we can all do is return the favor and fuck them back ..."

Both Brett Gurewitz of Epitaph Records and Jello Biafra of Alternative Tentacles offered sponsorship for a 'Rock Against Bush' tour while Wayne Kramer of MC5 and Billy Gould of Faith No More also took leading roles in the campaign. Though he had generally eschewed interviews about NOFX, Fat Mike now found himself a likeable figurehead and spokesperson for youth resistance. He made no bones about Punkvoter's goals, or the fact that, though only a fraction of the voting populace, the punk scene could conceivably make a difference.

"Our goal is to educate, register and mobilize over 500,000 of today's youth as one voice," said the Punkvoter mission statement. "This is not about who is a sell-out, who is too hardcore or who is from the West Coast, etc ... This is about getting everyone to mobilize as a block of concerned voters. Punk bands, punk labels, and punk fans must form a union against the chaotic policies George W. Bush has put in place. He must be exposed." Whatever happened, at least finally after years of songs about girls and surfing and farting, punk rock had linked up with politics again.

"I can understand why someone wouldn't want to vote," said Billie Joe of the apathetic apolitical malaise that had permeated into the American youth. "The last election, voting didn't count. How can you send a message to people that every vote counts, when obviously people voted and the loser got elected? We've always been active in different political things, like doing benefits for Food Not Bombs. When someone was looking at the [new album's] lyrics, they were like, 'You're probably going to catch some shit.' I was like, 'I hope I get assassinated for it.'"

With all this going on around them and a last album that had been a collection of acoustic-driven ditties whose sole sense of protest was confined to the odd oblique statement, to say that Billie Joe Armstrong was inspired by world events is an understatement.

In the wake of the stolen album and their all-new weekly confessionals, Billie Joe got down to business. It was as if a spark had been ignited. "We live in times of terror and now is the time to speak out," Billie Joe explained. "We wanted to face danger, put it on the line and tell people what we think. Rock 'n' roll is supposed to be dangerous, that's where we come from. For us, our education wasn't what we learned in school, it was what we learned on Dead Kennedys records, Clash records. We're a part of that."

A broad theme was already there – modern American life. Soon, these new songs began to coalesce into a more refined portrait, one of a nation ruled by an idiot, misinformed by a media, and subjugated to a worldwide "redneck agenda", all seen through the eyes of an everyman (the forthcoming album's main disenfranchised voice, Jimmy), modern icons ('Jesus Of Suburbia') and leaders (the aforementioned 'American Idiot', the zeig-heiling 'President Gasman' of 'Holiday') alike and set against a backdrop of shopping malls, empty suburban streets, booze, cigarettes and burning flags. The songs spoke of a country asleep, numbed by narcotics (as on the maudlin 'Novocaine'), soda pop and Ritalin and subliminal advertising, awakening just long enough to tap into a nationwide paranoia – what the BBC termed the Republican-spun 'Climate of Fear' in a 2004 documentary series of the same name – all perpetuated through continuous, carefully presented news broadcasts of Muslim 'crackpots', suicide bombers, unseen terrorists threats and hidden weapon caches.

The new collection of music was turning into – whisper it – a concept album. The trick was how to distill all these ideas into an album accessible enough to take Green Day right back to the top …

"One day we were just sort of messing around at the studio and I said to Mike, 'Write a thirty-second song, it doesn't matter what it's about,'" recalls Billie Joe. "So he wrote this thirty-second piece and we were all laughing about it when we came back into the studio, and I said 'I want to do one!' So I ended up putting in another thirty-second song, and then Tre ended up putting in another thirty-second song. And he's all, 'Oh, this is funny, it's kinda like a rock opera …'"

Blame the progressive rockers of the Seventies, but the general preconception is that a concept album is one long cohesive work, when in fact it's far more likely to be a collection of fractured musical suites brought together by the same themes or part of a broader idea – or concept. The conceptual work that Green Day had pieced together was indebted to a wider variety of works. Indeed, mirroring their heroes The Who before them, Green Day seemed to have come full circle – from releasing a punked up version of 'My Generation' at the turn of the Nineties to constructing a multi-layered work reminiscent of The Who's Seventies pinball tale *Tommy* or indeed its precursor, the mini rock-opera

'A Quick One While He's Away' on their 1966 album *A Quick One (Happy Jack)*.

But a lot had happened since the heyday of The Who and a whole plethora of influences can be felt on Green Day's sonic return to their punk rock roots that came in the form of their 2004 album, *American Idiot*. From second generation UK bands such as Conflict, Crass and Subhumans, who attempted to explore their own lyrical themes in greater depth, though often at the expense of the music (Subhumans' 1983 release *From The Cradle To The Grave* being a fine – if tuneless – example) to, in more recent times, NOFX's eighteen-minute, one-song address to the nation, *The Decline* that showed a desire to express more ideas than a standard punk-pop song could contain and perhaps acknowledged that complicated issues required more than a three-minute analysis. Green Day's choice title of *American Idiot* spoke volumes about its content.

"Writing it was kind of like writing a script and a score at the same time," said Billie Joe. "We embrace the 'punk rock opera' term because it's never been used. People have tried and even joked about it, but for us we're trying to do something spectacular."

As the recording sessions progressed and the album moved nearer to completion, it was becoming clear that while *American Idiot* may have been entrenched in an alluring combination of punk protest, pop music and a strong sense of social place, musically its reference points were broad, unashamed and less than subtle. Not that that had ever stopped Green Day before ...

The 'City Of The Damned' section from the five-part epic 'Jesus Of Suburbia' for example reminded me of the same melody and intonation of pock-marked soft rocker Bryan Adams' 'Summer Of '69' – and, amazingly, sounded all the better for it. Once the band had developed the tricky idea of combining songs into one homogenous work of various key and tempo changes, as on 'Jesus Of Suburbia', the scene for the rest of the album was set.

"We sort of looked at each other and said, 'Now we're onto something,'" said Armstrong. "At the same time, there was no looking back. It was scary. You can't go, 'Now I want to make a regular record.' You have to keep going. As soon as you make the big leap, you're looking at a bigger mountain to climb. It was really exciting and scary at the same time."

Elsewhere, anyone *au fait* with the overblown but nevertheless stirring songs of Meatloaf will certainly feel the presence of his rock-opera arias upon the album (check the horn-laden *Rocky Horror*-esque boogie of one of the album's weaker moments, 'Rock 'N' Roll Girlfriend' for proof). In an hilarious article entitled 'Green Day vs Meatloaf: Who's the real Punk Pavarotti?' Detroit paper *Metro Times* expanded the idea: "Green Day programmed in two nine-minute medleys, lots of unison 'hey' shouts reminiscent of Handel's *Messiah* and plenty of Wagnerian strum and drag. But c'mon, when have you ever heard anyone say, 'It ain't over till the skinny guy scowls'? What's more operatic than 300 pounds of beef stewing beneath a cummerbund, mopping his forehead with a red handkerchief and yelping like he accidentally inhaled Mario Lanza?"

But given that most pop and rock music is based on theft of sorts, these comparisons registered as observations rather than criticisms. In less than an hour of music on *American Idiot*, there are also hints of Queen, Husker Du's *Zen Arcade*, Motley Crue, David Bowie's *Ziggy Stardust* (particularly on 'City Of The Damned'), the expansiveness of The Clash's *London Calling* and *Sandinista* albums, anthemic Eighties balladeers such as Pat Benetar and Laura Brannigan, Cheap Trick, and the aforementioned The Who. And you couldn't say that about many albums.

Everything about *American Idiot* was steeped in American iconography – right down to the inspiration for the title of one the record's hit singles 'Boulevard Of Broken Dreams', taken from a painting by Gottfried Helnwein which itself pastiched Edward Hopper's iconic 'Night Hawks' picture by depicting Marilyn Monroe, Humphrey Bogart, James Dean and Elvis Presley hanging out in a bar (though Eighties glam rockers Hanoi Rocks had beaten Green Day to the appropriation of the title, and Oasis's 'Wonderwall' had seemingly beaten them to a similar chord progression).

Green Day had made an album that could be described as conceptual, progressive and political, but one that also worked as just a great collection of songs. The structure of the album and its many overlapping voices ensured that the band crammed in enough musical peaks and troughs to make it feel like a ride on a rollercoaster that spanned the entire emotional gamut, as on songs such as 'Tales Of Another Broken Home' or the glorious call-and-response, lighter-waving anthem, 'Are We The Waiting'.

"He's just trying to figure out why he's become this underachieving glorified version of himself," Armstrong says of the latter song's protagonist. "He's trying to figure out whether he's getting fat and drinking in a bar or saying, 'Do you want fries with that?' or playing in a rock and roll band, just what his identity is, his individuality. That song is just so bittersweet 'cause it just captures a guy in the city who really doesn't know where he's going."

'When September Ends' meanwhile was a song that went all the way back to the early Eighties, when Billie Joe lost his father, Andy Armstrong. "It's the first time I've written about my father dying when I was ten-years-old," he said. "But so there is continuity, I wrote it so it seems like the character is sort of crushed about something, a part where you're looking on your past and you're coming of age at the same time."

And that's all without taking into consideration the album's thumping title track and fist-raising lead single, a song aimed squarely at the Bush administration as Billie Joe spat the lyrics over a raucous blast of poppy power chords and nifty drum fills delivered with greater brio than ever before. 'American Idiot' – the song – was the paradigm of pop, punk and protest music, a perfectly realized reaction to a sick world that, crucially, acknowledged that a protest song is nothing without a hook to ensnare the public. Many of those who heard it almost instinctively knew that this was a song that, in years to come, would likely epitomize the state of the world in 2004.

Upon the album's completion, the band had major cause for celebration. They knew they had made a great record – but would the world? By the end of the night, they would barely care.

"Rob Cavallo [their old producer back at the helm] and us went to this restaurant in Los Angeles, where we got a huge feast and he bought two $1000 bottles of wine," remembered Mike. "It was unbelievable. And then we drank a whole bunch of cheap wine, too. Then we continued to drink back at the hotel. And then we drank some more. And then we drank at a friend's house. It ended up with a bunch of people naked in the pool, I think…"

And why not. Just when their career was on the down-turn, Green Day has just done the unthinkable and made arguably their strongest work to day.

Then things went ballistic.

Green Day's seventh studio album was released on September 20, 2004 in the UK and a day later in their native US. They had started their

American Idiot campaign as they meant to go on, by posting a free anti-war song written by Aaron 'Cometbus' Elliot and Pinhead Gunpowder, entitled 'Life During Wartime' online. Judging by the reaction from certain areas of the press, Green Day were embarking on the comeback of the decade, the irony of course being that they hadn't ever been away (seeing that they had little new to offer, some people had just stopped paying attention). Others scoffed at the idea of a 'punk opera' without ever stopping to consider the complexities of what such a thing entails.

Then of course, there was the small matter of half of America – only about 140 million or so people – who happened to think that the American Idiot in question was the greatest thing since John Wayne, capable of kicking foreign ass with the same grit, determination and mincing swagger. It's easy to forget that not everyone is open-minded to the type of criticism of America on offer. Criticism breeds doubt and doubt breeds questioning and questioning breeds insurrection, and then all hell breaks loose – or at least, that's what the pro-Bush patriots would have had the world believe.

So while the right wing, anti-rock 'n' roll types criticized the band – it would have been worrying if they hadn't – a lot of the older punk fans founds themselves drawn back to Green Day, either because of the strength of the songs or the fact that, at last, here was a band to divide opinion, beliefs and generations, even if it was in a relatively safe way (though, in a time when FBI watch lists, phone taps and secret dossiers is the norm for rock stars, you can still never underestimate the danger involved when a person as potentially powerful as Billie Joe Armstrong decides to speak out against the government in trying times).

Just to cement their status as leaders of the liberal vanguard in modern rock music, in the same month that they released the album, Green Day appeared on CBS' *Late Night With Letterman* show where they performed the buffoon-baiting title track from the album. The other guest was the Presidential challenger John Kerry, who the band met after the show.

When election day came around, *American Idiot*-mania was in full swing. Though they had played a number of festivals in Japan and the UK (including a show-stealing headline set at Reading before the album was even released), it wasn't until November that they toured the US and Canada playing to full arenas night after night. It was while out on the road that they turned in their absentee votes in the presidential election.

It's a pretty safe guess as to who they *didn't* vote for.

Though the polls had been close after hard fought election campaigns, George W. Bush and the Republicans prevailed once again when he won by a greater margin than had been expected. The dreams of rock music being able to change the world were crushed, the US election of 2004 a fine reminder that no-one but the select few truly has any power. A country settled in for four more years of bombing/democracy spreading.

Away from the cut-throat world of politics though, Green Day had not only played a major part in the largest youth and student voter turn-out in recent history but had soundtracked it too. They were at an all-time career high, having gained more critical respect than they had ever previously been granted and sold more copies than any of their previous albums. Yes, even *Dookie*. Out of nowhere, it seemed, Green Day were the band on everyone's lips … again. At the time of writing, every news-stand has a magazine with their faces on the cover; every radio seems to be playing either 'American Idiot' or 'Boulevard of Broken Dreams'; and every ticket agency is straining to get hold of a quota for anything resembling a Green Day show.

American Idiot was, simply put, an absolutely *massive* album. Even with 50 Cent topping the *Billboard* album charts and having four singles in the US Top Ten (a feat matching The Beatles), the honours still seemed to be heading Green Day's way. Recently, the music world had seen a remarkable comeback from the Red Hot Chili Peppers as well as an almost unthinkable transition from the lead singer of the world's biggest boy band, N*Sync's Justin Timberlake, into the 'new Jacko'. Yet somehow, Green Day and *American Idiot* topped all of this.

"I think what *American Idiot* has done for us is really change our own history in a lot of ways," Billie Joe said in February 2005. "It created a new future for us. It made all of our albums since *Dookie* make sense for people who weren't really up to speed with what we were doing. And the fact that we have the experience of this happening before just takes the edge off. It's all good. Obviously having all this critical acclaim is a first, but that's all …"

In the early days of 2005, Green Day were Europe-bound once again. It was a little less than fifteen years since they had first flown to the continent armed with little more than their guitars and home-made T-shirts.

When they arrived to play Berlin, things were a little different this time around. This time Green Day were *the biggest rock band in the world* [for those doubters, a generous cover feature by *Q* magazine confirmed this]. But things hadn't changed that much – it was still the same three core members, all older, worldlier and wiser, though not necessarily *adult*. They were still chasing the good times, the next thrill, the next perfect song.

The *American Idiot* roadshow moved through Europe, first to Holland then Italy and France before hitting the UK. That same month, Billie Joe Armstrong, the people's punk, turned 33, the same age as Jesus when they had crucified him.

Green Day were back.

Postscript

It's fucking freezing in London, make no mistake.

Lots of people I know – regular gig-goers one and all – hate heading south of the river to Brixton's grand Academy venue just off the High Street. I think it's due to some form of inverted north London snobbery, but I love the place. It's close enough to where I live now to call home. Very rarely do truly great bands play a mile or two down the road, but this place has seen them all. Gigs at Brixton Academy seem to guarantee drama and a sense of occasion.

Brixton is also former Clash territory. Guitarist Mike Jones and bassist Paul Simonon both went to school within pissing distance of here, and the reggae and dub music of the local sound systems and record stores infiltrated their music early on. The punk-ska-reggae hybrid was partially born out of this area, with its strange mix of poverty and gentrification, drugs and crime, community and celebration – and ever-changing vibes.

I mention all this on this most frosty of January evenings because without Brixton there would have been no Clash – or at least not The Clash recognized and loved by millions – without The Clash there would have been no Operation Ivy and without Operation Ivy there would have been no … yeah, you know where this is going. It all feels like it ties in somehow, if you care to delve deep enough.

Brixton features heavily on the psycho-geographical map of the punk rock world; and it still feels like it has an outlaw element today. The mix of rich and poor and an ever-changing cast of transients makes for an interesting and potent frisson. It's also an area that has seen its fair share of rioting, as an oppressed community bites back over poverty, race issues or police brutality. Brixton does what it wants to do.

So it's a punk kinda place.

It's where Green Day have chosen to do two 'intimate' – as intimate as five thousand people can be – London shows, their first in this city in which they've spent so much time since *American Idiot* hit the top spot here. It's a wise move, not least because Brixton Academy lends itself to career-defining performances, replacing as it does the low-rent, watery lager feel of a toilet venue with the grandiose, once-plush surroundings of an old time theatre. The original 1920s proscenium arch, the thirty-five foot bronzed 'semi-dome' and magnificent Art Deco interiors are all still in place. Even the two towers flanking the Academy's stage and the terrace above it are based on the great Italian masterpieces in the Colonna Palace. It's a strange mix of fading old world opulence and, given the great unwashed masses who regularly inhabit the place, modern street grime. Combining the best of the past with the present day and with a sloping floor which enables even the shortest of punters to get a decent view of proceedings, it is, as a couple of fans near me are enthusiastically discussing, the perfect venue to see Green Day. Not too big, not too small.

Later: after a show that has seen the first half-hour solely dedicated to play the opening *American Idiot* tracks in order, complete with pyrotechnical bangs, changing back-drops, glitter canons and all the other trappings of a big-time rock show – the best I've ever seen Green Day – I'm dodging plain clothes police, fervent bootleggers and mini-cab drivers aggressively touting for business as a mass of bodies spill out the front door and into the sub-zero night air, a torrent of sweat and steam and excitement.

It's freezing but I'm not yet cold.

I cut across the high street and down along beneath the railway arches of Brixton market and onto a side street where I hurriedly parked my car earlier. I turn on the radio and they're playing Minor Threat – on Radio 1! Huh? I've never heard Minor Threat on the radio before. Ten, fifteen years ago such a thing would not have been possible. I know that somewhere in there, Green Day are in some way responsible for such musical shifts.

A little over sixty seconds later and the track is over and I'm heading along Coldharbour Lane past the odd shivering crackhead hooker, and their pimps loitering a few steps behind them in the shadows, recognizable only by the glowing embers of a cigarette.

The DJ cuts to the news where the lead story is the release of two British men from America's infamous human rights-contravening Camp X-Ray at Cuba's Guantanemo Bay early today. It has only taken over three years – three years lacking in any standard legal rights *whatsoever* – for the American government to decide these men actually had no connection to Osama Bin Laden and the events of September 11, 2001. Or Iraq. Or North Korea. Or the French. Or whoever the fuck is the latest unseen enemy of America.

Upon arrival back in the UK a few hours earlier, the report tells us, the men were promptly arrested by MI5. It's a move that reeks of procedure – that the UK government had to be seen to be doing something, now that George W. Bush had finally foisted this embarrassing situation and diplomatic disaster back to Downing Street.

The point being – until the little man stands up tall, party politics will always be a load of cloak and dagger bullshit. But what does this have to do with Green Day and punk rock 'n' roll music?

Nothing. Nothing and everything.

Nothing because they just play dumb three-chord pop songs. Everything, because what they said tonight encapsulated the feelings of millions – the sentiments of we, the dispossessed, disenfranchised and powerless. Their anti-imperialist, anti-Republican stance is a small but necessary contribution – and, in many respects, a brave one.

Because the *American Idiot* is alive and well. So is the British Idiot.

Sometimes it feels like idiocy is taking over and only music and dancing and a raised fist can save us now.

Only in opposition does rock 'n' roll retain its potency.

But, hell, you probably know that already …

Some things don't need explaining.

Telegraph Avenue looks a lot like everywhere else in America these days. Just south of that great place of learning, protest, dissent and liberalism, the Berkeley college campus, Telegraph is a place where, as journalist Gina Arnold put it, "Nineties iconography – Starbucks, Benetton, Towers Records – mingles uneasily with all that Sixties flotsam: head shops, dope dealers, stringy-haired chicks selling crystals and whole contingents of grotesque-looking homeless people with hair, bright red eyes and a truculent veneer."

Such a display of people is still, of course, far from the norm. For while Berkeley might have certainly been affected by the slow creeping spread of corporate, chain-stored front street uniformity typical of America over the past decade or two, it still retains its spirit of independence. It has suddenly seen a big change nevertheless, as have the streets of Oakland behind it.

Over in Rodeo though – the true heart of Green Day – little has changed since the early Seventies. Stores and hang-outs such as nearby Rod's Hickory Pit have come and gone, as have families, but the general population and amenities available to them remain small and limited. Rodeo hasn't got unexpectedly wealthy, as has happened in the past (and more recently to two of its former inhabitants) nor has it had its heart and soul ripped out, as has also happened before. Willets, Mendocino, meanwhile remains as remote and ever-so-slightly eccentric as it always has been. Pinole Valley School remains, as does John Sweet High.

But then it's only a decade-and-a-half since Billie Joe Armstrong, Michael Pritchard and Frank Edwin Wright III left here to embark on their journey. Because the rise of Green Day is very recent history. And it's a history that is changing every day as the story writes itself, continually adding new backdrops, cameo characters and statistical milestones, but still more or less about the same people doing the same things they always did.

Last night I stayed up and watched the 2005 Grammys, where Green Day were nominated for six awards and saw off the likes of Billie Joe's favourite Elvis Costello to win an award for 'Best Rock Album'. The band's acceptance speech was completely edited from the proceedings – either because something controversial was said or more likely because Jennifer Lopez was up next to perform a duet with husband number sixteen or something. No matter. No speeches were needed – *American Idiot* had already said it all.

Even in their tailored suits, America's biggest rock band still seemed strangely out of place at such a glitzy, bullshit event. And that's a good thing. Because as soon as Green Day get too cosy with American music's ruling elite, they'll be finished. Fifteen years into their career that looks highly unlikely.

In the past week I've also watched them perform live on the UK's two biggest music shows, *Top Of The Pops* and *CD:UK*. I've watched them at the Brit awards, chuckling as the presenter points out that they were here ten years ago, when they lost out on 'Best International Act' to Bon Jovi. I've been bombarded with album sales statistics by friends and colleagues and last weekend saw the band's name mentioned in two separate news stories in the main section of a broadsheet newspaper. Not a review or a gig listing, but actual pieces alongside ones about rigged elections and bombings and the environment going to shit. This morning when I turned on the TV there they were, Tre telling Sunday morning kid's TV viewers the benefits of drinking dog's milk. I tuned in the radio and 'Holiday' was playing. Yesterday it was announced that Green Day are headlining, amongst others, the T In The Park festival this summer. And there's the small matter of selling out Milton Keynes Bowl in June 2005 – the biggest ever punk show in the UK. Another statistic.

But ultimately it still feels weird seeing a band that was once from the underground now sandwiched between soap opera and dog food adverts. It's rock music as another product ... *but* there's no need to feel bitterness.

If you hate Green Day for what they have become then it is you that has changed and not the band. But that's okay too.

Tomorrow there'll be something else to add.

This story keeps unfurling.

CD BRINGS BOY OUT OF COMA

A schoolboy was woken from a coma after he heard a CD by his favourite band. Corey George, from Aberaman, south Wales, was unconscious for two weeks on a life support machine after being knocked down by a car on his ninth birthday. His mother Tina, played him American Idiot *by Green Day and within an hour he had opened his eyes.*

The Daily Telegraph, March 2005.

GREEN DAY DISCOGRAPHY

Where appropriate I have included certain US releases which were available on import in the UK, though this discography is weighted more towards UK releases – or those more freely available on import. To that end I have included as many limited and collectable items as possible, though cannot claim that this is the definitive discography. Because certain singles were re-released in limited or alternative formats, releases are placed in chronological order, rather than by song, to give a better impression of the development of the band. The website www.greendaysweetchildren.com proved to be a particularly valuable research source and should be visited by any Green Day fan wishing to know more about the band's back-catalogue … and more. Thanks also to Andrea Graham.

Singles

1000 Hours
1000 Hours / Dry Ice / Only Of You / The One I Want
(Seven-inch, Lookout!, 1989)

Slappy EP
Paper Lanterns / Why Do You Want Him / 409 In The Coffeemaker / Knowledge
(Seven-inch, Lookout!, 1990)

Sweet Children
Sweet Children / Best Thing In Town / Strangeland / My Generation
(Seven-inch, Skene, 1990)

Longview / On The Wagon
(Seven-inch, Warners / Reprise, June 1994,

Longview / Going To Pasalacqua (live) / FOD (live) / Christy Road (live)
(CD, Reprise, June 1994)

Longview / Going To Pasalacqua (live) / FOD (live) / Christy Road (live)
(Ten-inch green vinyl, Reprise, 1995).
This release was highly limited and the only known Green Day ten-inch release

Basket Case / Tired Of Waiting For You
(Seven-inch green vinyl, Reprise, August 1994).
This was released twice as a single

Basket Case / Tired Of Waiting For You / 409 In Your Coffeemaker (unmixed)
(CD released in a clear or green case, Reprise, August 1994)

Welcome To Paradise / Chump (live) / Emenius Sleepus (live)
(Twelve-inch green vinyl, Reprise, October 1994)

Welcome To Paradise / Chump (live) / Emenius Sleepus
(CD released in a clear or green case, Reprise, October 1994)

Basket Case (album version) / 2000 Light Years Away (live)
(Seven-inch on black or green vinyl, Reprise, January 1995)

Basket Case (album version) / Longview / Burnout / 2000 Light Years Away
(CD, Reprise, January 1995)

Longview / Welcome To Paradise / One Of My Lies
(CD, Reprise, March 1995)

Longview / On The Wagon
(Seven-inch, Reprise, March 1995)

Longview / Welcome To Paradise
(Seven-inch, Reprise, March 1995)
US release only.

When I Come Around / She (live)
(Seven-inch picture disc, Reprise, April 1995)

When I Come Around / Coming Clean (live) / She (live)
(CD, Reprise, April 1995)

Geek Stink Breath / I Want To Be On TV / Don't Want To Fall In Love
(CD, Reprise, 1995)

Geek Stink Breath / I Want To Be On TV
(Seven-inch red vinyl, Reprise 1995)

Stuck With Me / When I Come Around / Jaded (live)
(CD, Reprise, 1995)

Brain Stew/Jaded / Do Da Da / Good Riddance / Brain Stew (Clean Radio version)
(CD, Reprise, 1996)

Hitchin' A Ride / Sick / Redundant
(CD, Reprise, 1997)

Good Riddance (Time Of Your Life) / Desensitized / Rotting
(CD, Reprise, 1997)

Redundant / The Grouch / Paper Lanterns (live)
(CD, Reprise, 1997)

Redundant (Richard Dodd medium wide mix) / The Grouch (live)
(Seven-inch, Reprise, 1997)

Minority / Brat (live / 86 (live) / Jackass
(CD, Reprise, 2000)

Minority / Brat (live) / Jackass / 86 (live)
(Seven-inch on black, red, green and peace vinyl, Adeline 2000)

Warning / Scum Bag / Outsider
(Seven-inch on gold and yellow vinyl, Adeline, 2000)

Warning / Suffocate
(Seven-inch green vinyl, Reprise, 2000)
Alternative release to the above.

Waiting / Maria
(Seven-inch pink vinyl, Reprise, 2001)

Waiting / Macy's Day Parade (live) / Basket Case (live) / Waiting (video)
(CD, Reprise, 2001)

American Idiot / Shoplifter / Governator
(CD, Reprise, 2004)

American Idiot / Too Much Too Soon
(CD2, Reprise, 2004)

American Idiot / Too Much Too Soon
(Seven-inch picture disc, Reprise, 2004)

Boulevard Of Broken Dreams (album version) / Boulevard Of Broken Dreams (clean version)
(CD, Reprise, 2004)

Boulevard Of Broken Dreams / Letterbomb
(Seven-inch, Reprise, 2004)

Holiday / Minority (live edit)
(CD, Reprise, 2005)

Holiday / Holiday (live) / Boulevard Of Broken Dreams (live)
(CD2, Reprise, 2005)

Holiday / Minority (live)
(Seven-inch, Reprise, 2005)

ALBUMS
Green Day's first two independently-released albums on Lookout! were also released (and later re-released) on CD, containing bonus tracks from their early singles, hence the slightly different titles on occasion. Reprise Records is a subsidiary of the Warner Music organisation (also known as WEA) – where applicable and for the sake of simplicity, I've simply listed it as Reprise.

39/Smooth
At The Library / Don't Leave Me / I Was There / Disappearing Boy / Green Day / Going To Pasalacqua / 16 / Road To Acceptance / Rest / The Judge's Daughter
(vinyl, Lookout!, 1990)

1039/Smoothed Out Slappy Hours
At The Library / Don't Leave Me / I Was There / Disappearing Boy / Green Day / Going To Pasalacqua / 16 / Road To Acceptance / Rest / The Judge's Daughter / Paper Lanterns / Why Do You Want Him / 409 In Your Coffeemaker / Knowledge / 1000 Hours / Dry Ice / Only Of You / The One I Want
(CD, Lookout!, 1990)

CD release of the band's debut, with added tracks from their early EPs,

Kerplunk!

2000 Lights Years Away / One For The Razorbacks / Welcome To Paradise / Christie Road / Private Ale / Dominated Love Slave / One Of My Lies / 80 / Android / No One Knows / Who Wrote Holden Caulfield? / Words I Might Have Ate

(vinyl, Lookout!, December 1991)

Kerplunk!

2000 Lights Years Away / One For The Razorbacks / Welcome To Paradise / Christie Road / Private Ale / Dominated Love Slave / One Of My Lies / 80 / Android / No One Knows / Who Wrote Holden Caulfield? / Words I Might Have Ate / Sweet Children / Best Thing In Town / Strangeland / My Generation

(CD, Lookout!, December 1991))

CD release of the album, with added tracks from their 'Sweet Children EP'

Dookie

Burnout / Having A Blast / Chump / Longview / Welcome To Paradise / Pulling Teeth / Basket Case / She / Sassafras Roots / When I Come Around / Coming Clean / Emenius Sleepus / In The End / FOD

(vinyl, cassette and CD, Reprise, April 1994)

CD versions also contained a secret track of 'All By Myself' featuring Tre Cool on vocals.

Insomniac

Armatage Shanks / Brat / Stuck With Me / Geek Stink Breath / No Pride / Bab's Uvula Who? / 86 / Panic Song / Stuart And The Ave. / Brain Stew / Jaded / Westbound Sign / Tight Wad Hill / Walking Contradiction

(vinyl, cassette and CD, Reprise, October 1995)

Nimrod

Nice Guys Finish Last / Hitchin' A Ride / The Grouch / Redundant / Scattered / All The Time / Worry Rock / Platypus (I Hate You) / Uptight / Last Ride In / Jinx / Haushinka / Walking Alone / Reject / Take Back / King For A Day / Good Riddance (Time Of You Life) / Prosthetic Head

(vinyl, cassette and CD, Reprise, October 1997)

Warning

Warning / Blood, Sex And Booze / Church On Sunday / Fashion Victim / Castaway / Misery / Deadbeat Holiday / Hold On / Jackass / Waiting / Minority / Macy's Day Parade / 86 (Live In Prague)

(vinyl, cassette and CD, Reprise, October 2000)

American Idiot

American Idiot / Jesus Of Suburbia: I. Jesus Of Suburbia, II. City Of The Damned, III. I Don't Care, IV. Dearly Beloved, V. Tales Of Another Broken Home / Holiday / Boulevard Of Broken Dreams / Are We The Waiting / St. Jimmy / Give Me Novacaine / She's A Rebel / Extraordinary Girl / Letterbomb / Wake Me When September Ends / Homecoming: I. The Death Of St. Jimmy II. East 12th St. III. Nobody Likes You IV. Rock And Roll Girlfriend V. We're Coming Home Again / Whatsername

(CD, double gatefold vinyl, cassette, Reprise, September 2004)

COMPILATIONS

International Superhits (Greatest Hits)

Maria / Poprocks & Coke / Longview / Welcome To Paradise / Basket Case / When I Come Around /

She / J.A.R (Jason Andrew Relva) / Geek Stink Breath / Brain Stew / Jaded / Walking Contradiction /
Stuck With Me / Hitchin' A Ride / Good Riddance (Time Of Your Life) / Redundant / Nice Guys Finish
Last / Minority / Warning / Waiting / Macy's Day Parade
(CD, twelve-inch purple and pink vinyl, cassette, Reprise, November 2001)

Shenanigans (B-sides compilation)
Suffocate / Desensitized / You Lied / Outsider / Don't Want To Fall In Love / Espionage / I Want To
Be On TV / Scumbag / Tired of Waiting For You / Sick Of Me / Rotting / Do Da Da / On The Wagon /
Ha Ha You're Dead
(CD, twelve-inch blue vinyl, cassette, Reprise, July 2002)

VIDEO / DVD
International Supervideos!
Longview / Basket Case / When I Come Around / Geek Stink Breath / Stuck With Me / Brain Stew /
Jaded / Walking Contradiction / Hitchin' A Ride / Good Riddance (Time Of Your Life) / Redundant /
Nice Guys Finish Last / Last Ride In / Minority / Warning / Waiting
(DVD and VHS, Warner Vision, November 2001)

OTHER COMPILATION AND SOUNDTRACK APPEARANCES
As well as Green Day's many soundtrack and compilation appearances, this list includes a number of
international compilation curios.

The Big One (1990) *Flipside* magazine compilation features 'I Want To Be Alone'
Can You Break Though (1990) Twelve-inch vinyl compilation on Skene that features 'Best Thing In
Town'
Gilman Street Block Party (1993) features 'Sweet Home Alabama', 'Eye Of The Tiger' and 'Rock
You Like A Hurricane'
Fuckin' Groovin' Fahrvergnügen (1993). Compilation of US punk bands who toured Germany circa
1993. Features '2000 Light Years Away'
Jerky Boys official soundtrack (1994) features '2000 Light Years Away'
SNL 25 Vol.2 (Performances from Saturday Night Live) (1994) features 'When I Come Around'
Built To Blast (1994) Fierce Panda Records' punk/hardcore compilation that features a live version
'Christie Road'
Crossing All Over Volume 3 (1994). Metal-leaning (Soundgarden, Rollins Band etc) sampler
compilation that features 'Basket Case'.
In Ya Face Contents (1994) Sampler that features 'Longview' along with a track each from
grunge/stoner bands Kyuss, Down and Candlebox.
Woodstock (1994) features 'When I Come Around'
Guinea Worm S&M magazine (1995) Newport punk compilation/magazine features 'At The Library'
(live at TJ's, 1991)
American Punk Invasion (1995), includes live versions in Germany of 'Welcome To Paradise', 'One
Of My Lies', 'Chump', 'Longview', 'Basket Case' and 'Burnout' alongside tracks from the Offspring,
Bad Religion and NOFX.
American Punk Invasion Vol II (1995), includes live versions in Germany of 'Basket Case', 'When I
Come Around', 'F.O.D.', 'Paper Lanterns', 'At The Library', 'The Judge's Daughter' and ' Going To
Pasalacqua'. Also includes tracks by NOFX, Foo Fighters, Pennywise.
Megamix (1995) four-track sampler of ill-advised 'megamixes' of Green Day, Pearl Jam, Nirvana and
The Offspring.
Live USA (1995) features a live version of 'When I Come Around' (alongside the likes of Huey Lewis

& The News and Lionel Ritchie!)
Angus - Motion Picture Soundtrack (1995) features 'J.A.R.'
Musical Chairs - Reprise Alternative sampler (1995) label compilation features 'J.A.R'
Brit Awards (1996) Britpop-heavy awards compilation that features 'Basket Case'.
*Generations I: A Punk Look At Human Rights (*1997) features 'Do Da Da'.
Godzilla - Motion Picture Soundtrack (1998) features 'Brain Stew (Godzilla remix)
The All Time Greatest Rock Songs Volume 1 (1998) bargain bin comp that features 'Basket Case'.
Varsity Blues - Motion Picture Soundtrack (1999) features 'Nice Guys Finish Last'.
Short Music For Short People (1999) Excellent 99-track Fat Wreck Chords compilation that features 'The Ballad of Wilhelm Fink' (Fat Wreck Chords, 1999)
Austin Powers: The Spy Who Shagged Me - Motion Picture Soundtrack (1999) features 'Espionage'
MTV Fight For Your Rights - Take A Stand Against Violence Compilation (1999) features a 'Billie Joe Soundbite'
SNL 25: Saturday Night Live The Musical Performances Volume 2 (1999) includes a version of 'When I Come Around' from 1994.
Friends Again – Original TV soundtrack (2000) features 'The Angel And The Jerk'
American Pie 2 – Motion Picture Soundtrack (2001) features 'Scumbag'.
Freddy Got Fingered – Motion Picture Soundtrack (2001) features 'Blood, Sex, And Booze'.
*The New Guy Soundtrack - Motion Picture Soundtrack (*2002) features 'Outsider'.
Every Dog Has Its Day (2002), Adeline Records compilation features 'Ha, Ha, You're Dead '.
We're A Happy Family: A Tribute To The Ramones (2003) features 'Outsider'.
Rock Against Bush Volume II (2004) features 'Favourite Son'.

LIVE ALBUMS
There are hundreds of unofficial Green Day bootlegs available. Though the band have never released a worldwide live album, the following are decent quality official live releases for specific Green Day 'territories'. All are available in UK record stores and are worth investigating.

Bowling Bowling Bowling Parking Parking
Armatage Shanks / Brain Stew / Jaded / Knowledge / Basket Case / She / Walking Contradiction
Live tracks recorded in the Czech Republic, Russia and Japan in 1994 and 1996.
(CD, Reprise / WEA International, 1996)

Foot In Mouth
Going To Pasalacqua/ Welcome To Paradise / Geek Stink Breath / One Of My Lies / Stuck With Me/ Chump / Longview / 2000 Light Years Away / When I Come Around / Burnout / F.O.D
More live tracks, recorded in Sweden, Russia, Czech Republic and Japan, 1994-1996
(CD WEA Japan, 1997)

Tune In Tokyo
Church On Sunday / Castaway / Blood, Sex and Booze / King For A Day / Waiting / Minority / Macy's Day Parade
Live recording of Japanese dates from March 2001
(Reprise Records 2001)

SIDE-PROJECTS AND GUEST APPEARANCES

Billie Joe Armstrong
Look For Love / Interview With Billie Joe
(seven-inch vinyl limited to 800 copies, Fiat Records, 1977)

The Lookouts
Featuring Tre Cool on drums

Albums
One Planet, One People
Why Don't You Die / The Mushroom Is Exploding / Friends Of Mine / Mendocino County / Downtown / Catatonic Society / The Last time / Death / I Wanna Love (But You Make Me Sick) / Recycled Love / It's All Over Now, Baby Blue / Miss Trendy Burrhead / My Mom Smokes Pot / Nazi Dreams / Fuck Religion / Thank The Lord / Fucked Up Kid / CAMP Get Out / Fourth Reich (Nazi America) / Don't Cry For Me Nicaragua / One Planet One People / Sometimes
(Lookout!, 1986)

Spy Rock Road
That Girl's From Outer Space / Wild / Alienation / Generation / The Green Hills Of England / Living Behind Bars / Red Sea / Sonny Boy / Trees / Life / Friends
(Lookout!, 1989)

Singles / EPs
Mendocino Homeland
I Saw Her Standing There / Judgement Day / Relijion Aint Kul / Mendocino Homeland
(Lookout!, 1989)
NB: Though they released further records, this was The Lookouts final release to feature Tre Cool.

IV
Story / Dying / Gape / Out My Dope
(Lookout!, 1990)
Also featured Billie Joe Armstrong on guitar and backing vocals.

Compilation appearances
Bay Mud (Very Small, 1986) features 'Why Don't You Die' and 'California'
Lethal Noise Vol. II (Very Small, 1987) features 'Recycled Love'
The Thing That Ate Floyd (Lookout!, 1988) features 'Outside'
Make The Collector Nerd Sweat (Very Small, 1989) features 'Big Green Monsters'
More Songs About Plants And Trees (Allied, 1990) features 'Once Upon A Time'
Can Of Pork (Lookout!, 1992) features 'Kick Me In The Head'

Pinhead Gunpowder
Featuring Billie Joe Armstrong on vocals/guitar

Albums
Jump Salty
Future Daydream / Freedom Is / I Wanna / Losers Of The Year / Big Yellow Taxi / Dull / Keeping Warm In The Night Time / Beastly Bit / Benicia By The Bay / MPLS Song / In

Control / Hey Now
(Lookout!, 1995)
Note: this is a compilation of the 'Fahiza' and 'Trundle & Spring' singles

Carry The Banner
Find My Place / Before The Accident / I Used To / Reach For The Bottle / Walkin'
Catastrophe / I Am An Elephant / I Am The Stranger / Certain Things / Mahogany
(Lookout!, 1995)

Goodbye Ellston Avenue
Life During Wartime / Without Me / High Maintenance / Backyard Flames / Song Of My
Returning / Once More Without Feeling / I Walk Alone / Train Station / Homesick Hopes /
Work For Food / Brother / Swan Song / The Great Divide
(Lookout!, 1997)

Compulsive Disclosure
Buffalo / 2nd Street / Landlords / Porch / New Blood / Letter From AOF / Black Mountain,
Pt. 3 / Crazy Horse / At Your Funeral
(Lookout!, 2003)

Singles / EPs
Trundle & Spring
Dull / Keeping Warm in The Night Time / MPLS Song / No Control
(No Reality, 1991)

Fahiza
Future Daydream / Freedom Is / Hey Now / Big Yellow Taxi
(Lookout!, 1992)

Shoot The Moon
Cabot Girl / My Boot In Your Face Is What Keeps Me Alive / Asheville / Junkpile / 27 /
Kathleen / Achin' To Be (Adeline, 1999)

Split single with Dillinger Four
At Your Funeral / Porch Song / Second Street
(Adeline, 2000)

Pinhead Gunpowder
Buffalo / Crazy Horse / New Blood / Letter From An Old Friend
(THD Records, 2000)

8 Chords, 328 Words
Landlords / Black Mountain Pt. 3
(Lookout!, 2000)

Compilation appearances
Very Small World (Very Small Records, 1991) features 'Losers Of The Year'
Can Of Pork (Lookout!, 1992) features 'Benicia Of The Bay'
Misfit Heartbeat (Take A Day/Ineration, 1993) features 'I Wanna'
Vinyl Retentive (Very Small, 1993) features 'Beastly Bit'
The Last Great Thing You Did (Lookout!, 1997) features 'Life During War Time;
Down In Front (No Idea, 1999) features 'Beastly Bit', 'Reach For The Bottle', 'Swan

Song'
Blind Herd Of Sheep (El Sabado, 1999) features 'Before The Accident'
Might As Well…Cant' Dance (Adeline, 2000) features 'Porch Song'
Bored, Lonely And A Little Pissed Off (KALX, 2000) features 'Life After War Time' (Billie Joe Acoustic)

Rancid
Single
'Radio Radio Radio' single (Fat Wreck,1993)
Co-written by Billie Joe Armstrong who also played in the band for one show.

Screeching Weasel
Albums
How To Make Enemies And Irritate People album (Lookout!, 1994)
Featured Mike Dirnt on bass / backing vocals.
Planet Of The Apes / 99 / I Hate Your Guys On Sunday / Jonny R U Weird? / Time Bomb / Burnout Girl / If I Was You / Nobody Likes You / Degenerate / Surf Goddess / Kathy Isn't Right / Kathy's On The Roof / I Wrote Holden Caulfield.

The Frustrators
Featuring Mike Dirnt on bass/vocals

EPS / singles
Bored In The USA
I Slept With Terry / Then She Went Away / Living In The Real World / East Bay Or Urden Bay / We're Only Human / West Of Texas / The Great Australian Midget Toss / Brown Mercury Comet
(Adeline, 2000)

Achtung Jackass
*Hide and Seek / Stupid / Frustrators Jingle / 25 / The Crasher / My Best Friend's Girl / Pirate Song / AAA / The End / Tuort (*version of *'Trout'* … played backwards*)*
(Adeline, 2002)

Compilations
Might As Well…Can't Dance (Adeline, 2000) features 'Trout'

The Network
Featuring Fink, Van Gogh, Captain Underpants, Snoo and Z

Album
Money Money 2020 (Adeline, 2003)
Joe Robot / Transistors Gone Wild / Reto / Supermodel Robots / Money Money 2020 / Spike / Love And Money / Right Hand-A-Rama / Roshambo / Hungry Hungry / Spastic Society / X-Ray Hamburger

Miscellaneous / related releases
Various Artists *A Different Shade Of Green* (Skunk Ape Records, 2003).
Features various obscure bands covering Green Day. The only band of note are Weezer, who cover 'Worry Rock'
Honeywagon *Pickin' On Green* (CMH Records, 2004) features bluegrass version of Green Day songs.

BIBLIOGRAPHY

The following publications were consulted in the writing of this book. The author recommends each of them.

Arnold, Gina, *Kiss This: Punk In The Present Tense* (Pan, 1997)
Edge, Brian (Editor), *924 Gilman: The Story So Far* (Maximum Rock 'n' Roll, 2004)
Harris, John, *The Last Party: Britpop, Blair And The Demise Of British Rock*, (Harper Collins, 2004)
Myers, Ben, *American Heretics: Rebel Voices In Music* (Codex, 2003)
True, Everett, *Live Through This: American Music In The Nineties* (Virgin, 2001)

INDEX OF ARTICLES REFERENCED

All quotes are taken from the author's own interviews unless otherwise credited. Where applicable the author has taken every care to reference all sources used. Specific attention must be drawn to the following excellent articles: 'Green Daze: It's Official: Green Day Are The Best New Band In The Land' by Chris Mudy, *Rolling Stone*, January 1995; 'An American Family' by Craig Marks, *Spin*; 'A Lean, Green, Rock Machine' by Neal Weiss, Yahoo Launch, 2000; 'It's not easy being Green Day' by Frank Meyer, Yahoo Launch, 1998; 'Intimate Portrait' by Caryn Ganz, *Spin*, September 2004;

The following publications proved to be particularly valuable sources of information: *Kerrang!, NME, Melody Maker, Maximum Rock 'n' Roll, Flipside, Rolling Stone, Spin, Alternative Press, Big Cheese, Rock Sound, Metal Hammer, Sky, Q, Select, The Face, The Times, The Guardian, The Daily Telegraph*, Chris Mudy, Alex Foege. An extended Green Day biography simply entitled 'Band Biography, 1987-1994' issued by Warners was also particularly helpful in documenting the band's earlier days. Special thanks to Warners UK for graciously providing access to the Green Day press archives.

WEB SITES

The author would like to acknowledge and direct your attention to the official Green Day website, (www.greenday.com); the meticulously-compiled www.greendaysweetchildren is essential, as is www.greendaycellar.com; as well as the hundreds of other enthusiastic fan sites around the world.

Specific band and label sites worthy of a visit are most definitely www.operationivy.com and www.lookoutrecords.com.

Other web sites which proved very useful in researching this book include:

www.tomeryclan.com, 'A History of Rodeo, California.'
www.sanfran.com/archives/view_story/96/*San Francisco* Magazine's Rock 'n' Ribs Beginnings, by Andrew Nelson, September 2005,
www.greenday.net/basement/livermore.html
www.onstagemag.com <http://www.onstagemag.com/
www.billiejoebaby.tripod.com/Greenday/id26.html
www.outyourbackdoor.com (Al Sobrante interview)
www.taxi.com/faq/ar/cavallo.html (Rob Cavallo interview)
www.livedaily.com <http://www.livedaily.com (interview with Bad Religion by Christine Fuoco
www.greendaycellar.cjb.net/

www.nyrock.com/interviews/greenday.htm (interview April 1998)
www.warnermusic.com (news story)
www.nme.com
www.launch.com
www.nyrock.com
www.mtv.com
www.jam.canoe.ca/Music/Artists/G/Green_Day/2004/09/24/745527.html
www.musicmoz.org/Bands_and_Artists/G/Green_Day/Concerts/U.K._Tour
www.http://musicmoz.org/Bands_and_Artists/G/Green_Day/Concerts/U.K._Tour
www.mtv.com/bands/g/green_day/news_feature_040913/index2.jhtml

PHOTO CREDITS

To request a catalogue or find out more about
our other music titles, including books on
The Streets and Mike Skinner, Dave Grohl,
The Cure and Robert Smith,
John Lydon, Muse, Two Tone, Mick Ronson,
Stereophonics, Shaun Ryder, Prodigy and
numerous subculture classics, please visit:

www.impbooks.com